The Global System

The Global System

Economics, Politics and Culture

BARRIE AXFORD

St. Martin's Press
New York

THE GLOBAL SYSTEM: Economics, Politics, and Culture

Copyright © 1995 by Barrie Axford

St. Martin's Press, Scholarly and Reference Division,
175 Fifth Avenue, New York, N.Y. 10010

First published in the United States of America in 1995

Printed in United States of America

ISBN 0–312–15828–9
ISBN 0–312–15829–7

Library of Congress Cataloging-in-Publication Data
Axford, Barrie.
    The global system : politics, economics and culture / Barrie
Axford.
        p.   cm.
    Includes bibliographical references and index.
    ISBN 0–312–15828–9 (cloth). — ISBN 0–312–15829–7 (pbk.)
    1. International economic relations.   2. International
cooperation.   I. Title.
HF1359.A96   1995
337—dc20   95–34537
                                                                      CIP

Printed in Great Britain

Contents

Preface

This book occupies the somewhat uncomfortable space where a number of disciplinary concerns and intellectual traditions intersect. I started it as a political scientist with an interest in politics beyond the nation-state, and with a regard for some of the insights of Immanuel Wallerstein's world-system analysis, and I have finished it convinced that disciplinary parsimony obscures an understanding of the processes of globalization and the constitution of the global system. As a result of this growing realization, I have found myself drawn into areas of literature and fields of study – in cultural studies, in social and cultural anthropology and in some segments of management theory, to name but a few – all previously foreign to me. I have benefited greatly from reading the works of scholars in these fields, and in what follows I hope that I have done justice to the richness and subtlety of their arguments.

My further hope is that the book will make a contribution to the growing debates on globalization as a complex process and not one driven by single, ineluctable logics. Rather, globalization should be construed as a multi-dimensional process and analysed by making connections between the personal and the global, even where that requires abjuring conventional levels of analysis. In this endeavour, I have been guided by the insights of those often called 'structurationists', as well as by work in some strains of 'institutionalist' analysis, from both sociology and international relations. Although some writers believe that it is impossible to reconcile agent-centred accounts of the constitution of social life with structural interpretations, I have sought to do this in an attempt to come to a better understanding of the nature of global *systemness* in a time of rapid and massive change in many areas of life and in all parts of the world.

At the same time, this book should be read not only as a contribution to a theory of globalization, but as a means of exemplifying it through the breadth and richness of illustration. Here, I have allowed myself a good deal of licence in raiding the treasury of anecdotes, media stories and official publications, as well as drawing on more learned discourses to illuminate my themes, and I hope that reference to such exotica as the American 'wigger' phenomenon, the Islamic banking system and the characters from the motion picture *Sleepless in Seattle* will all serve to vivify the idea of a globalized world.

While writing this book I have incurred many debts, some indirectly but many directly. In particular I would like to thank my colleagues in Politics at Oxford Brookes University, who listened (sometimes unwittingly) to fragments from the book, and whose own work has helped to clarify my thinking, especially with regard to the debates on postmodernity. Parts of the argument have appeared in various conference and seminar papers over the last couple of years, and I am grateful to all those who responded to my requests for comments: their advice has proved invaluable. Tony Giddens first asked me to write the book too long ago for safe memory, and when the world was very different. His forbearance and advice, and the ready help of Gill Motley at Polity Press, have been worth a great deal. Finally, and because in every way but the actual writing, they lived with the book for as long as I did, I would like to dedicate it to Frances and Bethan.

1 Conceptualizing the Global Condition

Introduction: all change?

It is entirely in vogue these days to talk about the rapid pace and the unpredictable direction of social and political changes in the world. Like Bunyanesque characters, Dislocation and Discontinuity are abroad and learned journals and media commentary are all full of attempts to come to terms with this 'age of unreason', reflecting the current intellectual preoccupation with the alleged crisis of modernity (Handy, 1989). In Peter Drucker's (1989) mordant phrase, the notion that we have crossed a great 'divide' over the past couple of decades weighs heavily, as familiar social, political, cultural and geopolitical landmarks are not so much eroded as blasted away. Change, runs the by now familiar refrain, is not what it was.

This book is about the constitution of the global system, about the processes which are reproducing and transforming the structures of global *systemness* built around the great themes of Western modernity. Let me just note these themes here because they reappear in detail throughout the book. First there are the institutional forms of *market capitalism*, wherein goods and services are produced and then sold for profit and where capital is privately owned. Then there is *industrialism*, which at its most basic involves a transformation of nature through the use of machinery in the production process (Giddens, 1990, pp. 55–6). Capitalism is only one variant of modernized societies, but some lines of thinking about the make-up of the modern world suggest that a 'world-system' of capitalism has been developing since the sixteenth century, and that not even the 'alternative' version of modernity, Soviet communism, has been exempt from its embrace (Wallerstein, 1974). Third is the territorial *nation-state* as a generic form of rule and as the foremost actor in world politics. Fourth is the *international system of states* which, through warfare and alliances between its members, has drawn and redrawn the map of global politics. Finally, there is the whole corpus of *cultural and philosophical knowledge* which provides the under-pinning for the 'Western cultural account', a phrase I shall use throughout the book (Meyer et al., 1987, p. 29). Primarily this account emphasizes the possibility of individual and social progress through the application of universal rationality and empirical science, goals which involve the mastery of nature for human ends. Then there is the status of the individual human being, who is at the onto-logical centre of the Western idea of modernity. The significance of the individual is reflected in debates about the sources of moral and political authority, in conceptions of free will versus determinism, and in accounts seeking to explain the dynamism of market societies by reference to the purposive behaviour of rational consumers.

In every sense of the term these are 'grand narratives' but, while there has been a tendency to see them as part of a teleology in which the 'modernization' of societies is an evolutionary process ending in full modernity or the 'end of History' (Meyer et al., 1987, p. 31; Fukuyama, 1992), they have never constituted what Anthony Gid-dens calls 'totalizing orders' of sufficient power to obliterate alter-native world views, or the means by which to integrate the global system in some hierarchical or uniform fashion (1993, p. 8). I return to these questions in a number of subsequent chapters in order to challenge the claims of those who have depicted the global system as being integrated by different but ineluctable single logics, for example market exchanges or power relations, and in order to establish the still contingent nature of global systemness (Wallerstein, 1974; Gilpin, 1981; 1987).

The question of the constitution and transformation of the global system, indeed of any social system, must perforce deal with the varied relationships between institutional orders and human agents, where agency can be individual or collective. In the global system there are a wide variety of actors – individuals, voluntary associa-tions, ethnic groups, formal organizations, nation-states and so on – whose status has been legitimated during the modernization of Western societies and during the spread of the Western cultural account to other parts of the world. Ways of theorizing these relationships and of dealing with the perennial 'agent–structure' problem in social theory are taken up later in this chapter and in greater detail in chapter 3. There an attempt is made to integrate aspects of structurationist accounts of the active constitution of social systems by agents (Giddens, 1981; 1984; 1990; 1991b; 1993; Cohen, 1989; Archer, 1988; Dessler, 1989) with some of the insights from institutionalist analyses applied to the study of global systems, of the extent to which individual identities and actions are 'anchored' in social and cultural 'scripts' of greater generality and longevity. This version of institutionalist analysis is closely associated with the work of authors like John Meyer et al. (1987), whose conception of the social construction of reality owes much to the insights of action-centred theorists like Berger and Luckmann (1966). In its most general form, the main thrust of this analysis has been to show that while actors can and do 'construct reality', they do so in what Dessler, with proper deference to Marx, calls 'concrete historical circumstances' which give meaning to their actions (1989, p .443).

It is clear that the translation of these sorts of argument to the global 'level' presents its own difficulties, since it is often said that a concern with the 'everyday practices' of individuals as they go about 'constructing' their own lives (Giddens, 1993) cannot possibly connect with or influence the warp of global trends and processes, which are ordered increasingly without constraint of place or time. But the question of whether local subjects are not only influenced by global scripts, but also able to influence them, has to be treated as an empirical matter and not one to be settled by mere stipulation. Evidence for different sorts of mediation is reported in chapters 4 to 8. In much of what follows the theme of massive, even epochal change is rehearsed at length. I hope that an emphasis upon both the routine reproduction and the transformation of social relationships and structures will qualify the impulse to see the world as Sean O'Casey's Joxer Daly saw it: in a state of irredeemable chaos, or as he would have said, 'chassis'. In other words it will be important to recognize continuities in the reproduction of self and other identities as well in encompassing structures, stressing discontinuity or entropy in modernist narratives only where this is appropriate.

This is a hard injunction to observe, for any litany of recent events does reveal dramatic changes and a growing disorder, notably in the period since the mid 1980s. Then we lived in the 'shadow' of a potential nuclear holocaust, with the threat of possible species death. Now, the end of the Cold War and the promise of peace dividends have replaced that risk, not with a greater sense of security, but with new sources of uncertainty, prompting a curious nostalgia for that moment of global stability. Then, state socialism seemed a permanent fact of life; now Soviet communism lies dead in its heartland, even if it has still to be interred, and the constituent units of the Soviet empire fragment into more elemental parts as they search for new identities. In 1986, the member states of the then European Community put in place a rather prosaic measure called the Single European Act, trying to relaunch the Community on a voyage it should have completed more than a decade earlier. By 1995 it was still not entirely fanciful to depict the completion of the internal market in Europe and the Maastricht Treaty on European Union as harbingers of a new, fully institutionalized regional polity, with some of the attributes and core functions of stateness transferred to a supranational level, or else reconstituted in a non-territorial policy space. But in our more confused reality a number of different futures remain possible for Europe, and even the word 'Europe' itself conjures up a battery of conflicting definitions and prescriptions.

I will return to ways of 'reading' European unity in chapter 5. For now I want to suggest that the 'disorder' widely spoken of as characteristic of these 'new times', and evident in some of the illustrations used above, is itself a systemic phenomenon and should not be confused with a burgeoning chaos but be seen as a property of dynamic systems and of the transformative capacities of agency (Friedman, 1993).

The illustrations used above are all part of big events, headline news in fact, but the danger of canvassing big events is that of either isolating them from the wider contexts and processes in which they are situated, so that each is treated as *sui generis*, or else presenting them as a further twist in a teleological or an evolutionist view of history. As such it will be necessary to pay attention to the more mundane and incremental processes of change which are in train. These may form part of longer-term transformative processes which may not be apparent to those whom they affect most, because they are hidden by the sheer taken-for-granted-ness of routine actions and interactions. Less dramatic and certainly less visible than the cymbaline clash of great events, these processes and flows, whether of people, material objects or signs and images, are nonetheless important, for they too are expressions of the growing pace and intensity of globalized life.

Much of what is discussed in this book under the broad rubric of globalization falls into this category, where the term 'globalization' refers to those processes which are serving to 'compress' the world in David Harvey's (1989) sense, and thus help fashion a single global space. The richness and diversity of various 'transnational practices' (Sklair, 1991), which are serving to broaden and deepen the extent of global interconnections between individuals or groups, are seen in many areas of life. The television viewer whose conscience is pricked by pictures of African famine becomes a fringe player in the *virtual* reality created through the medium of satellite technology and may experience, however fleetingly, a common humanity, even an intimation of global citizenship. If this seems too whimsical, it is difficult to quarrel with the more obvious if mundane evidence available. Britons 'make' motor cars whose component parts are sourced from around the world; Hungarian managers learn the arts of general management from Western business school professors, who in turn may be influenced by Japanese philosophy or practice. McDonald's and Sonic the Hedgehog are depicted as icons of the global consumer culture, and Japanese interests are more dedicated lobbyists on Capitol Hill than many American organizations (Choate, 1990).

In all these examples it is often the unintended or unconsidered consequences which carry the most potent charges, because they reveal that, as a process, globalization can be indirect and unconscious as well as overt. Of course not all facets of globalization take place indirectly. Many are the product of the conscious and intentional actions and interactions of agents who have been 'constrained to identify' or to come to terms with globalized conditions (Robertson, 1992). This is noticeably true of different forms of collective agency which can channel individual concerns in directions far removed from their starting point and original identity (Meyer et al., 1987). For example, the activities of environmental groups which carry a message about aspects of global ecology and which predict eco-doom might serve to raise the consciousness and the global awareness of individuals whose concerns and politics were once entirely parochial.

In this book I want to deal with both big events and mundane processes in so far as each bears on the theme of 'globalization' which, following Robertson (1992), I interpret as the 'processes by which the world is being made into a single place with systemic qualities'. From a social-scientific standpoint the perennial difficulty is not only to identify these events and processes but to locate them, whether as bit players in some grand narrative of history, as data in a nomothetic theory of social change, as unique historical events, or as moments in the transition from a modern to a notionally postmodern order (Chase-Dunn, 1989). These are contested issues because they reflect disagreements over the rules under which knowledge of the world is possible. For although we may be living in what Heidegger (quoted in Smart, 1993) called the 'age of the world picture', it is by no means accepted that this requires the concept of a *global* system, partly because much social theory is still limited in its preoccupation with societal levels of analysis, and partly because the term 'system' sets alarm bells ringing through its association with utilitarian and functionalist accounts of social life and teleological explanations of social change.

In the following pages I will argue that it is possible to conceive of a global system, or rather of relations between what I will call global scripts, actors and processes and those operating at lower levels of generality, which display features of *systemness* and thus offer a frame of reference that permits us to conceive of the world as a single place. The notion of global 'systemness' is crucial to this formulation because it emphasizes the contingent and dynamic nature of these relations instead of assuming a neat functionality between parts of a system which promotes its survival (Parsons, 1966; 1968). In other words, I am concerned to show that a system is only possible through the practices of agents. At the same time, the idea of a 'single place' will be treated with some caution, in order to avoid the impression of a homogenized space in which global structures and global processes have sufficient integrative power simply to meld localities and individual subjects. As Roland Robertson says, this is a matter of recognizing both a growing 'concrete interdependence' in and a greater 'consciousness' of the world, but insisting that neither of these should be taken as complete or uncontested (1992, p. 8).

In a paper on the nature of global systems, Jonathan Friedman (1993) argues that within such systems, global processes affect the reproduction of local units and local identities, and this argument seems unobjectionable. But his further point, that the disorder fed through global processes produces disorder in localities and among local subjects, but *not* vice-versa, seems to underestimate the recursiveness and reflexiveness of the relationships involved (pp. 208–9). For example, North Korea's attempts to manufacture a nuclear bomb may be taken as a 'world crisis', and this is not just hyperbole on the part of politicians but a recognition of the regional and global impact of local decisions and particular world views. I will take up the question of the relationships between local and global directly in chapter 6.

Let me reiterate: the idea of global systemness employed here refers to the reproduction and transformation of a system through the conscious and the routine practices of agents. In a globalized world these practices are conducted increasingly without constraint of time or space and may lead to either the reproduction or the transformation of that system (Giddens, 1990; 1991a; 1991b). The component elements of the global system – individuals, voluntary groups, localities, regions, ethnic groups, nation-states and all kinds of transnational actors – will be construed as socially constructed features of a global 'reality', which becomes meaningful for them through practice. Thus, and here Friedman (1993) is right, the 'order' in the global system should be seen not as evidence of its organic unity, or as the result of a functional 'fit' between parts of a system, but as a negotiated and contingent condition arising from the articulation of local subjects and structures with more encompassing global ones. The growing number and complexity of these connections intimate the possibility of a systemic *dis*order as much as they confer a functional order, since the connections constitute new sites for potential conflict and new opportunities for structuration, including the possibility of individual and systemic transformation. The processes of globalization not only make it more difficult for societal and individual systems to effect closure but, as we shall see, also open up new imaginaries, 'new practices and new institutions' (Friedman, 1993).

Attempts to theorize the global system and the processes of globalization which are making it are still very much in their infancy. Roland Robertson (1992) has provided a detailed and erudite discussion of the intellectual provenance of the concept of globalization and pointed, rightly, to the continued reluctance to transcend the 'sequestered national societies' of conventional social science. Yet the *idea* of the world-as-a-whole is canvassed widely, albeit informally, in popular discourse and in some more specialist narratives. Managers are advised to 'think globally and manage locally' and products which are 'global-homogeneous' rather than 'national-specific' are marketed through the use of generic strategies (Colchester and Buchan, 1990). The concept of the 'borderless world' (Ohmae, 1990) strongly pervades much strategic thinking in what, until recently, would have been described as *international* management. Even our moral panics now take on a global reach, so that we worry about the threat of *global* warming and the allegedly pandemic character of the AIDS crisis (O'Neill, 1990).

However, much of this sort of usage is peripheral to the task of understanding the qualities of global systemness, either because the concept has been appropriated in support of some political strategy or world view, like that espoused by devotees of the Gaia philosophy (where the earth is treated as a single, living organism), or because those who use the term are content with useful but more anodyne descriptions of global 'interdependence' or 'interconnectedness'. This is not always so, of course, as witnessed in the recent attempts to establish the provenance and to map the contours of the 'modern world-system' systematically, through the spread of unequal market relations between societies located at the core, the semi-periphery and the periphery of the world capitalist economy. World-system analysis, particularly that associated with the pioneering work of Immanuel Wallerstein, developed in the 1970s out of a critique of the then dominant paradigm of modernization as a theory of large-scale, long-term social change, and as an attempt to refocus much social theory (most notably in Wallerstein, 1974; 1979a; 1979b). Wallerstein's thesis has been roundly attacked as reductionist (Skocpol, 1977) but in fact his work demonstrates a tension equally familiar to a good deal of neo-Marxist analysis: that between a theoretical reductionism, wherein 'essential' features or dynamics are held to account for the nature of social life, and a strategic voluntarism, which in Wallerstein's (1991a; 1991b) case involves the impact of 'anti-systemic' political and cultural forces on the dominant 'geoculture' of the world-system of capitalism.

These issues are taken up at length in chapters 2 and 3, but here I want just to distinguish between Wallerstein's conception of a world-system configured by the needs of an expanding capitalism, and one of the concerns of this book and of Roland Robertson's *Globalization: Social Theory and Global Culture* (1992), which is to demonstrate the systemness of the globe without recourse to essentialist propositions or reductionist arguments. Wallerstein's world-system of capitalism has a single system identity, but the idea of global systemness implies no such single, implacable logic or holism but denotes a fluid and contingent state which is the expression of interactions within and between societal and intersocietal systems. In other words, this is a systemness which is made rather than given. The characteristics of global systemness are revealed in what Anthony Giddens has called 'the chronic structuration of agents and institutional orders' (see for example 1984; 1990; 1991b; 1993). In Giddens's version of structuration theory the structural properties of social systems have no reality independent of their 'instantiation' by knowledgeable agents, but along with some lines of 'institutionalist' thinking I argue that the sociological 'realism' of actor-centred accounts understates 'the difficulties associated with the question of whether social life is socially constructed, or enacted in relation to broader institutional scripts' (Meyer et al., 1987, p. 13).

The attempt to integrate theories of agency and structure is one of the main philosophical problems facing social theory, and occupies a region of great and often abstract debate (Dessler, 1989; Archer, 1988; Clegg, 1989). Neither structural explanations for action, which, as Dessler says, 'bracket' the capacities and intentions of agents, nor action-centred accounts, which treat structures as 'mere' environments in which action takes place, are sufficient on their own for understanding the links between the conditions for action and action itself (1989, pp. 452–3). These issues are discussed more fully in chapter 3, but the message is that once such ways of thinking about the constitution of social life are grasped, it is impossible to work from an essentialist standpoint on the functioning of social systems, of from one common to the more radical of postmodernist theories of social life, in which the world is infinitely pliable and there are no limits to human action or to the ways in which individuals can construct and deconstruct their identities. Rather I want to stress the significance of institutions in contextualizing social life, in making it intelligible, and the importance of practice for the reproduction and transformation of structure.

The concept of structuration

The concept of structuration does present some difficulties for any attempt to understand the social world. Without doubt it directs attention to the qualities of systemness and to the dynamics that make a system possible, but in a rather abstract and 'free-floating' manner (Urry, 1991). Moreover, the attempt to apply it to concrete research endeavours receives no endorsement from Giddens himself. Robertson, too, cautions against the conflation of the factors that have facilitated the shift towards a single world, like the spread of capitalist market mechanisms and consumer ideology or the increasingly globalized communications order, with the general global agency–structure theme (1992, p. 55). This is a salutary warning against excessive abstractionism, but the danger in what seems to be a conventional expression of the analytical separation of process from structure is that process itself floats free, supplying a dynamic that is somehow independent of the actual relationships between agents and structures.

I take it that this is the burden of Lash and Urry's insistence that we should not just concentrate upon what they call the 'global sociology of flows – of migrants, tourists, communications, money, images, information and time' (1994, p. 7) but pay close attention to the reflexivity in the relationships between local subjects and global structures and processes. Otherwise, as in Robertson's account, the question of the systemness of the world is simply posed in another way. Of course it is necessary to treat with the concrete circumstances in which structuration takes place, including historical circumstances, for these are the contexts in which the world is being made into a single place (Robertson, 1992, p. 54). It is precisely the ways in which globalization processes are refracted in relationships between actors and institutional orders during different periods of world history that demonstrates what Robertson calls the 'concrete structuration of the world', but which is perhaps better seen as its indeterminate structuration.

The global condition then has to be mapped over variable terrain. From rather different perspectives, Anthony Giddens (1990) and Roland Robertson (1992) both write of the need to offer a multidimensional approach to the analysis of the global system, and for the purposes of this book I take that injunction to mean paying close attention to the relationships between social, economic, political and cultural elements in the constitution of global systemness and being at least agnostic on the value of the conventional separateness of micro and macro levels of analysis. The relationships between the constituent elements of the global system display no neat functional unity but, as Arjun Appadurai suggests, often demonstrate that there are 'fundamental disjunctures' between economy, culture and politics (1990, p. 296). These disjunctures are the product of different integrative 'logics' – for example the universalistic logic of world capitalism versus the particularistic logics of nation-state – and are seen too in the perspectives of actors engaged in quite different 'life-games'. Because of this they exacerbate the 'disorderly' characteristics of the global system and substantially qualify any trends towards unicity.

The concept of multi-dimensionality also clarifies ways of looking at the connections between the personal and the global, and between the local and the global, where the main points at issue are the reproduction and transformation of identities. One-dimensional versions of globalization often depict a world becoming whole through the assimilation or the evisceration of individual and local identities. But an understanding of the making of the global system as active along a number of dimensions, and as answering to different and competing logics of integration and disintegration, must allow for messier results and outcomes and not just global homogeneity. For example, it is true that the increasing density of global–local connections and the dissolution of the 'time–space edges' around individuals and social systems have eroded the physical and cultural barriers which protected once coherent identities and traditional forms of life (Giddens, 1984; 1990). They have also afforded greater scope for self-realization, and for human agents to develop more influence over both self- and collective development. Of course apparent liberation from the bonds of tradition or locality may also increase the scope for doubt, relativism and anxiety, fracturing old allegiances and helping to forge 'new' political identities, like ethno-nationalism, which are the antithesis of a progressive, inclusive modernity.

The search for both old and new identities under powerfully transformative conditions are critical themes in the examination of global systemness. To explore them more fully, I want to begin by looking at the relationship between modernity and globalization, beginning with the concept of *reflexive modernization* (Beck, 1992a; Giddens, 1990; 1991a; Lash and Urry, 1994; Beck et al., 1994) which allows us to link the personal with the global and to examine the ways in which agency can affect the reproduction and transformation of social systems. Furthermore, the concept of reflexivity modifies teleological interpretations of social change, because of its insistence on recognizing what may be called a 'critical subjectivity' in the constitution of social life.

Modernity and reflexivity

The idea of reflexivity, or 'self-monitoring' in the sense that Giddens (1993) suggests, is central to the concept of modernity as this has developed in much Western social theory. Giddens says that reflexivity is 'that quality of human action that subjects social practices to constant examination and reformation in the light of incoming information about these practices, thus constitutively altering their character' (1990, p. 38). He uses the extent and intensity of reflexive practices to distinguish traditional from modern cultures (Giddens, 1985; 1990; 1993). He argues that traditional cultures display a sort of reflexivity, in the sense that their members routinely 'keep in touch' with or monitor what they do, but in relation to an order which is extant and either God-given or entirely natural. In traditional societies social interactions are more likely to be face-to-face than mediated by formal institutions and abstract systems.

In such cultures, says Giddens, the past is honoured and symbols of the past are venerated because they carry and exemplify the experience of generations. The present is given meaning through reference to the past and reflexivity is narrowed to reinterpreting and clarifying tradition (Giddens, 1990, p. 37). Thus in the holy city of Qom, in Iran, Islamic logic and rhetoric are taught, but learning consists of an ordered life of commentary and interpretation of articles of faith, not of investigation and scientific scepticism. In societies which are in all other respects 'modern', fundamentalist religious groups and denominations still debate the literalness of truths revealed through interpretation of holy writ. Even so, there may be no such thing as 'perfect' literalism, or truth which is so perfectly revealed that it confounds all further interpretation.

Modernity on the other hand entails not natural order but 'natural contingency' (Lash, 1993, p. 4). In modern social orders, reflexivity consists of an 'interminable interrogation' of institutions and social practices by rational subjects (Castoriades, 1987). The world is not given but made, and made through the choices of actors engaged in a reflexive monitoring of all areas of life. Modernity thus makes possible 'active processes of self-identity' (Giddens, 1990, p. 150) and what is usually called modernization involves the 'detraditionalization' of cultures and the replacement of natural order (cosmos) with what Scott Lash calls a 'subjective ordering of natural contingency' (1993, p. 4). Now whether the notionally 'postmodern' also represents a break with modernity, or just a further intensification of contingency with even greater scope for individual reflexivity, remains a matter of much debate. In terms of the disordered feel of the contemporary world, it may be that contingency and exposure to incalculable risk are, as Lash says, 'far more characteristic of the predicament of the contemporary self than notions of ontological security', or indeed of the reflexive and protective self-monitoring of the world by individuals (p. 3).

Now if this is true, it has considerable implications for the temper of the global system. The possibilities of a transformation of modernity and the substance of this putative shift are taken up in chapter 8, but the theme of transformation runs throughout the book. In fact the distinctions between tradition and modernity, and between modern and postmodern, are better viewed as analytical constructs rather than descriptions of an infinitely more complex reality (Arnason, 1990). Modern identities, both individual and collective, reveal hybrid features, and residues of tradition subsist with and are part of the constitution of modernity, as well as vice versa. To take Giddens only slightly out of context, we are rarely 'cut from whole cloth'.

Let me take the question of 'order' versus 'disorder' a little further by offering a few thoughts on just how these themes are reflected in some new forms of cultural politics and in certain theories of social organization. An obvious starting point is the general agreement that the processes of modernity are likely to be experienced as dislocating, and may produce uncertainty and loss of identity. The order associated with traditional forms of life gives way to the disorderliness of modern conditions, in which the rootedness of place, the comforting weight of history and a belief in the divine or the cosmic are all threatened. So modernity is at least unsettling for individuals and groups having to confront its momentum, and at worst it is totally destructive of whole ways of life. The destruction of order and a growing sense of personal anxiety are often the soil in which cultist organizations, fundamentalist movements or forms of redemptive politics are seeded. Despite the apparently religious overtones of many such phenomena, their appeal may owe less to spirituality than to the promise of security they offer in 'timeless' rituals which are a world away from what Lyotard (1984) calls the 'fracta', the fragments of contemporary life.

There are parallels here with attempts by citizens in Russia, Poland or Romania to come to terms with a difficult present and an uncertain future by invoking myths and traditions from a reinvented past (Kumar, 1992). In these countries people have seen the socialist order dissolve, but the prospects for a transformation to a full consumer culture and pluralistic polities still seem very distant. In the vacuum left by the collapse of one utopia and amid frantic attempts to construct another, there is ample room for political and cultural appeals which seek to establish a cognitive and a moral order based on 'natural' ties and 'authentic' traditions. The basis of such appeals is that they hold out a promise of whole identities, but often at the expense of the toleration of difference, or of 'otherness' (Parekh, 1994). In contemporary Russia this has taken the form of the assertive 'Russianness' seen in the ultranationalism of Sergei Jirinovsky and his oddly named Liberal Democratic Party; and elsewhere in Central and Eastern Europe the movements of the post-communist right indulge their fantasies of racial and ethnic purity and national exclusiveness (Hockenos, 1993). These same forces are at work in the West too, although more benign versions of the anti-modern ethic are also on offer. These include invitations to bury individuality in the collective idyll and embrace a communitarianism where 'small is beautiful' and where it is still possible to rediscover more authentic 'habits of the heart' (Bellah et al., 1985).

From the standpoint of different strands of social theory, the tension between a prescribed or a predicted order and the recognition of natural contingency and complexity is obvious. For example, Francis Fukuyama's (1992) version of Hegelian universal history, mediated through the writings of Alexander Kojeve and Friedrich Nietzsche, reasserts a directional theory of history. But even here the teleology of the argument is diluted somewhat because the march of history displays not smooth but punctuated evolution so that, although the denouement is the triumph of liberal democracy and the market society, progress towards it remains contingent and crab-like.

Of course, for Fukuyama the 'end of History' is only postponed by the breakout of little local and historical difficulties, by moments of arrested modernization, such as that which occurred in the former Soviet Union. Hobbesian world views see the solution to the natural war of all against all in an imposed order, although in some versions this appears as a form of civil contract, where Leviathan, whether as an individual or a collective subject like the state, prevents humankind from realizing the chaotic outcomes of its own brute nature. On a much narrower front, some strains of organization theory which have explored the relationships between organizations and their environments also suggest that, in the face of inevitable contingency, organizations seek to restore equilibrium through closer management of social systems, cognitive processes and informal group norms (Pascale, 1986, p. 113).

Modernity, contingency and postmodernity

Now my purpose here is not simply to endorse any of these conceptions of large-scale, long-term social change or of organizational dynamics, but to point up the contrast between them and those which counsel the impossibility of order and the triumph of chaos or disorder in these 'new times'. Clearly it is not difficult to attach this description to many of the features of contemporary life, and therein lies its appeal. Zygmunt Bauman, thinking of the disorder seen in the wrack of south-eastern Europe, envisages a falling off into a new kind of chaos, visible in the 'unanticipated flourishing of ethnic loyalties . . . and the continuous redrawing of boundaries in contemporary cultures' (1990, pp. 167–8). Indeed it is the prospect of increased contingency, greater risk and threats to secure identities that supports the claims of those who see a new kind of social order in prospect, called the *postmodern condition* or sometimes just *postmodernity* (see Harvey, 1989; Giddens, 1990; 1991a; Smart, 1993).

For individuals, but for collective identities too, attempts to elimi-

nate or ameliorate the personal anxieties and the disorder exacerbated by a 'voracious' modernity often require some reworking of
identities, and a variety of possible solutions to identity problems
are available. These range from what might be called 'regressive'
solutions – in which exclusivist forms of collective identity, like
ultranationalism or militant gender identities, construe a world in
which the 'other' is by definition alien and untrustworthy – to the
creation or 'purchase' of 'designer' selves to suit fashion and to meet
individual circumstances (Bauman, 1992).

Interpretations of these processes of identity formation work with
different conceptions of reflexivity. One version is heir to the Enlightenment tradition of the rational self, and stresses the cognitive dimensions of selfhood. It involves taking control of self-development
through rational processes of self-monitoring and the monitoring of
one's surroundings. A rather different usage suggests that reflexivity
also has a strong aesthetic and interpretative component. The latter
consists of attempts to construct meaning and identity from what
Lash and Urry call the 'expressive components' of different aspects
of life (1994, p. 6). This may be seen in a growing concern with quali-
tative notions like 'empowerment' in the workplace, a concept that
emphasizes a sense of self-esteem as much as it prescribes any constitutional means for giving workers more clout. Aesthetic reflexivity
appears too in reinterpretations of self-identity following exposure to
advertising images of approved lifestyles, which are either morally or
aesthetically pleasing. In this type of reflexivity, 'choice' is the key
term. Individuals 'choose' or 'choose not' to do or to be something
or somebody, and identity can be as fickle or as enduring as the winds
of fashion. Aesthetic reflexivity can be glimpsed in attempts to take
greater control over the body in the manner of 'right to choose'
movements like the pro-abortion lobbies, or in the attempts to make
bodily concerns like 'fatness' a political issue (Lash and Urry, 1994;
and also Bauman, 1992; Giddens, 1991a; 1993; Beck, 1992b;
Mauss, 1979a; 1979b).

To reiterate, modernity is said to be distinguishable from traditional cultures by virtue of the predominance of reflexivity or self-
monitoring, and from the notionally postmodern by the excess of
flux, contingency and complexity which characterizes the latter.
These changes may not be subsumed under the reflexive subject, at
least where this is understood as the capacity of agents for critical
reflection and as the institutionalization of this faculty as a constitutive framework within which action takes place (Lash, 1993, p. 2).
Of course, a world in which everything is contingent summons up
the prospect of greater autonomy for agents, but also may erode their

sense of 'ontological security', where this refers to a 'sense of continuity and order in events' (Giddens, 1991a, p. 243). Thus the burden of most discussions of modernity is that it tends to produce ambivalence rather than wholeness of identity, in some cases leading to a perpetual state of anomie and anxiety. Possible resolutions to ambivalence may involve a search for more secure identities, for example those based on faith and tradition, or the creation of contingent but not necessarily pathological redefinitions of selfhood. So the question of how people come to terms with or are 'dismembered' by the experience of modernity is of central importance when discussing the notional crisis of modernity.

Risk and modernity

The flavour of these debates is conveyed in Ulrich Beck's attempt to distinguish between *simple* modernity and the idea of *second* modernity, through the use of the concept of the *risk society* (1992a; 1992b; Beck et al., 1994). Both versions of modernity are distinguished from pre-industrial societies in terms of the kinds of risks incurred. Pre-industrial societies harboured risks, but for the most part these were 'natural' rather than man-made and were not subject to any sort of critical reflexivity from people who were accustomed to treat hazards fatalistically, as being outside their control. On the other hand, industrial societies produce hazards which are 'artificial', in the sense that they spring from the use and the misuse of industrial technology by human beings.

Beck regards simple modernity as coterminous with the industrial society within the bounded nation-state. The main feature of such societies is reflexivity both by individuals and by parts of a social system with the object of minimizing risk. This goal is achieved in modernity's first, simple phase through the instantiation of the 'insurance principle', whereby risk, though largely incalculable, is rendered manageable or tolerable through the forms of private insurance schemes and state welfare services, in other words by way of reflexive monitoring of an open and uncertain future (1992b, pp. 97–120).

The second modernity, which Beck calls the risk society, is, by contrast, global and not national in scope. Because of this the risk factor increases, while the opportunities to insure against risk diminish. The basis of the insurance principle is that risks are foreseeable, subject to limitation through intervention by individuals and collective agents like governments, and thus compensatable. In the past, for most people, hazards had their roots in local circumstances; or in primitive and traditional societies, they could be imputed to cosmic occurrences. But the second modernity brings with it hazards which make the insurance principle much less tenable. For example, issues like global warming, AIDS, widespread famine, overpopulation, large-scale migration, periodic crises in the world financial economy, or the collapse of the 'stable' Soviet world empire and the environmental and strategic risks which flow from that collapse, are risks 'largely without boundaries, not limited in space, and because they are also likely to affect future generations, not limitable in time either' (Lash, 1993; Lash and Urry, 1994, pp. 32–7).

In such circumstances it might be argued that the scope for contingency, doubt and relativism increases vastly, almost to the point where the reflexivity characteristic of simple modernity founders altogether and modernity becomes a more plural, fluid and altogether more unmanageable *postmodernity*. But Beck does not reason in this way. Rather, the second modernity does not make reflexivity untenable, but provides the conditions for a more pervasive monitoring (interminable interrogation) and for the achievement of true reflexivity that is grounded in the spread of formal education, the popularization and demystification of scientific knowledge and the routine use of expert systems like medical care, public access data bases and, who knows, personal banking services. Because of their own extension across space and time these provide a more effective, though still very imperfect, means of monitoring global risk and managing global contingency.

At the same time Beck holds a relatively jaundiced view of the role of technical and scientific elites in the modernizing process, seeing them as potential sources of decisions which degrade the quality of life, for example in areas like the poor management of pollution control and the regulation and use of nuclear power. Technical elites must be subject to democratic controls and the requirement of accountability, through reflexive monitoring by more attentive publics and the attention of new kinds of political forces. The latter include social movements concerned with the quality of life, but also the shock tactics of the new media, which through the techniques of electronic news gathering and dissemination have 'immediatized' forms of suffering around the world for ever-growing audiences and made it more difficult for public and private authorities to escape culpability for their action and inaction. However, it is important to emphasize that, like Anthony Giddens, Beck sees the routine encounters of individuals with experts and expert systems basically as empowering.

There is no Foucauldian pessimism here, with the reduction of people to passive consumers or 'loose change', but an Enlightenment belief in the possibility of mastery of circumstances and of hard-won democratic control.

The theory of reflexive modernization as developed by Beck has much to commend it. It does, however, appear to be rooted rather firmly in what Lash and Urry see as an 'astonishingly orthodox notion of modernity and modernization' which is in direct line to the stern Enlightenment tradition of 'cognitive critique' . . . as a means towards moral and political change' (1994, p. 37). Yet it is the very continuity of that tradition which is in question, or, more accurately, it is the continuing power of rational, cognitive reflexivity which is in doubt, in a world characterized by growing uncertainty and risk. It is partly because of this that Lash and Urry draw attention to the importance of the aesthetic dimension of reflexivity and its part in the construction of the self, as well as to the hermeneutic tradition of modernity in which this is grounded (1994, pp. 44–59).

Following Charles Taylor (1989) they see the aesthetic dimension of modernity as a reaction to the cognitive aspect of modernization, with its strong rational and moral overtones. Aesthetic reflexivity consists of a search for the authentic, the expressive and the natural components of selfhood as a basis for identity. They argue that it is precisely these qualities that have been eroded by the rationality and abstractionism of the Enlightenment tradition. Nonetheless, individuals are able to 'connect' much more directly with these expressive 'symbol systems' or meaning systems than with those which have to be mediated by technical experts or abstract systems. So, as havens of security in a risk-laden environment, or as potential solutions to identity problems, the appeal of aesthetic sources of self-identity remains strong, or at least immanent. New social movements – of indigenous peoples, ecologists, communitarians and feminists – all invoke elements of this romantic-aesthetic tradition. In a more robust form, so do appeals to collective sentiment and attachments which tribalize relations between groups, often to the point of violence and sometimes to the point of genocide. Now whether at this point reflexivity has been left behind in favour of more atavistic and seemingly elemental sources of identity and their attendant forms of politics is open to question. I take up this issue later in the book, in chapters 8 and 9.

At this stage of the argument it can be said that the aesthetic dimension of reflexivity intimates a politics influenced more profoundly by personal and cultural factors, and one in which the conventional forms of political mediation and identity formation – bureaucracies and modern political parties, perhaps even the nation-state – have less and less purchase when faced with demands for 'authenticity'. Some of these changes seem distinctly emancipatory, offering challenges to what Mongardini (1992) calls 'the dark side of modernity' – bureaucratization, the dehumanizing effects of technology and the sense that moral values can be relativized out of existence. But for other observers they suggest a growing and systematic uncertainty, in which the prospects for loss of control and for social chaos are rife. Anthony Giddens (1990) however is more sanguine about the 'juggernaut' of modernity, which is still accelerating but safe to ride, at least to the extent that paradox and uncertainty become routinized, so that, in a nutshell, we come to expect the unexpected and learn to live with it.

This adjustment is already in train in some quarters. Some management gurus counsel the wisdom of 'living with chaos', not just as a way of making life tolerable, but as a means of achieving a competitive edge (Pascale, 1986; Peters, 1987). For Giddens, security lies in the 'empowerment' offered by reflexivity and in the returns on the trust that we place in abstract systems and forms of accounting, indeed in expert advice of all kinds. For all this, he treats the idea of a transition to postmodernity with some circumspection, preferring to talk of a modernity that has become 'radicalized' and is struggling to come to terms with its own intense reflexivity. This accommodation is achieved by individuals reappropriating fragments of knowledge and experience previously expropriated by modernity's expert systems, thus countering the tendency of such systems to commodify, impersonalize and, in the most draconian forms of social engineering, to threaten human existence. There are strong links here with Beck's interpretation of reflexivity, and because of this they share some of the same strengths and weaknesses. While Giddens is not impressed by the same Enlightenment evolutionism that informs Beck's work, he may be accused of offering an alternative brand of optimism, wherein subjects make convenient accommodations and execute 'leaps of faith' in line with the changing content of expert knowledge, and this athleticism is sufficient to sustain coherent self-narratives (Lash and Urry, 1994, pp. 37–44).

Mongardini (1992) is much less optimistic. He acknowledges that radicalization of modernity involves greater contingency and uncertainty, but the result is a massive loss of stability that entails a loss of history, tradition and culture – in other words the breakdown of all those factors which secured whole individual and collective identities. On this interpretation modernity is not so much radicalized, or in the process of benign transformation, as swallowed by its own spawn. In sum, the distinction here is that between a picture of a radicalized or 'late' modernity, in which the processes of modernization have made possible 'active processes of self-identity' (Giddens, 1990) and expanded the scope for the interminable interrogation of institutions and practices, and one where the self is 'dissolved or dismembered by the fragmentation of experience' (p. 150). In the latter scenario, putting Humpty back together again can produce pretty brutish behaviour and unusual forms of politics.

Modernity as red in tooth and claw

Beck's argument falls within the optimistic camp and also in the mainstream of continuist versions of modernity in direct line from the Enlightenment, primarily because of its emphasis on the importance of cognitive reflexivity. On a global scale, the Enlightenment tradition makes it tempting to adopt a teleological view of modernity as involving a necessary unfolding or diffusion of the features of Western 'civilization', not simply through the mechanisms of global industrial and commercial capitalism, but also through the transformative capacities of the Western cultural account. To reiterate, these features include a belief in the possibility of order, in the progressive and liberating qualities of rational science and in the rationalization of life through the application of impersonal norms and formal rules governing behaviour (Meyer et al., 1987). They also stress a belief in the goals of justice, and in the ontological status of the rational individual as the key social actor.

The global spread of this account has gone some way to making these cultural properties part of a world-wide cultural 'order', but it would be a mistake to read this as part of a simple diffusion, or as the staged evolution of a set of universal modernizing imperatives, or as likely to produce a homogenized world order. On the contrary, as much of the recent literature on the cultural aspects of globalization has argued, a great deal of negotiation continues to take place between more generalized or global sources of meaning and local subjects and contexts (Appadurai, 1990; Friedman, 1993; King, 1991). Appadurai (1990) has spoken of the disjunctions between the various 'scapes' created through globalized flows – mediascapes (images, communications), ethnoscapes (immigrants, workers, tourists, refugees), technoscapes (flows of technology), finanscapes (currency markets, commodity markets, investment and speculation) and idioscapes (ideas, often diffused as images) – which move along non-isomorphic paths, and the 'indigenization' or 'localization' of universal cultural flows by particular cultures and societies. Taken together these disjunctures contribute to the making of a highly pluralistic world, rather than a simple model of cultural centre and periphery.

Of course it might be argued that indigenization merely constitutes a backs-to-the-wall response to ineluctable forces and that, in Emilio Paz's brooding phrase, all cultures are 'condemned to modernity' because of the overwhelming integrative power of the nation-state system, the global capitalist market and increasingly the world-spanning power of mediascapes (Paz quoted in Robertson, 1992, p. 170). Certainly this seems to be the theoretical burden of Wallersteinian world-system theory, although, as we will see in chapter 3, Wallerstein's own position seemingly is now more equivocal on the question of culture as the site for anti-systemic tensions or oppositional politics. Even in Fukuyama's account of the triumph of the West there is a sense that the 'end of History' may only be a prolonged interlude. The essentially continuist slant of his thesis does retain much of the optimism of the Enlightenment 'project', but tempered by disquiet about the possible degenerative effects of the final act of historical 'progress' on the human spirit. At the 'end of History' the visceral and morally taxing quality of life in traditional cultures gives way to a modernity that is intensely reflexive and highly relativized. In 'post-historical' (Western) societies we are condemned, but only to the boredom of successful modernizations. Interestingly, Fukuyama offers the vision of a unified and bureaucratized European Union as an intimation of this state of affairs (1992, p. 311). The same qualified concern can be found in other continuist accounts of the modernization process, notably those of Jurgen Habermas, wherein modernity is in danger from its own logic and success. Both Fukuyama's 'men without chests', who are the inheritors of the bland side of reflexive modernity, and the denizens of Habermas's 'formal democracy' of passive consumers, are candidates for a crisis of motivation and identity which is at the root of all crisis phenomena in what Habermas (1972; 1987) calls 'late' capitalist societies.

So in different ways, continuist accounts like those of Beck and Habermas rehearse the Enlightenment themes of change and progress, but tempered by consideration of the darker consequences of modernity. By contrast, discontinuist versions of modernity, like that of Giddens, paint sharp distinctions between traditional and modern societies, in the ways outlined above. As I have indicated, Giddens (like Beck) does not subscribe to the chaotic image of what he calls late modernity, but paints a picture in which extreme contingency and doubt are ameliorated through the benign intervention of expert systems. For Giddens (1990), modernity does not imply settled relations and unfolding progress so much as a constant state of insecurity with which actors are continually required to come to terms. This profoundly discontinuist character beggars any attempt to impose a grand narrative or single story-line of historical change, whether teleological or evolutionist.

Time, space and modernity

At this point it will be useful to introduce two related dimensions of modernity, again through the insights of Anthony Giddens, the more so as both are crucial to an understanding of the processes of globalization and of the constitution of global systemness. The first of these is the idea of 'time–space distanciation' and the second is the concept of the 'disembedding' of social relations (Giddens, 1981, chapters 4 and 6; 1990, chapter 1). Although strictly speaking these are not institutions themselves, along with reflexivity, they constitute what Giddens calls 'facilitating conditions' for the historical transitions of modernity. The thrust of Giddens's argument again turns on the dissimilarities or dicontinuities between the premodern and the modern world, primarily because the technological changes typical of modernity, notably in the fields of communications and production, have transformed social relations from those requiring physical presence to those which can be carried on across very large distances.

The effects of this 'stepping out' of time and place are to 'disembed' social relations from local contexts of interaction and to reorganize or to 'stretch' them across much larger spans of time and space. In other words, it has the effect of globalizing social relations, and this is the basis of Giddens's claim that modernity is 'inherently globalizing'. He defines the latter as 'the intensification of worldwide social relations which link distinct localities in such a way that local happenings are shaped by events occurring miles away and vice versa' (1990, p. 64). There may be many illustrations of these phenomena, but for now perhaps a rather frivolous example will suffice. In the motion picture *Sleepless in Seattle* the principal characters, who do not meet until near the end of the film, nonetheless conduct a 'virtual courtship', broadcast by a radio show which goes out across the time zones. Place and time are insignificant in this relationship until the need for physical presence makes the airwave connection seem too ersatz. More substantively, the dissolving of time and space raises two more important points which will be introduced here and taken up at greater length in chapters 3 and 6. The first concerns the 'authenticity' of global cultural flows as opposed to local contexts as a means for anchoring identities. The second questions the need for face-to-face interaction as the medium through which social integration is effected.

Modernity and globalization

For now, I want to return to the relationships between globalization and modernity, where two issues are often raised (Robertson, 1992, p. 142). The first concerns the implied causal link between modernity and globalization. It is quite true that the main institutions of Western modernity – industrialism, capitalism and the nation-state – have become truly global (McGrew, 1992), but it is also important to recognize that globalizing forces, for example the universalizing concept of 'Christendom', existed prior to the modern period as this is conventionally understood. In Wallerstein's (1974) account of world-historical processes, politically unified 'world-systems', for example world empires like the Alexandrian or the Chinese, also predate the onset of modernity, and in the case of the latter retained strong elements of identity under Western tutelage. The idea of a single (Western) process of modernization is also difficult to sustain in face of powerful evidence of the various routes to modernity travelled, or now being travelled, by such countries as Japan, China and parts of the former Soviet Union.

The partial and admittedly short-term evidence from recently successful modernizers like Singapore or South Korea is that it is perfectly possible to achieve and sustain a dynamic market economy alongside an authoritarian system of rule and that, in the short term at least, the 'spillover' effect is minimal. On the other hand, some writers have argued that Parsons's (1966; 1971) claim to have identified the 'evolutionary universals' of modernization through which all societies must progress – social stratification, cultural legitimation, money and markets, bureaucracy, a universalistic legal system and democratic association – is reinforced by the experience of the former Soviet Union, marginalized in a world-economic sense because of its failure to achieve a breakthrough to the higher levels of evolution, particularly that of a functioning pluralist democracy (Mouzelis, 1993; Fukuyama, 1992; Sagan, 1992).

The second and related question is whether the processes of making the world into a single place have to be seen as a Western project. In fact Giddens is at pains to point out that the consequences of modernity involve more than a diffusion of Western institutions across the world with the elimination of local cultures, and this is a proper enough claim when set in the context of the heterogeneity of an increasingly globalized world and the continued vitality of alternative 'metaphysical presuppositions', like Islam or even ecologism (1990, p. 175). The question of a global 'order' is clearly of theoretical and practical importance, but it should not be treated in a functionalist manner, to support a simple evolutionary view of history or to suggest the successful completion of an exercise in systemic closure.

While modernity has supported a progressive globalization of human affairs (McGrew, 1992, p. 65), this is not to say either that globalizing tendencies or global 'visions' are unique to modernity, or that these processes under modern conditions are homogenizing to the extent of producing a neat global totality. To argue thus merely transposes societal functionalism and all the problems associated with it to the global level. But I do want to argue that globalization in its current phase is part of the radical transformation of Western modernity, making societal closure all but impossible, most clearly in economic matters, but also increasingly in aspects of culture and politics. Recent transformations in the shape of modernity undermine its totalizing aspect and 'destructure' the cardinal tenets of order, progress and rationality, replacing them with risk and greater contingency. As such it may be more appropriate to say that the processes of globalization have not so much enlarged modernity as acted as a quickener in its transformation. As Robertson and Lechner observe, 'many of the themes of modernity – fragmentation of life worlds, structural differentiation, cognitive and moral relativity, widening of experiential scope . . . have been exacerbated in the process of globalization . . . the problem of modernity has been expanded to – in a sense subsumed by – the problem of globality' (1985, p. 108).

In practical affairs, the major force of Euro-centred modernization has been vitiated in recent years, to the extent that Europe, the European Union in particular, is seen as losing out to the economic power of other trading blocs and as being under threat from cultural imports as various as American meat patties and Japanese cartoon styles (Kennedy, 1993; Porter, 1990). In one sense this loss of centrality is the direct result of the successful and rapid modernization of other parts of the globe, of Western modernity globalized, but it is also the outcome of a conscious reversal of the 'power geometry' (Massey, 1991) of Western modernization, whereby the forces of globalization are indigenized, localized and 'played back' on their progenitors (Featherstone, 1990, p. 2). As such, the *single* global space turns out to be extraordinarily plural and the *totality* associated with the idea of the spread of modernity is shown to be remarkably fragile. For some social theorists these conditions suggest not modernity but postmodernity, an excess of contingency over order and the end of all grand narratives. Globalization now appears less as the hand-maiden of totalizing modernization, and more as the convener of disorder and global restructuration.

Globalization: the concept

So we come directly, Robertson would no doubt say rather late, to the question of globalization. There is by now a substantial and growing literature on the concept but much of it is allusory, despite a substantial amount of empirical work in certain areas (Chase-Dunn, 1989; Ramirez, 1987; Modelski, 1983; Held, 1992; Soysal, 1995). The appeal of the 'idea' of globalization lies in the belief that a proper understanding of the complexities of social life can no longer be extracted from an analytical focus on 'society', especially where that is seen as equivalent to the quintessentially modern form of the nation state (Smart, 1993, p. 135). Yet being agnostic or even hostile to treating the concept as a 'paradigm shift' is understandable. Unbelievers and sceptics display a suitable social-scientific caution, a wariness about faddist notions and contentless concepts. Further-more, there may be disciplinary, even paradigmatic objections to the use of the concept, where, as in more traditional forms of inter-national relations theory, the dominant analytical focus is still that of interstate relations or the construction of international regimes.

The most profound difficulties lie in the extent to which social theory is still dominated by society-centred models and theories, which take the boundaries of the territorial state as the given unit of social analysis, thus making it problematic to admit of more than intersocietal connections or, in a stronger form, intersocietal systems (Giddens, 1981). The idea of intersocietal systems is a useful develop-ment of the societal paradigm, since it allows for the existence of potentially 'world-wide' systems that are both interpolity and inter-organizational (Heintz, 1982), but we must be wary of any implied or assumed dominance of either societal subsystems or a global suprasystem, and recall Giddens's injunction to see such systems as formed through the intersection of multiple systems with power differentials but where no one level or component is assumed to dominate.

My concern in this book is to emphasize points already made strongly by Roland Robertson and others, namely that the global system is not reducible to a 'scene consisting merely of societies, and/or other large-scale actors' (1992, p. 61), and also to insist that the idea of uniquely global features does not obscure the extent to which all social systems are embedded in or otherwise overlap with other such systems. Consequently it is a mistake to see the global system as one that in some autonomous fashion 'imposes' its imperatives unmediated on national and societal units, as well as on groups and individuals. By the same token a conception of the 'global' as little more than a utilitarian framework created out of the random or patterned exchanges between states and societies will not do service. For while there may be a global dimension to social relations, what Robertson calls a 'specifically global point of view' (1992, p. 61), we should hesitate to explain the making of the global system through a focus on particular levels of analysis, whether global or subglobal. Instead, understanding the complexity of the global system requires a multi-dimensional approach that deals with the mediated connections between actors and institutional orders, at whatever 'level' they are to be found. These will include conventional units of analysis like individuals, intra- and international groupings, and the independent nation-states, singly or in concert. But in addition there is the increasing variety of actors whose consciousness and *raison d'être* are transnational or global, and who may have quite different prescriptions for world order.

So globalization is just a convenient term for the multi-dimensional processes by which the global system is being made. While it is clear enough that these processes involve what Lash and Urry (1994) call flows of 'objects and subjects' – money, services, goods and people – and the creation of transnational institutions, it is less obvious that global cultures and non-territorial identities are being fashioned. On a final note of caution, globalizing processes must not be seen as the expression of the ineluctable power of a single deep 'logic', despite the fact that there is an appealing parsimony about those theoretical accounts which see the 'genetic code' of the global system manifested in such factors as the international division of labour created by unequal exchange, or see ideas as the engines of history (Wallerstein, 1974; Fukuyama, 1992).

None of these qualifications are damaging to the proposition that globalization processes are creating a single world, but they do focus attention on what is meant by that claim and on the actual processes through which that 'single place' is being created. Most attempts at defining globalization are tentative at the same time as they are sweeping. This is hardly surprising, given the scope of the enterprise, but it does leave room for a good deal of confusion, as well as the suspicion that practically anything might qualify as a possible indicator. The core of the idea is that the world is undergoing a process of ever-intensifying interconnectedness and interdependence, so that it is becoming less relevant to speak of separate national economies, or separate national jurisdictions founded upon principles like the sovereignty of the territorial nation-state. The idea of a global system suggests that this interconnectedness and interdependence is making it increasingly difficult for social units like nation-states, localities and even individuals to sustain identity without reference to more encompassing structures and flows. At the same time, diversity is still rife in what is undeniably a pluralistic world; indeed it may be heightened by a sharpened awareness or consciousness of global pressures and expressed in forms of cultural resistance or attempts at economic and political autarky.

Overall, the effect of globalizing forces – for example the increasing irrelevance of 'place' for purposes of production, the boundary-spanning and boundary-dissolving character of communications technology and media, and the movement of migrant populations across national and 'zonal' boundaries (Kennedy, 1993, p. 129) – is to promote a cognitive global order. While this is some way short of a global political system and a long way short of a global moral order or a world society, such consciousness is serving to redefine the experiences and the perceptions of more and more actors. As one consequence the 'fragile unity' of national societies (Touraine, 1991) comes under threat from a variety of transforming global processes and also from ostensibly 'internal' pressures – demands for regional autonomy, cultural and political separatism – that have been galvanized by regional and global pressures.

In many instances the challenge to existing identities at least coincides with a growing consciousness of the world on the part of aggrieved minorities or subjugated populations. For example, the Iranian Revolution of 1979 was a struggle to overthrow the authoritarian and 'fascist' rule of the Pahlavi dynasty, but it was also the expression of a militant reinterpretation of Islam against the depredations of 'Westernization' and the corrupted and fragmented lifestyles of Euro-America. Perceptions may be either positively oriented to the 'global circumstance', for example in the ideologies of those groups promoting the idea of 'one world', or negatively disposed towards it, as seen in various 'fundamentalist' and local responses. But quite often the idea of being 'constrained to identify' with the global system involves little in the way of conscious, globe-oriented behaviour or affective responses, because the processes are threaded into the routines of daily living (Robertson, 1992, chapter 1).

Perhaps most visible of all, the processes of globalization render the territorial boundaries of the nation-state less and less coincident with the changing patterns of life, because of the significance of various transnational media, both economic and cultural, in constituting the ways in which people live. This is the barb in Giddens's disarmingly simple conception of globalization, namely that it serves to link people and collectivities previously separated and insulated by time and space. Social relations are no longer configured entirely by the need for face-to-face encounters and are not limited in time or across space. In this they reflect the 'stretching' of economic and other social processes across the world space. Local settings for action and interaction remain important; and not just residually, but because of the 'world-embracing' character of modern institutions and the 'disembedding' of social relations, the conventional distinctions between local and global or between micro and macro levels of analysis look increasingly threadbare.

The axial features of globalization

There is a good deal of debate and uncertainty about the historical origins of the global system, largely fuelled by the internecine arguments about the provenance and timing of the long cycles of mercantilist and then capitalist expansion, which are the structural features of the modern world-system identified by some branches of world-system analysis (Wallerstein, 1974). During the early phase of capitalist expansion, which in Europe may have lasted from the fifteenth century until the mid eighteenth century, but which on some accounts may be traced back to the thirteenth century, aspects of earlier, medieval transnational arrangements and identities were eroded and replaced by the nascent national communities and state-like forms of the modern period (Wallerstein, 1974; Abu-Lughod, 1989; 1991). This shift was consolidated, again primarily in Europe, between the mid eighteenth and the late nineteenth centuries, and during this phase the concept of international society became more firmly established. Industrialization of the economies of the core states of Europe and then America also transformed social relations to those based primarily upon industrial market principles.

Globalizing trends and tendencies were intensified over the critical period between the late nineteenth century and the latter part of the second decade of the twentieth, when the standardization and spread of the nation-state form, more intensive exploitation of the non-European world by European powers, the spread of industrialization and the growing sophistication of communication techniques all contributed vastly to global compression and to the opportunities for reflexive experience of that process. During these early and 'take-off' phases of globalization (Rostow, 1960) the independent nation-state increasingly occupied centre stage as a locus for identity and legitimacy and as an actor in the world political economy. In fact, along with market capitalism, it became the paradigmatic form through which globalization has proceeded. Since then, developments have both reinforced the status of the nation-state, not least as a desired goal for various nationalist and ethnic movements, and weakened its ability to keep control of areas critical to its prosperity and autonomy. Rightly or wrongly, the dominant motif in some accounts of the condition of the global system is that of the 'decline' of the nation-state, and this issue is taken up in chapters 4 and 5.

The long wave of capitalist expansion after 1945 saw remarkably high levels of prosperity in the countries of the West, at the same time as the underlying fragility of the global order was exposed by the tensions of the Cold War. In the wake of the ending of superpower rivalry on a global scale there seem to be even fewer absolutes. The Second World of state socialism has fallen apart, and capitalism as a world-wide economy continues to transmute under the pressures for 'flexible' production and the 'knowledge revolution'. The Third World, only recently 'discovered' and given status in official discourse, also languishes in a kind of post-hegemony tristesse. Global institutions and movements multiply and the concern with 'humanity' as a whole is perhaps greater now than ever before, as witnessed in the wide appeal in the West of environmental causes and humanitarian concerns. Tolerance of difference also seems more firmly rooted: in some respects the 'other' may be less alien in a world made more familiar by global communications and global cultural products. Yet at the same time communities seek to destroy each other in the name of ethnic purity, and we rehearse the Eloi's fear of the Morlocks in our dealings with the underclass in our major cities.

In the middle chapters of this book the following key features of globalization are extracted for attention.

The world economic order and the new world division of labour   The global expansion of capitalist, market-driven economic activity has produced a truly world-wide economy, now expanding directly into the old Soviet empire and established in newly dynamic areas like southern China. To all intents there is a 'borderless world' in financial markets and in foreign direct investment (FDI), and the completion of the single market in Europe and the messier resolution of the Uruguay Round of the General Agreement on Tariffs and Trade (GATT) talks in April 1994 signal the end of national protectionism in key sectors. Even if such predictions prove illusory, the logic of the global marketplace is increasingly indifferent to exactly where a product or a service is produced; and through the application of flexible working practices and high technology, even the social relations of production are being transformed. However, it is still a matter of debate as to the continued salience of national factors in achieving global competitiveness (Porter, 1990; Ohmae, 1990). These questions are explored in chapter 4, but it is clear that these and other broadly economic processes are having a significant impact upon the second institutional component of globalization, namely the nation-state.

The world political order   The nation-states are still seen as the principal actors in this order, but it must now include a plethora of suprastate and non-state transnational actors and networks of actors. In the wake of the Cold War, the making of a world democratic order has assumed a growing significance, as the emergence of trans-societal policy networks, large-scale migration and the prospects for democratic transformation in the former state-socialist countries raise issues about the meaning of key 'modern' concepts like citizenship and accountability (Bryant and Mokrzycki, 1994; Offe, 1991). In other respects new and old forms of politics which are centred on questions of identity intimate either a 'new dark age' or a more benign restructuration of politics which have transcended the left–right dimension of much modern political conflict (Cable, 1994; Minc, 1992). These issues are taken up in chapters 5, 6, 7 and 8.

The global military order   This grew out of the conflicts between nation-states or alliances of states and produced two 'world wars' in the twentieth century. It has undergone something of a transformation since the demise of the Soviet Union as a global superpower and the emergence of post-communist regimes within its former sphere of influence. The threat of nuclear proliferation rather than superpower conflagration remains high, and the global arms economy is still dangerously volatile in this period of 'peace dividends', as 'new', less manageable conflicts have broken out in the vacuum caused by the ending of superpower geopolitics. Signs of a new global military order in a much more fluid, multipolar world are visible in the Gulf War alliance, but the role of global peacekeepers or brokers of human rights sits very uneasily on bodies like the United Nations (UN) or the European Union (EU) when they are faced with conflicts like those in Bosnia, Rwanda or Haiti. These issues and the question of global governance are examined in chapter 7.

Global or cosmopolitan cultures   The emergence of such cultures, spread by the faster circulation of consumer products, by the information carried on the burgeoning global communications 'super-highway' and by the movement of people, is contributing to the spread but also to the modification of the Western cultural account. Global cultures have been portrayed as rather brittle when compared with more 'authentic' local or traditional cultures, while still having the power to empty them of meaning. I look at these matters in chapter 6, where one of the concerns will be to examine cultural factors as constitutive of the global system and to relegate talk of culture as a superstructural phenomenon to the sidelines of social theory.

Following Featherstone (1990, p. 2) I want to suggest that there are a number of 'opposed tensions' to bear in mind when thinking about the making of the global system. These tensions must be read not as neat antinomies but as 'frames of reference' through which to understand the contested making of the global system. They can be summarized as follows: the increase in the scope for reflexivity implied in the process of globalization, set against the conscious attempts to limit and amorphize experience seen in fundamentalist responses to globalizing pressures; the familiar dichotomy of the local and the global and of the emergence of what Featherstone (1990) has called 'glocal' identities; and the antinomy of apparent homogenization versus visceral difference or of integration versus disintegration.

These processes of globalization will be presented as contested, and thus the concept of system employed here will owe little to those intellectual traditions that have stressed the self-regulating and closed nature of social systems, or that treat the dynamics of system formation as a hierarchical ordering of suprasystem dominance. In the light of recent critiques of functionalism and systems theory, this is not a radical departure but a necessary antidote to one-dimensional and reductionist accounts of globalization and the making of the global system. While it is easy to caricature alternative positions from the literature on systems analysis in general and on world-system analysis in particular, my point is that what is needed is a fuller explication and treatment of the systemness of the global system, both in terms of its structuration (how the system is possible, how it can be reproduced) and in terms of the more dynamic concern with how it can be transformed.

As I have suggested, this requires a multi-dimensional approach to the understanding and mapping of system characteristics and dynamics, one which is sensitive to the relations between the features of the global system, in the areas of politics (steering, power), economics (production) and socialization (socio-cultural), and to the reflexive interaction between a growing variety of agents and structural and cultural forms which are becoming ever more global in scope. In other words it is as concerned with the personal as it is with the global. An understanding of the systemness of the global system must traffic carefully between psychological and phenomenological accounts of the constitution of actors and institutional accounts that often marginalize the role of agency. This is difficult terrain. I begin in chapter 2 with an excursion through a number of important strands of thinking about the global condition as a way of laying down some markers and issuing some health warnings about the contribution of different intellectual traditions. I proceed in chapter 3 both to a critique of recent theorizing about the constitution of social life, and to an elaboration of how global systemness might be grasped through a modified treatment of structuration theory and institutionalist analysis.

2 Ways of Thinking about the World

Introduction: a science of the global system?

We can understand the complex systemness of the world as this has developed during the modern period by paying attention to the ways in which actors reproduce and transform increasingly global scripts. Despite problems with the definition of globalization and some difficulties in establishing indicators of that process, there is at least a diffuse sense that it is far advanced in many areas of economic life, but less symmetrically in the political and cultural realms. For at least one commentator there is little doubt about the power of globalizing trends; indeed, he says that the last three centuries have been an 'apprenticeship for living in one world' (Heintz, 1982, p. 7).

To be a useful concept, globalization has to be seen as a multi-dimensional process, and that implies cutting across levels of analysis to grasp the reflexivity in relationships between actors and various institutional forms, whether local or global. By implication this approach rejects the argument that the global system is being integrated by a single causal logic. It also questions one of the key assumptions of over-systematized accounts of the global system, whereby the 'internal' attributes of actors are given by assumption and are not treated as variables. In such interpretations of systemness, changes in the behaviour of actors and system outcomes are explained on the basis of changes in the attributes of the system itself. One of the purposes of this book is to contribute to a breaking down of the tendency to perceive the individual and the social as different and opposed entities, and to see them as reflexively linked (Mendes, 1992).

In this chapter I want to look at the ways in which various strands of thinking from within the social sciences are dealing with questions about globalization and the making of the global system. As we proceed it will become clear that there is no standard position. Some accounts stress the cyclical and rhythmic integration of a 'world-system'; others predict more or less complete disintegration and emphasize the historicity of social relations and forms. Social change is seen either as cyclical and rhythmic or as disjunctive and transformative; explanations are either teleological or historicist. There is clearly a major division between those positions that describe a global system which in Bergesen's phrase 'has a life of its own' (1982, p. 23) and those that hold a more utilitarian picture of the world political economy, in which 'globalness' is no more than an aggregation of the activities of nation-states and national economies. I am not agnostic in this debate but, while leaning to the former, I will argue that the systemness of the globe cannot be understood in terms of the simple autonomy and dominance of privileged levels or units of analysis.

There is clearly a growing fascination with global dynamics and the perceived compression of the world, but it may be something of an exaggeration to say, as Mendes (1992) does, that there is an 'emerging science of global processes' (see also Bergesen, 1982). In fact a growing preoccupation with the global has yet to produce any overall agreement in theoretical terms, and the emerging 'science' of the global system is, in Kuhn's (1970) sense, pre-paradigmatic. The purpose of this chapter is to set out some of the main intellectual positions on the global system, taking note of the fact that it is identified in quite different ways depending upon what sort of dynamics or logics are deemed to be most powerful and what sort of images are being used (Kegley and Wittkopf, 1993). The perspectives canvassed reflect quite different intellectual concerns and disciplinary traditions. What follows is not meant to be an exhaustive treatment of highly developed and complex accounts, nor is it entirely comprehensive in the range of positions covered. Thus there is no mention here of the growing literature on globalization found in international and strategic management, or in international economics. I will return to these areas in chapter 4, but in each of the following approaches I want to take up:

1 the extent to which the argument is oriented to the global circumstance, that is, uses the idea of a global system (or some synonym for it) as a point of reference rather than societal-level phenomena or other spatial-temporal forms

2 the nature of the global system being discussed, its main features and structural properties, and the relations between actors and structures

3 the extent to which the system is seen as integrated by single or multiple 'logics'

4 how, if at all, the system is being transformed, and whether this change has to be seen as evolutionary or disjunctive.

There is no generally accepted way to classify these materials. I have grouped arguments around quite broad themes, some of which address the idea of a global system more directly than others. The idea that there is, as Peter Heintz says, a 'worldwide field of inter-action' (1982, p. 12) is generally understood, but interpretations of it are more or less inclusive: an international or intergovernmental system of states, a sectoralized world economy, the routine and dramatic intersection of individuals, communities, societies and civilizations, or an integrated 'world-system'. I begin by looking at some of the main strands in international relations theory, which until recently was the only area of political science to pay anything like careful attention to matters beyond the societal level of analysis.

A world of states? Theorizing the international

The area of academic study usually called 'international relations' is, like all disciplines, riven by canonical disputes. At root these differences still turn on the extent to which the territorial state remains at the heart of explanations of international politics, or whether its centrality has been eroded by the rapid development of non-state actors, by transnational forces and global processes. These are issues which are central to an understanding of globalization and in addition to a more general discussion here; I will return in chapters 5 and 7 to some of the issues raised. In the 'realist' school of international relations theory, which until recently enjoyed the status of an orthodoxy, the idea of global politics is predicated upon the more or less conflictual relations between independent nation-states. The realist view of international politics developed as a response to the frailties of idealist solutions to the problem of order in international life, and as an alternative to early Marxist attempts to theorize the international system through concepts like imperialism.

In fact there are a number of 'realist' positions, but for our purposes a core of common assumptions can be identified (Carr, 1939; Morgenthau, 1948; and see Strang, 1991). In place of the idealist world view, which was full of opprobrium for the ravages of war and its distortion of humankind's essentially moral nature, the realists, or rather those of the older or classical school of realism which dominated thinking in the 1940s and 1950s, drew heavily upon the political philosophy of Niccolò Machiavelli and the evolutionary *realpolitik* of Charles Darwin to ground their conception of international politics (Kegley and Wittkopf, 1993, p. 22; Krasner, 1994).

For realists the core dynamic of the international system is the passionately self-interested or egoistic behaviour of nation-states, many of which are endowed with resources sufficient to prevent or to limit the possibility of that system being dominated by a single ruler, even though pretenders abound (Krasner, 1994). As a result, the system is characteristically anarchic. By definition, a combination of rational state actors and systemic anarchy produces a highly conflictual form of international relations, in which the pursuit of power is the *raison d'être* of statecraft. But the system that results is said usually to be 'in balance', even stable, because the pursuit of rational self-interest still requires states to counter the threat posed by potentially dominant system members by forming alliances, often with weaker states. By the same token, rationality also demands that attempts by dominant states to annex a small, weak state need not be countered by others, since annexation may not add significantly to the power of the aggressor, relative to the costs incurred through intervention. As Wendt says, the realities of 'power and human nature preclude significant cooperation' between states (1994, p. 384).

At this point, realist essentialism fades into what are generally called 'neo-realist' accounts of international politics (Waltz, 1991; 1979; 1954) in which the unambiguous and passionate lust for power is mitigated by the demands of rational behaviour imposed by the constraints of the international system of states – and where reason overcomes desire. As well as these core assumptions concerning the wiles of statecraft by rational actors, neo-realist positions adopt a strictly utilitarian stance on the motivations of states as actors. States, like rational individuals in classical economics, are assumed to have 'given' utility preferences *as states* regardless of other attributes they may possess, or variability they may show. The result is an interesting conflation of theoretical perspectives. On the one hand, the *givenness* of actors' preferences makes the idea of an institutional or structural constraint upon actor behaviour highly unlikely, because institutions are simply 'arenas' or contexts in which action takes place (Krasner, 1988; 1994). At the same time, these are undeniably systemic conceptions of international politics in that, as Kegley and

Wittkopf suggest, differences in the characteristics of the international actors are seen as irrelevant to an understanding of recurrent behaviour in international politics (1993, p. 36).

Such utilitarian-systemic accounts make the otherwise difficult question of the relations between agents and structures appealingly unproblematic, because the preferences of actors derive from the properties of a system in which self-interested strategies in pursuit of optimal outcomes are the only rational behaviour, especially when viewed from the point of view of the need to survive (Olson, 1965). Because it is the survival of states which is the keystone of the international system, states possessing few resources justifiably may fear for their survival, especially if they are new. A sense of insecurity may dictate the need for greater cooperation with other states, but the rational actor must always weigh the possible advantages of mutual cooperation against the disadvantages, namely, increased dependence upon others with a consequent loss of power and autonomy.

Political realism, and the more systemic variants found in the neo-realist tradition, came under increasing attack during the 1960s and 1970s, largely because of two phenomena, which taken together challenged both the main assumptions of the realist *oeuvre*. First, one of the major difficulties with realist perspectives, and to some extent with those of the neo-realists too, is the assumption of the centrality of state actors who are reluctant to cooperate with each other, save from fear of destruction by a more resourceful competitor bent on regional or even global domination. During the height of the Cold War and at points in the 1980s when the rhetoric of the 'evil empire' coloured international discourses, this Hobbesian view of world order retained some currency. To some extent it still provides a purchase on the continued importance of national security as a crucial factor in the behaviour of states, not least because the relaxation of superpower dominance of world politics has left many states feeling more vulnerable (Gilpin, 1987; Krasner, 1994). The pursuit of power and the need to balance the distribution of power remain strong as motive forces in the international system.

Second, the strength of the state-centric view of political realism has been eroded by the rapid growth of genuinely transnational phenomena of an economic kind, for example in the operation of global financial markets, in the conduct of global companies, and also through the relatively pacific networks of travellers, business people, academics and so on who now populate a more robust global civil society. In the political realm too there are challenges to the realist orthodoxy, and two may be mentioned here. First there is the extent to which the European Union may be creating a qualitatively new sort of political space not tied to territory and built upon mutual cooperation (Agnew, 1994; Hix, 1994; Wendt, 1994). The second is the sense in which realist assumptions about the inevitability of conflict between states are controverted by the apparently unambiguous evidence that democracies do not appear to fight each other (Krasner, 1994, p. 17; Mearsheimer, 1990; Fukuyama, 1991; 1992).

The realist/neo-realist conception of states as actors with given preferences also underestimates the extent to which the internal qualities of individual states, their domestic politics and the concerns of their citizenry, have a bearing on the functioning of international relations (Keohane, 1983). 'Low politics', in Kegley and Wittkopf's (1993) phrase, have increasingly clear implications for national policy agendas, but in discussions of European integration, to take an obvious example, they have scarcely figured in the constitutive account which until recently was dominated by an international relations problematic (Hix, 1994). My point here is that the demeanour of states cannot be inferred just from the given quality of their stateness – or, to employ a much-worked analogy, by treating them as billiard-balls with no internal politics or ideology and no history.

Realism, as Francis Fukuyama says, holds that the struggle for power among nation-states is universal across time and space, and that it is only the shape of the international system – either bipolar or multipolar – which determines the likelihood of war or peace (1991, p. 662). Thus realist arguments have a curiously ahistorical feel about them. History is not important: there are only environments and optimizing actors with given preferences, whose behaviour adapts, or sometimes fails to adapt, to changing environmental circumstances. In reality historical processes like the collapse of the Soviet empire cannot be seen solely as the outcome of environmental factors but must take account of 'domestic' conditions, like the legitimacy of the regime and its capacity to deliver value to an increasingly demanding and less trusting citizenry (Kennedy, 1993; Offe, 1991).

Further modification of the billiard-ball analogy has occurred in recent years as the idea of states as 'unitary' actors has given way to arguments which suggest that the state is either an amalgam of forces or an arena for struggle between contending societal interests, rather than a unity clearly demarcated from civil society and obeying its own laws and logic (Jessop, 1990, pp. 292–3). In their most anodyne form such reinterpretations merely stress the domestic sources of foreign policy (Rosenau, 1967), but in more radical versions the very idea of the state undergoes major revision, appearing, as Halliday says, less as the dominant actor on the world stage and more as a social force which 'relates to other social and economic forces, both within and between societies' (1989, p. 353). The willingness to see states as 'genetic-cultural' entities, or to emphasize their diverse character rather than the givenness of their ontology as rational actors, owes much to the growing popularity of late of comparative macro-history, with its mission to 'bring the state back in' to social theory (Miliband, 1985; Skocpol, 1978; Evans et al., 1985; Mann, 1986; Nordlinger, 1981), and to the reworking of international relations theory under the influence of varieties of institutionalist analysis.

Broadly speaking, institutionalist positions argue that actors follow and to that extent are conditioned by institutions, that is, by rules or 'history encoded into rules' (March and Olsen, 1984), and that self-definitions and policies are the outcome of engagements or interactions with institutionalized rules rather than the expression of raw self-interest. The question of just how actors engage with institutions in the constitution of a social system is rather more problematic than many institutionalist accounts suggest, and this is the subject of greater reflection in chapter 3. For now, it will be enough to outline the main strands of institutionalist thinking as applied to international relations and the global system.

Institutionalist perspectives trade on the idea that an institutional framework of cultural rules and norms exists prior to and thus is constitutive of an actor's identity, rather than, as in realist accounts, the other way around (Young, 1986; Keohane and Nye, 1988; Krasner, 1988). Actors are thus conditioned by 'complexes of rules and norms' (Keohane and Nye, p. 9) but the relationships between them and institutions are reflexive, where this implies that they rely upon 'history encoded into rules' for at least some aspects of their self-definition and thus for legitimation of their behaviour. In this repect some forms of institutionalist arguments are closer to the concerns of structuration theory, with its attempt to reveal the mutual constitution of agency and structure, than to the actor-centred accounts of both realism and neo-realist liberalism, which are simply more catholic on the range of actors which populate the international stage (Dessler, 1989; Wendt, 1987; Koslowski and Kratochwil, 1994).

Overall, this leads to a rather more systemic view of international relations than is found in utilitarian-realist and even in neo-realist theories. But the notion that institutional rules shape behaviour implies not just that the system constrains actors but that it constitutes them at the same time as it is enacted by them, although such a 'dualistic' view does not find its way into all institutionalist positions (Hix, 1994; Giddens, 1990; Wendt, 1992; Krasner, 1988). For example, on Krasner's rather stark reckoning there are two interrelated characteristics of the institutionalist perspective, namely the derivative character of actors and the persistence of rules – behavioural patterns, roles, organizational charts, ceremonies and so on – over time. Now this is a much more one-sided picture of the relationships between agents and structures than is appropriate to the attempt to understand the complex structuration of the global system, largely because it leaves little room for agency and for reflexivity in the relationships between agents and structures. Some structurationist or 'constructivist' accounts of the social construction of international institutions and processes, like sovereignty or the Cold War, come much closer to filling this gap (Wendt, 1987; Gusterson, 1993; Koslowski and Kratochwil, 1994) and I will return to their contribution in chapter 5 when discussing the nation-state and the international system of states.

While institutionalists tend to concentrate upon the international system, rather than on the actors that comprise it, their collective reflections on the changing nature and dynamics of that system also reveal other important departures from the realist genre. A number of themes are apparent. The first, sometimes called 'complex interdependence' or 'international political economy' (Kegley and Wittkopf, 1993, p. 31; Keohane and Nye, 1977; 1988), challenged the basic assumption of realist thinking, namely that national security issues dominate the policy agendas of states, and that military force is the most important instrument of such policy. In simple terms, the emphasis in institutionalist thinking shifted to international and transnational economic processes, in which the main actors and forces are not just states but banks, multinational corporations and, in a more diffuse sense, markets. The power of these actors and forces suggests not only a more complex milieu for the working out of conflicts, but a world in which the state no longer appears as the dominant form of political organization, or the most important actor in a world-economic sense. Instead it is the interaction of security and military processes, still structured at the level of the state or in alliances between states, with the increasingly global economic forces and institutions like the General Agreement on Tariffs and Trade (GATT) and the International Monetary Fund (IMF), which are the engines of the international system.

The second theme, which builds on this idea of a growing interdependence effected through both functional links and institutions, rests upon the concept of 'international regimes', a term borrowed from international economics but which for these purposes refers to arrangements covering rules, norms, principles and decision-making procedures (Keohane and Nye, 1988). Regimes are institutionalized systems of cooperation in a particular issue-area, and they may or may not be elaborated in organizational form. Activity is regime-governed to the extent that the behaviour of actors conforms to the rules laid down by, or the expectations implicit in, the regime, even though these may not be binding in a strictly legal sense. Examples of international regimes which govern behaviour include the IMF and the GATT, or the Climate Agreements which followed the Earth Summit in Rio in 1991.

In other respects, the institutionalist reworking of the traditional model of international relations draws attention to the ways in which interdependence, or mutually accepted constraints which may arise from market failure (Keohane, 1984; Stein, 1990), can breed coopera-tion and perhaps a growing trust between states, sufficient to encourage the 'surrendering' or 'pooling' of key areas of sovereignty (Wendt, 1994). This is seen most obviously in the history of the European Union, but would apply presumably to many situations in which cooperative behaviour produces outcomes that are more pre-ferred or less costly than individual, self-interested action (Stein, 1990). Thus regimes may appear not just as pragmatic responses to insecurity, but as institutional anchors in a turbulent world. The moral overtones of this line of argument are in some ways akin to idealist solutions to the problem of international anarchy.

The problem of world order, or the lack of it, informs the third strand of institutionalist thinking, and in this respect it shares some of the concerns of traditional realism. For realists, the existence of an international system composed of self-interested states both increases the scope for economic development and dynamism, because the possibility of closure by a dominant power is proscribed, and for the same reason increases the risk of war as states wrestle for position. In this scenario, the threat of hegemonic power and the fear of unbridled anarchy are the engines of the state system, and thus cooperation is the 'unnatural' corollary of a 'natural' state of conflict. Some institutionalists, on the other hand, have chosen to address the issue of hegemonic power in a rather different fashion, seeing it as a source of stability and, *contra* realism, as a vehicle for the promo-tion of cooperation in the form of international regimes. The position of the United States as a global hegemon has prompted much of this debate, along with the consequences for international cooperation which flow from its putative decline as a 'manager' of the world order (Gilpin, 1987) or as a relatively benign facilitator of interstate cooperative behaviour (Keohane, 1984). Needless to say, the concept of hegemony is capable of a variety of interpretations, from those (like Gilpin's) that use the term to denote the dominant military and/or economic power, to others that adopt a neo-Gramscian view of the state and of class forces operating both within and between territorial jurisdictions (Gill and Law, 1988; Gill, 1994).

Of course, as Halliday (1989) points out, at least part of the growing confusion in international relations theory arises from the treatment of the concept 'state', in which the tradition has been to deal with state behaviour only as 'determined' by the nature of an international system made up of other state actors, rather than based on a calculus which includes 'internal' factors, for example the balance of political and class forces within a society, as well as non-state regional and global forces. Taken to its limits this revisionist argument removes territorial states from the theory of the global system altogether, or leaves them as shadowy entities, hardly actors at all, simply sites for or vehicles of class antagonism and other societal and trans-societal conflicts. These are only conveniently and fleetingly expressed through the martial or diplomatic guise of the territorial state. If this seems a particularly reductionist line of argument, it may be no less so than one which explains structures and institutions as 'manifestations of the preferences and capabilities of states' (Krasner, 1994, p. 14).

Much of the debate about the 'decline' of the state turns on the threats to its sovereignty. As we shall see in chapter 5, the institutional order of sovereignty that legitimates the independent nation-state is hardly in tatters, so that institutional persistence rather than radical change or major deconstruction might still be held up as the defining characteristic of the global political system. The power of the 'idea' of the nation-state also remains strong, as witnessed in the continuing appeal of statehood as a symbol of recognition in the global system and of 'sovereignty' as a badge of privilege and legitimacy (Ruggie, 1993). Of course this is not the same thing as saying that the territorial state still functions as the optimal way to organize political life, or even that it enjoys unrivalled legitimacy as the focus for loyalty, obedience and the aspirations of citizenry. Much of the discussion about the decline of the state in a globalized world turns on the speed with which environmental changes have overtaken the capacity of states to adapt, and assumes a Darwinian world in which fitness to survive continues to provide the evolutionary logic.

The persistence of the institutional order of sovereign states cannot, however, be taken for granted as the mainspring of an international system increasingly caught up by 'turbulence', in Rosenau's phrase, where institutional inertia and adaptation give way to volatility and politics 'cascades' rather than evolves (Rosenau, 1988; 1990). In such a world, the paradigm form of the nation-state is becoming 'hollowed out', its powers shifted upwards and outwards to alliances, regimes and supranational bodies, and downwards to regions and localities as well as to non-accountable quasi-governments in the form of boards, trusts and quangos (Rhodes, 1994). Moreover, in recent years a more radical critique of international relations theory has been mounted using poststructuralist or postmodernist concepts (Der Derian and Shapiro, 1989; Wendt, 1992). The main burden of this critique has been to question further the canonical status of concepts like international 'order', realist icons like the territorial state, and even the 'male-centredness' of much theorizing (Enloe, 1989; Gusterson, 1993; Tickner, 1992; Peterson and Runyan, 1993). Contingency, fluidity and the fundamental redrawing of the international system by a host of non-state actors and forces are given much greater emphasis in this literature. In chapter 3, it will be seen that the radical deconstructionism of the postmodernists also leaves unasked too many questions about the relationships between actors and institutions, their structuration, even though a postmodern turn in the theorizing of European unity, for example, has much to recommend it (Axford, 1994).

Modernization theory

International relations theory uses a historical special case, that of the nation-state, and the post-Enlightenment concept of sovereignty, to construct an essentially state-centric view of the global system, albeit one which has been modified considerably to reflect the growing interconnectedness and interdependence of the world. The spread of the ideology of the sovereign state and the idea of an international system of states based upon the principles of territoriality, sovereignty and a monopoly of 'internal' force are themselves part of processes through which the world has become modernized and globalized. Looked at from a state-centric position, modernization has been an ambivalent process, serving to institutionalize states in all parts of the world while contributing to the diminution of the power of individual states, where this implies the 'loss' of sovereignty and of decisional autonomy. Interpretations of these processes are very contested, not least because the very concept of modernization is associated with particular world views and the desirability of particular trajectories of national development (Peet, 1991).

A crisis of interpretation arises over the treatment of modernity as a predicted and prescribed moral order and of modernization as the process by which it is to be achieved. In chapter 1 I explained that there are both continuist and discontinuist versions of the path to modernity, but that both involve the effective destruction of traditional world views and institutional forms. Modernization theory gives this destruction a particular gloss, and in so doing takes on a pronounced ideological hue. This ideological tinge appears in its attempt to explain the making of the modern world as a progress through a number of 'required' stages of development (Parsons, 1966; Parsons and Shills, 1951; Smelser, 1959). The rapidity with which societies master changing environmental conditions is held to turn upon factors internal to those societies, like the degree of economic specialization, the physical isolation of the society, the extent of 'social mobilization' (Deutsch, 1961) and the mindset of political and other elites which might be more or less favourable to societal innovation (Weber, 1976; 1978).

As explanatory variables for why some societies 'modernized' earlier than others, these conditions were soon branded as ethnocentric and tied to a markedly 'Western' view of development (Frank, 1969a; 1969b; Gouldner, 1970). However, it was the shift to apply modernization theory to patterns of global development, and in particular to explain the development of Third World societies in the aftermath of colonialism, which crystallized the opposition. Apart from the notion that modernization theory painted too simple a picture of the transition from broadly traditional *Gemeinschaft* to forms of modern *Gesellschaft*, the main criticism was that the image of modernization on offer was often stereotypic in suggesting an evolutionary model of national development made in the image of successfully modernized countries in Europe and North America.

In fact the literature on modernization does show some catholicity and debate on the convergence of societal paths of development (see Peet, 1991). In particular the convergence–divergence debates of the 1960s turned on the possibility of different paths to modernity, and more recent accounts offer historically sensitive treatments of the survival of 'civilizations' or their re-emergence as 'furrows' across world history (Eisenstadt, 1987; Huntington, 1993). But overall, there is little which allows for the idea of modernization as a thoroughly reflexive process that allows scope for subjectivity and difference to reveal itself in outcomes as well as in processes.

One of the defining characteristics of modernization theory, which it shares with Marxism, is the idea of social and societal evolution (Gouldner, 1980; Sagan, 1992). Evolutionist positions were often incorporated by functionalist theoreticians to impart a more dynamic quality to their analysis, which on some accounts are incapable of explaining social change given their concern with those factors which reproduce and stabilize social relations (Smith, 1973). For example, Walt Rostow's *Stages of Economic Growth* (1960), which was a deliberate alternative to Marx's theory of history, argues that societies can be located along one of five universal dimensions of economic growth, ranging from traditional and largely agricultural societies, through a stage in which the preconditions for economic take-off are laid down, to actual take-off – the key stage of the modernizing process – towards the mature and high-mass-consumption stages of growth. In this evolutionist account, high-consumption modernity is the fulfilment of social evolution. Stage theories of modernization, whether Marxist, Parsonian or Rostowian, outline a necessary path of development and historical change from which deviation is possible but probably at some considerable cost. The jumping of stages of development or attempts to circumvent history by radical modernizing elites, as happened in the former USSR, or in Cambodia under the Khmer Rouge, produce at best short-lived historical anomalies, at worst major social pathologies.

Evolutionism and its frequent bedmate, historical directionality, have generally received a bad press. In such accounts, says Giddens (1990, p. 5), complex histories become simplified and totalized stories that can be told only through a grand narrative, and which unfold to a happy ending. The evolutionist would answer that evolutionism does not imply linearity, only that there is always a skew towards an 'authentic track', or a 'directionality', which history must follow. For Fukuyama (1992), branded as a teleologist, there is in fact no 'end of History', if that means the end of conflict, or debates over the means of politics, but 'History' does achieve its denouement in the triumph of global liberalism and global liberal democracy, because there are no longer any serious alternatives to these features of the Western cultural account.

The convergence theories of the 1960s and 1970s predicted that pretty nearly all societies were moving towards the same point, though at variable speeds. When applied to the 'convergence' of East and West, this implied that the two 'sides' were moving towards some hybrid model of industrialized society. The collapse of state socialism has led some theorists, Fukuyama included, to suggest that what was presented as convergence was only ever a one-way flow (Offe, 1991) and that, because of this, modernization theory has been vindicated in the face of the attacks both of those he describes as 'Nietzscheans' – who believed that modernization theory was a Western prejudice – and of those designated as Marxists, who saw it as an ideological front for an exploitative system of global capitalism secured under American dominance (Fukuyama, 1991, p. 660).

The writing on modernization from within conventional political science, especially from some areas of comparative politics, described the processes of economic development, from the preconditions for 'take-off' to full mass-consumption maturity, as tightly bound up with the processes of political democratization (Lerner, 1958; Lipset, 1959; Binder, 1971). However, the waves of partial democratization which have followed the breakup of the Soviet empire on the European and Asian landmass cannot be explained simply by reference to levels of economic development, and there are also other examples of the lack of isomorphism in political and economic modernization. Substantial economic growth in places like Brazil, the Republic of South Korea and Taiwan during the 1960s and 1970s did not produce the expected democratic breakthrough, and in the 1980s and 1990s even more spectacular growth on the part of Pacific Rim countries like Singapore has not been accompanied by 'matching' democratization. Of course, as Fukuyama says, it may be that democracy is ultimately a matter of choice, a measure of the maturity of the polity in question, or of the intensity of the aspirations of people under adversity and subalternity. More prosaic interpretations of these revolutions are also available, in which the urge to be more whole-hearted consumers of the products of Western capitalism weighed more heavily than any love of democratic values (Offe, 1991; Zaslavsky, 1994).

Classical Marxism and theories of imperialism

At heart, modernization theory paints a relatively optimistic picture of the relationships between liberal capitalism and liberal democracy, with economic development sometimes presented as a precondition for the achievement of a functioning and stable liberal democracy (Lipset, 1959; Almond and Verba, 1963). Where the historical record has modified if not completely undermined these sorts of predictions, local factors, both historical-cultural and socio-genetic, have been offered as intervening or explanatory variables in the processes of democratization (see Barry, 1970; Lipset et al., 1993). Increasingly a more 'pragmatic' view of the relationship is allowed, in which authoritarian regimes are seen as compatible with both achieving and sustaining high levels of economic development, especially on the part of states newly launched on to the world economy.

The compression and major reordering of the world caused by the collapse of state socialism, and the consequent slackening of the bonds of subalternity in parts of Central and Eastern Europe (Bahro, 1981), have made the question of how to achieve and sustain democracy once again a critical matter for theorists of modernization and for national and international decision-makers. For Marxists, issues like constitutionality, accountability and democratic procedures have usually been subsumed in treatments of the functions of the state in maintaining exploitative relations between social classes. However, one area in which both modernization theory and various strands of Marxism share a common concern is the role of capitalism in developing the Third World, both economically and politically. The key difference is that, in some interpretations from orthodox Marxism and in most neo-Marxist writing, the concepts of imperialism and underdevelopment replace those of development or modernization at the core of the analysis.

Even within the Marxist canon there are genealogical disputes, since it is now commonplace to identify 'two Marxs'. The one was a proponent of universal history and a believer in historical, dialectical progress, for whom the stages of history unfold in no less evolutionary a manner than for modern functionalists. Stage succeeds stage in the shift from less to more developed modes of production, each with more technologically proficient forces of production and, in the more technologically advanced stages, different means for extracting economic surplus. For this Marx capitalism is a progressive stage in the march of history, and modernity is entered through the gateway of bourgeois revolution. Both are the precursors of a socialist society, the alternative 'end of History'. For the other Marx, and certainly for generations of his followers, the attractive myth of the natural and transitional nature of bourgeois capitalism and its progressive nature is vitiated through the human misery caused by capital's ceaseless requirement for accumulation, and by the recognition that, in the case of peripheral societies at least, development does not mirror the course charted by countries in the core. The condition of capitalism as a global system is one of uneven and unequal development.

In fact, Marx himself has relatively little to say on the non-Anglo-American world of nineteenth-century liberal capitalism. His writings on colonialism are largely confined to India and Ireland, and on these his views differed considerably. In the case of India, Marx was convinced of the dynamic effects of progressive British capital on a society 'stagnating' under the burden of 'backward' oriental despotism (Carnoy, 1983). Ireland, on the other hand, experienced the immiseration which is the handmaiden of industrialism and capitalism, but without the benefits. The effect of British colonialism on Ireland, said Marx, was to turn that country into an agrarian offshoot of a rapidly industrializing Britain. In other words, Britain underdeveloped Ireland but, by destroying the old Asiatic society in India, laid the seeds there for rapid change and industrial development. The colonial state performed radically different functions in each of these cases. However, what we observe from both is that capital is inherently expansionist, needing outlets beyond those afforded by domestic economies to survive and prosper.

Imperialism and global capitalism

The idea of capitalism being inherently expansionist transforms Marxism from an evolutionist theory of history to a theory of the dynamics of a global system. This transformation is associated most notably with the writings of V. I. Lenin (1975), but also with luminaries like Luxemburg (1951) and most notably Bukharin (1917; and see Sklair, 1991). Lenin tells us that imperialism is a necessary phase of capitalism, driven by the law-like tendency of the rate of profit to fall and by the resultant need to seek out new sources of accumulation. The imperative to colonize arises not just from capital's need to annex new regions of exploitation, but out of the rivalry between the major capitalist powers in their search for hegemony.

   This political economy of imperialism displays some of the features of global *realpolitik* found later in realist accounts of the international system. It also conveys the contradictory logics of a global system formed out of the mutually exclusive imperatives of continuous and unfettered expansion for the forces of capital and the drive for systemic closure apparent in the attempts by powerful states to achieve hegemony. For Lenin, expansionist capitalism is the begetter of imperialism, which is itself the vehicle for the expansion of capital. For non-Marxists, notably liberal theorists like J. A. Hobson (1902) and Joseph Schumpeter (1952), the causes of imperialist expansion are not 'reducible' to economic considerations but lie variously in 'atavistic impulses' or other cultural-historical factors.

   Lenin's contribution to theories of the global system was to lift

Marxist analysis above its obsession with both capitalism and socialism in one country and to begin to refocus it at the level of capitalism as a global system. This refocusing has gone on apace, building on Lenin's conception of the uneven development of capitalist societies. In general, neo-Marxists (neo-Leninists) have been concerned with the implications of uneven development for colonial and post-colonial societies in the global system, exploring the theme of the systematic impoverishment of the Third World. At the same time, some revisionist accounts have revived Marx's 'Indian' perspective on the dynamic qualities of a globalizing capitalism (Warren, 1980) while others have sought to map out quite new schemes of capitalist development, either using 'neo-Smithian Marxism' as the cutting tool (Brenner, 1977; Wallerstein, 1974) or bringing the theory of imperialism into world-system analysis (Addo, 1984).

Dependency theories

Both modernization theory and, confusingly, orthodox Marxism-Leninism offer a particularly Eurocentric view of development and uneven development. Whereas the former worked largely with conventional Ricardian concepts of economic development, in which the terms of comparative advantage actually work in the longer-term interests of all countries, even where the industrialization of the periphery in the world economy remains limited, the Leninist theory of imperialism depicts peripheral economies and peripheral polities as pale reflections of the political economies of core states (Addo, 1984, p. 125). Dependency theory challenges both these assumptions, while still being wedded to a Marxist problematic.

The central concern of early dependency theorists was to find an explanation for the uneven development of different parts of the globe (Dos Santos, 1970; Amin, 1972; Frank, 1969a; 1969b). Setting aside the basic assumptions of neo-Ricardian economics and those of modernization theory, they argued that the phenomenon of uneven development, so central to explanations of capitalist expansion, had to be understood as a structural feature of the global economy, and thus was better seen as arising from a relationship between development in the core of the world economy and *underdevelopment* in its periphery, with both as aspects of a single historical process. The degree of underdevelopment varied with the extent to which the periphery was rich in resources of value to core powers. Thus the incorporation of Latin America into the world economy from the 1600s onwards shows no benign Ricardian process of development and incorporation, but a form of systematic underdevelopment geared to the demands of capital accumulation in the metropole countries. This argument was extended to the political and social structures of underdeveloped countries. In a radical departure from modernization theory, Frank and others insisted that 'social relations of production' in the periphery were primarily the result of the penetration of those regions by capitalism, and not the product of 'backward' or traditional societies which either had missed or were still waiting for the vivifying force of capital.

The outcome is a world-wide division of labour in which local development is stunted by the need for expansion of metropolitan capital. Originally, such needs were met through direct colonization, military intervention and forms of administrative rule. Of late, the primary agencies have been 'aid-for-trade' regimes, benefiting metropolitan producers and multinational or transnational corporations, often aided and abetted by a denationalized business class or bourgeoisie in the periphery. As a theory of the global expansion of capitalist relations, early dependency theory paints a rather stark and deterministic picture of centre–periphery relations. Capitalism develops one and underdevelops the other: there is no middle ground.

Revisionist positions (Frank, 1978; Amin, 1980; Emmanuel, 1972) qualified the despondency of the earlier writing, but only to suggest the possibility of a stunted form of 'dependent development', in which the industrialization of peripheral economies is encouraged, indeed required, by changing conditions in the metropole and, at least in Amin's version, by bourgeois movements of national liberation (Carnoy, 1983, p. 186). Principally, this change is caused by the transition to more technically efficient systems of production, and to the production and sale of higher value-added goods by firms based in the metropole. Such production as is shifted to the periphery is often that of labour-intensive and less profitable goods.

Although this shift undoubtedly modifies the international division of labour by relocating manufacturing capacity in the periphery, it does little to alter the dependent nature of core–periphery relations, which continue to be dominated by unequal exchanges between core countries specializing in the production and export of high value-added consumer goods, and peripheral ones still playing out their historical role as suppliers of raw materials to the metropole. Peripheral economies continue to be characterized by low agricultural wages, extended in the periods of development to the industrial sector, and any surplus generated by increased industrial production reverts either to the metropole or to the local bourgeoisie, to fund their purchases of the trappings of success. In terms of their consumption of surpluses, the local bourgeoisie now behave more as an arm of an international class alliance, purchasing goods produced in the metropole, while local industry wilts for lack of domestic investment and lack of domestic purchasing power.

Dependency theories of the sort outlined above see very little prospect of the autonomous or supported development of the periphery in a global capitalist system. Of late, work from within the Marxist canon and elsewhere has questioned the basic tenets of dependency thinking, including its rejection of the concept of dependency development. Some writers have even entertained the idea of 'dependency reversal' which admits the possibility of a 'breakout' from dependency (Sklair, 1991, p. 32). Warren's (1980) account of the 'powerful engine' of colonialism on Third World industrialization, and other treatments of 'import-substitution' industrialization of the sort debated by Landsberg (1979) and Barone (1983) and applied to the case of newly industrialized countries (NICs) like South Korea, are typical of this revisionism. More structuralist interpretations of the difficulties associated with dependency reversal are also available in the attempts by 'regulation school' theorists, like Aglietta (1979) and Lipietz (1987), to establish the uncompetitive basis of peripheral 'regimes of accumulation' still grounded in Taylorist and Fordist systems of production when compared with the efficient 'flexible production systems' of core economies (see also Piore and Sabel, 1984).

Apart from their merit as counterfactuals against the determinism of dependency accounts, these ideas sometimes offer a radical treatment of the functions of states and political classes in peripheral societies, seeing 'strong' post-colonial states in the periphery as engines and sponsors of social and economic progress, their functions contingent upon local circumstances and local history and not tied to class interests or, more abstractly, to the 'needs' of capital. While this notion is accepted readily enough when applied to Western development (Badie and Birnbaum, 1983) and has been used also to 'explain' the Japanese transition to capitalism (Trimberger, 1978), it is a concept alien to most dependency theorists. Even Cardoso and Faletto's (1979) 'structural-historical' approach to the analysis of peripheral societies does not go this far, though they too reject arguments that derive 'mechanically significant phases of dependent societies only from the implied logic of capitalist accumulation' (also quoted in Carnoy, 1983, p. 193), preferring to see systems of domination in the periphery as the outcome of 'internal' accommodations between class forces and state elites in peripheral societies, and between these and metropolitan interests. The argument here is instructive: different historical conditions produce variable outcomes, and the systematic underdevelopment of the periphery need not, and in fact does not, produce uniform and permanent stagnation of peripheral economies.

For all this, Cardoso and Faletto's 'particularistic' or 'historicist' version of dependency is at one with the basic tenet of the the 'dependinistas', namely that capitalist development in the periphery is not a mirror image of what took place in the metropole, but is conditioned by the spread of capitalism as a global system. It is however a view of global capitalist constraints substantially modified by local circumstances. The same tensions can be seen in the discussions about the form and the functions of the dependent state, and most clearly in arguments over the 'progressive' nature of 'bureaucratic-authoritarian' regimes in peripheral societies along with the prospects for the democratization of state structures which result from popular struggle (on the broader theme of transitions to democracy, see O'Donnell et al., 1986). Many such debates are little more than a reworking of the endless nuances of the Marxist *oeuvre*, but they do serve to highlight an important facet of globalization, namely the complexity of relationships between local and global, and to call into question the explanatory power of theoretically parsimonious but reductionist arguments applied to the 'real' logic and essential nature of the global system.

World-system theories

Dependency theories are a significant contribution to attempts to understand the functioning of the global political economy, despite their shortcomings and massive over-generalizations. Seeing centre–periphery relations as ordered through the systematic underdevelopment of dependent countries by those in the metropole not only provides a theoretical counterweight to theories of modernization, but offers a holistic conception of the global system of capitalism and its dynamics, albeit one heavily reliant upon broadly economic criteria. In reality, dependency theory is split by sectarian conflicts about the relative importance or definitional power of social class as opposed to exchangist conceptions of capitalism, and by divisions over the degree to which, historically, capitalism means only 'core' capitalism (Chase-Dunn, 1989, p. 29).

In Frank's (1969a; 1969b; 1978) spatial and holistic version of the underdevelopment thesis, peripheral societies are locked into dependency, and capitalism cannot develop the Third World; however, in positions which are more sensitive to history, place and culture, the prospects for at least dependent development are much more favourable. The theoretical pessimism of much dependency theory is not always translated into strategic considerations, and activism abounds, especially that which calls for political radicalism of one sort or another. Generally, dependency theory makes it very hard to entertain the idea of autonomous industrialization taking place in non-metropole countries. This failure prevents an open treatment not only of the 'tigers' on the Pacific Rim of the world economy – Taiwan, Singapore, South Korea and of course Japan – but also of the large and complex economies of countries like Mexico, Brazil, Argentina and Chile, all with 'strong' states and substantial evidence of indigenous manufacturing capacity.

World-system analysis, like dependency theory, grew initially from a critique of the modernization paradigm; but, most notably in the work of Immanuel Wallerstein, it is also an attempt to redirect the analytical focus of much social theory. The burden of this crusade lies in moving the analytic focus from a societal to a world level of analysis. It is important to note that there are various strands of world-system analysis: some of them are revisionist accounts of the ground-breaking arguments first set down in detail by Wallerstein in 1974 in the first volume of *The Modern World-System*, while others are attempts to gloss the Wallersteinian model through a 'strongly theoretical' reading of his basic concepts (Chase-Dunn, 1989, introduction). Still others adopt a quite different logic or set of key structures to explain the dynamic of the global system, including war and political factors (Modelski, 1983; 1988; Bergesen, 1980b), while of late the importance of cultural factors in the constitution of the global system has been given much greater weight (Rabinow, 1993; Robertson, 1992; King, 1991). I will start by outlining Wallerstein's position, itself widely caricatured by opponents, and move to related and alternative conceptions of the world-system.

World-system theory is rooted in the radical tradition of the dependency theorists, and displays some of the theoretical pessimism of that genre in its treatment of the possibilities of a non-capitalist world future. At the same time it is strongly influenced by the more historically grounded tradition of the Annales school, particularly that of Braudel (1972; 1975; 1977) and through historical geographers like Vidal de la Blache. It is from these provenances that it draws its concern with both the long term and the spatial as key organizing concepts in the social sciences. In short, the world-system perspective looks to analyse long-term, large-scale social change by treating world history as the emergence of a single system. It does this by combining societal and trans-societal perspectives (Chase-Dunn, 1989, p. 1) and challenges the assumption of much conventional social science that national societies can be analysed without recourse to the manner in which they are linked to and conditioned by extra- and trans-societal networks of exchanges, called world-systems.

Wallerstein distinguishes between two categories of world-system – world empires and world economies – and this distinction also serves to mark off many types of historical system from what he calls the *modern world-system*. Historical world-systems (mini-systems, world empires) were not global in their geographic reach, and often they were cut off physically and culturally from systematic exchanges with other systems. Each had a unified division of labour and an overarching cultural and political-administrative framework. In the past, proto world economies succumbed to attempts by dominant regional powers to achieve imperial closure, thus creating world empires like the Chinese, the Roman or the Egyptian that had a great deal of cultural heterogeneity and a geographical division of labour, but were held together by a single coercive administrative-legal framework.

By contrast, the modern world economy of capitalism has successfully resisted all attempts at closure by a succession of hegemonic powers to become the dominant, indeed the only, world-system of the modern era (Wallerstein, 1983). The modern world-system is a capitalist world economy, which by the end of the nineteenth century had achieved a global reach and established a virtual 'geoculture', based upon economic liberalism and the liberal doctrines of individual emancipation and human perfectibility. Unlike a world empire, a world economy is a world-system which contains multiple societies or cultures and many states, but only a single economic division of labour. For Wallerstein the capitalist world economy originated in sixteenth-century Europe, and spread out from there through the dynamic and exploitative activities of core states, like the United Provinces and Great Britain (but see Abu-Lughod, 1989, for an account of the earlier and non-European provenance of the modern world-system).

In turn, capitalism is defined by Wallerstein as commodity production in which there are different forms of class relations: wage labour in the core of the world economy and more repressive forms of surplus extraction in the periphery. A global capitalism is achieved through the establishment of 'commodity chains' between peripheral and core producers and consumers (Wallerstein, 1979b) while commodity production is itself defined as the production of commodities for sale in a price-setting market. Like the writers of the dependency school, Wallerstein is at pains to depict capitalism as a global system from the sixteenth century onwards, and not one confined to the 'advanced' economies and societies of the European landmass. The lack of conventional development in the periphery is thus explainable in terms of how such societies were integrated into the world economy, and not as a result of their separation from it or their genetic 'backwardness'. In sum, the modern world-system of capitalism constitutes an economic unity fashioned on the basis of unequal exchange in commerce and on an international division of labour between strong core states and economies and weaker ones in the periphery. The core–periphery hierarchy and the exploitation of the periphery by the core are thus key elements in the reproduction of the world-system.

Wallerstein's world-system perspective assumes that the essential feature of the system, its mode of production, exists at the level of the whole system. In other words, he is arguing that capitalism is a global system because it has become a distinctive and world-embracing mode of production. In Wallerstein's capitalism, the 'deep essence' of the mode of production is the network of uneven material exchanges between states located at the core and at the periphery of the world economy. These are the structural constants of the world-system of capitalism. The international division of labour between an exploiting core and an exploited periphery, embodied in the international system of states and in international markets, is a central feature of global capitalism. Market forces on a world scale affect and even condition the behaviour of states as well as that of other sub- or supranational actors. At the same time, Wallerstein (1979a; 1979b) acknowledges that capitalism is not always, even if ultimately, structured by economic relationships. It is also a set of power relations and thus subject to the vagaries of relations between social classes and states. Now it is open to question whether these qualifications make him less of an economic reductionist than he is sometimes painted. I return to this more directly in chapter 3.

Unlike the cruder and dichotomous Frankian model of global capitalism, based on a centre–periphery divide, Wallerstein's world-system exhibits a threefold division of labour between states located at the core, the semi-periphery and the periphery of the world economy. These are characterized by relations of unequal exchange and successively more repressive and labour-intensive systems of production for world trade (Wallerstein, 1984, chapter 8). In this zonal and hierarchical world economy the semi-periphery appears as something of an *ad hoc* category, and performs an almost Aristotelian function by ameliorating the destabilizing effects of an otherwise completely polarized world-system.

Within the global hierarchy, state structures operate as the means for particular groups to affect and distort the functioning of global markets, a state's 'strength' or capacity in this respect being reflected in its position in the global hierarchy. On the face of it, no individual state can break free of the toils of capitalistic exchanges, and autarkic solutions to the problem of incorporation are ruled out on the grounds that all areas of the globe are enmeshed (materially, if not culturally) in the logic of commodity markets. Where they are not, they are still heavily dependent upon various forms of largesse (for example in the form of aid-for-trade agreements) or subject to strategic controls and other means of ensuring subalternity. Thus premodern societies, former state-socialist countries and the vanguards of fundamentalist opposition to Western cultural imperialism in post-revolutionary Iran, or in Cambodia under Pol Pot, are or were unable to effect even local closure for any length of time.

In the favoured category of core states, the most successful may become hegemonic. But hegemony too is fleeting, at least in a world-historical sense, and states so endowed – to date the United Provinces, Britain (twice) and the United States – cannot do more than aspire to the status of a world empire, because competitors are able to exploit possibilities for development which are either not controlled directly or poorly controlled by the hegemon (Meyer, 1980b, pp. 263–6). As a result there is a decidedly cyclical quality about the structuration of the world-system. Not to be coy, the whole scheme is founded on the conception of global cycles, or long waves as these are sometimes called (Kondratieff, 1979). Originally, long waves were conceived as long, historical periods of sustained economic expansion, followed by periods of stagnation and depression. In Wallerstein's scheme of things the history of the world-system is periodized into waves of expansion and contraction, and by ascending and declining hegemonies. The stress on long waves as either self-regulating or, in an attempt to avoid reductionism, affected by an amorphous category of 'extra-economic' factors, like war or ecological disaster, reinforces the unfolding logic of the argument.

It is hardly surprising that all this fails to find favour with much conventional social science and with strains of Marxism. On the one hand, it is critical of the societal basis for much social theory; while with respect to Marxism, it is happy to invoke much of the litany of Marxist analysis but with scant regard for its epistemology. As a result there have been many criticisms of Wallerstein's interpretation of the modern world-system, most of them too well known to warrant extended discussion here. His attempt to fashion a 'historical social science' through the study of historical systems has met with a barrage of criticism, much of it, as Bergesen (1990) says, blind to the advances being made in establishing a truly global level of theorizing. On a different tack, Theda Skocpol (1977) objects that, while Wallerstein's scheme is rooted in both Marx and Weber, he is true to neither. Let us take the treatments of the state and of mode of production as exemplars of these debates.

Wallerstein is scarcely a minimalist on the question of the relationships between states and world-economic forces. Not only does world-system analysis involve a rejection of the territorial state and national societies as the starting point for social analysis and the primary locus of social action, but Wallerstein's heavily systemic view of the world-system has states as functional subunits of the global system (1983; 1984, chapters 3–9). For Wallerstein the function of states of varying strength is to act as forms of protection for national class interests (Chase-Dunn, 1989, chapter 6), and their relative economic strength determines the placement of states within world zones. The structural position of states in the core or the periphery of the world economy is directly attributable to their economic strength and also to their military capacity and bureaucratic efficiency. In all but name, this is a decidedly realist interpretation of the world-system.

Two consequences flow from his reasoning. The first is that states are reduced to the admittedly critical performance of a system-integrative function, since it is through their activities that the core–periphery hierarchy is reproduced. In fact Wallerstein is capable of being read as offering a more catholic interpretation of state autonomy than these observations would suggest (Axford and Deacon, 1984) but none of this revisionism finds favour with various critics, particularly those anxious to underscore the dynamic autonomy of state elites from a modified Weberian perspective (Skocpol, 1977; 1981).

The second result is, if anything, more significant for attempts to conceptualize the global system, because the emphasis on broadly economic forces as the organizational principles of the world-system leaves little room for a more voluntarist approach to the structuration of that system. Despite the inclusion of a globalized 'political structure of multiple sovereignties' (Rapkin, 1983, p. 237) as a key element in his conceptualization of a capitalist world-system, Wallerstein still has states as little more than transactors of unequal commodity exchanges. The global division of labour is only 'expressed' in political terms, and the state is a necessary adjunct of, but still subordinate to, the economic system. In other words, the genesis and functioning of the state system follows from the logic of capitalist development expressed in the global division of labour among different production systems. Capitalism creates the state system and states are cap-à-pie primarily because the processes of world-system competition sometimes have to take place through political and military action.

Other possible explanations of the origins of the modern state and of the modern state system are abjured in a treatment of core–periphery relations as being about economic exchange rather than power relations, land-lust and so on. This argument is possible only by treating states as tied to capitalist interests and by allowing a confusion about the connection between state 'strength' and economic success in the world-system. Both Badie and Birnbaum (1983) and John Meyer (1980b) have commented upon the inappropriateness of equating strength in terms of coercive power with the capacity of states to mobilize resources effectively. They point to the important historical fact that the only hegemonic powers in the capitalist world-system – the United Provinces, Britain and the United States – are all notable for their relative statelessness, at least in terms of the key attributes of centralization and institutionalization noted by Badie and Birnbaum (1983).

Wallerstein's conception of world capitalism is that of a chain of production locations in sovereign states linking the world through more or less complex commodity chains. As Bergesen (1990) suggests, this too looks like an unwarranted extrapolation from the European to the global experience, and one which ignores the absence of state forms in the non-European periphery during the critical early period of mercantile expansion. Wallerstein's argument also plays down the non-economic origins and dynamics of states and the system of states. Bergesen (1990) tries to redress this gap by pointing out the part played by *force majeure* in establishing the dominance of core states over peripheral territories, and in underpinning the resulting international division of labour (see also Bergesen, 1980a; 1980b; 1982). His argument, which relies heavily upon the establishment of a global system of unequal exchange through conquest and power relations, is still an attempt to substantiate the idea of a truly global set of social relations, but it stands in opposition both to Wallersteinian analysis and to varieties of orthodox Marxists, for whom the social relations of production are a societal or a regional phenomenon. Bergesen's (1990) account draws upon institutionalist analysis to ground the idea that both realist and utilitarian-functionalist conceptions of the international system of states are invalid. In fact he is suitably cautious about the vexed question of agency–structure relations, especially where difficult issues about the 'real' historical origins of the state system have to be addressed. On balance he prefers the notion that proto-global cultural scripts of various sorts pre-date and to that extent explain the origins of the modern state system.

For Marxists, one of the major difficulties with Wallerstein's formulation of the capitalist world economy is that his conception of a single world-system can be sustained only by clinging to a deviant interpretation of a mode of production (Brenner, 1977). The idea of a single, global capitalist mode of production works only if all factors other than networks of unequal exchange are ignored, and the division of labour becomes simply a description of the terms of trade, leading, says Brenner, to a kind of 'neo-Smithian Marxism'. Following the line of most orthodox Marxists, Brenner goes on to criticize Wallerstein for his failure to understand the centrality of class relations as the defining characteristic of a mode of production, and for failing to recognize that the totality of class relations exists only nationally or regionally, and so cannot be used to derive the existence of a single, global capitalist mode of production.

From a rather different theoretical perspective this is the position of those, like Peter Worsley (1990; 1984), who insist that the world consists of not one but many modes of production, and that the theoretical compression necessary to entertain Wallerstein's holistic argument distorts the characteristic pluralism and autonomy of political, economic and cultural factors. It might be said that the force of Worsley's ideas about the vitality of the Second World now looks a little threadbare in the wake of events in the former Soviet empire, but any autopsy of state socialism cannot be confined to the revolutionizing effects of world capitalist forces, even where, *pace* Wallerstein, these have to be understood as part of a global institution with which the state-socialist bloc was increasingly entwined.

Christopher Chase-Dunn, whose work stands as the most sustained attempt to develop and apply Wallerstein's ideas empirically, is also critical of the latter's holistic assumptions about the singularity of the world-system as a mode of production (Chase-Dunn, 1989; but see also 1988; 1981; 1979). Although he is still at pains to identify the 'deep structures' of world capitalism, Chase-Dunn is prepared to admit the possibility of two or more modes of production within a single world-system or *global formation*. On this reckoning, the world-system or global formation of capitalism subsists through the articulation of societal modes of production with the social institutions of the conceptually wider global social formation. The global formation may well contain the residues of historical modes of production, as well as the seeds of future ones (1989, p. 27). In other words, this is a spatial definition that locates the point of production as the kernel of the whole system, since that is where the reproduction of the system occurs through the exploitation of one class by another.

Chase-Dunn's global formation displays all the structural features of a world-system, namely constants (the interstate system and core and peripheral production), cycles (Kondratieff and hegemonic) and trends (for example, large-scale migration and the transnationalization of capital), and the defining features of both the core–periphery division of labour and the international system of states. Without doubt he goes some way to rescue Wallerstein from his critics, arguing that Brenner in particular misreads an argument whose main concern is not to develop an 'exchangist' or 'circulationist' version of a mode of production over one based on class struggle, but to point up that global commodity exchange takes place in a variety of institutional contexts, some of which are compatible with the continued reproduction of the system, others less so.

Chase-Dunn's account certainly gets Wallerstein off the hook of having to sustain the idea of a global mode of production. However, he still has the problem of translating an essentially societalist concept (mode of production) into a global system. Many Marxists of the dependency school have flirted with the idea of translating class struggle on to a global plane, removing it from the point of production and relocating it as a global relation, but from the point of view of providing a transformative energy for radical change in the system this has always seemed rather fanciful. Bergesen (1990) tries to get round this dilemma by suggesting that the core–periphery relationship is in reality a form of class relationship, based upon both unequal exchange and, more critically, structures of power, with the exploitation of peripheral by core states and their class cohorts. Of late, the concept of mode of production itself has received much critical treatment from within Marxism and from areas influenced by neo-Weberian historical sociology (Anderson, 1974; Hindess and Hirst, 1975).

Wallerstein's world-system theory and the variant provided by Chase-Dunn are basically economic in interpretation. Their analyses of the origins and development of the world-system of capitalism, although different in key respects, share the assumptions that the process of modernity is one of the 'globalizing' of capitalism as a system of unequal exchange. The world-system is integrated by market forces and, as these become diffused, the system becomes stronger through the interaction of its constituent parts in a global division of labour. For all that these arguments offer a 'historically detailed' (Robertson, 1992, p. 12) theory of the transition from *Gemeinschaft*-like social formations to some sort of global *Gesellschaft*, the main line of objection is that this is still too reductionist, particularly as regards the treatment of the state and what may be termed 'cultural' phenomena. As will be shown in chapter 3, Wallerstein's attempts to generate a more 'culture-sensitive' account of world-system formation and transformation centred upon the activities of anti-systemic forces do not, indeed cannot, liberate him entirely from the charge of reductionism.

Nor is the issue of reductionism resolved simply by recourse to more politically rounded positions. A more charitable reading of Wallerstein (1979a) than is allowed by some of his critics reveals an agnostic treatment of the relations between world-economic forces and political actors, such that he is loath to distinguish a logic of the world-economic system from a logic of the interstate system. Lang (1980) even suggests that by volume II of *The Modern World-System* the political realm is viewed as an independent source of world-systemic variation – an interpretation echoed in the claim that much of the opprobrium directed at Wallerstein over his equation of state strength with capitalist interests could be avoided by defining state strength separately from capitalist interests and making the linkage between the two subject to empirical investigation and not reasoned *a priori*. However, this does rather assume a willingness to surrender some key assumptions about the systemic qualities of the modern world-system, and still leaves the problem that Wallerstein has a basically realist presumption about the characteristics of the states operating on his world-economy stage.

The main 'political' rival to Wallerstein's holistic model of the world-system is Modelski's 'long cycle' of global politics approach, in which it is argued that since 1500 a modern, global political system has emerged, and where the systemic agenda is dominated by questions of order, security, territorial rights and trade stability (Modelski, 1978; 1988; 1990; and see McGrew, 1992). This shift of emphasis is reflected too in the increasing interest in the spread of the nation-state form as a global modern institution (Giddens, 1985; Anderson,

1983; Balibar, 1991; Bhaba, 1990) and in the attempts from both anthropology and geography to understand the increasingly global context of national and local cultures (Hannerz, 1990; Appadurai, 1993; Pred and Watts, 1992; Harvey, 1989; King, 1991).

Overall, it is possible to say that the strength of world-system analysis has been its sustained attempt to understand the systematic pattern of relations between societal actors, previously dealt with in isolation or only comparatively. The main difficulty with these attempts to map a 'world-system' consists in seeing the 'modern world' as being made largely under the organizing force of capitalist exchange, and as spreading outwards from the core to the periphery of the world-system. The systemic properties of such a world-system are seen as sufficiently powerful to prescribe the points at which and the ways in which societal entities are incorporated into the system, and there appears little room for what Robertson (1992) calls reflexive engagements between entities at different 'levels' of generality in the world-system, or for the possibility of 'defining' the world in different ways.

Where Wallerstein does allow for pluralism in the making of the modern world-system, empirical insights are rarely connected to the theoretical account. The track to modernity picked out by him is made to do service in the interests of his theory of world-wide system formation, with states and societies playing out their allotted role in the division of labour, and this too is a stark and limited treatment of a rich, varied and contested process, still in the making in many parts of the world. In short, world-system analysis is an important but only partial way of conceptualizing and understanding the making and dynamics of a global system, and of coming to grips with globalization as a process. In chapter 3, I will begin by looking at the ways in which cultural phenomena are dealt with in accounts of the modern world-system.

3 Treating the World as a Social System

Introduction: the cultural component of world-system analysis

From the preceding account it is clear that it would be hard to endorse fully any of the strands of world-system theory. Both the utilitarian-functionalist approach of Immanuel Wallerstein and the even more formal structural analysis offered by Chase-Dunn are flawed by their one-dimensional analysis of the constitution of social life, and thus of the 'systemness', of the world. This one-dimensionality is particularly noticeable in their treatment of cultural factors in the constitution of global systemness. Even the extensive references to cultural phenomena and to culture as the primary intellectual battle-ground of the modern world-system, found in Wallerstein's more recent work, are really only attempts to round out reductionist positions by reference to some semi-autonomous ideological and/or cultural dynamic. But he still retains the central theoretical thrust, which relegates practically all counter-cultural and 'anti-systemic' phenomena to the role of functional, or potentially dysfunctional, bit players in the reproduction of the capitalist world economy (Wallerstein, 1991c, chapters 10–15; 1994). Jonathan Friedman's injunction, that recent marked changes in the 'cultural state of the world' (1989; 1993) have contributed to a crisis of hegemony, finds parallels in Wallerstein's corpus; but, as I will show, the latter's theoretical economism still prevents him from seeing that this is having profound systemic consequences, fragmenting what Friedman calls the 'identity space of the hegemon', where that refers to the whole cultural corpus of Western modernity and not just a single hegemonic power (1993, p. 210).

For Wallerstein, culture is not constitutive in systemic terms, that is in 'creating or defining new forms of behaviour' (Searle, 1965), but only functional for smoothing out the dynamic contradictions in world capitalism. This is a road well travelled by legions of economic reductionists, but it will be useful to look at the revisionism in Wallerstein's recent thinking, since it underscores the continuing weakness in his conception of a world-system. Culture, says Wallerstein, is the 'ideas system' of the capitalist world economy (1991b, p. 166). In its most recent form, this ideas system has been the dominant ideology of liberalism with its individualizing and universalizing credos. Unlike Fukuyama, Wallerstein sees the collapse of the main alternative to liberalism, in the guise of Leninism, not as clear evidence of the triumph of 'Western' ideology, but rather as an augury of the latter's own crisis and ultimate demise. He is able to argue thus, since both Wilsonian liberalism and Leninism are seen as variants of the same ideological consensus, previously hidden by the 'façade' of superpower enmity but, in the aftermath of the Cold War, shown up as still ubiquitous although increasingly brittle (Wallerstein, 1991c, introduction; 1994).

Universalizing liberalism is still the 'geoculture' of the modern world-system, the cultural framework within which global capitalism subsists. It is thus analogous to the concept of 'geopolitics', but in no way a neologism for treating culture as the ideological superstructure of the world-system of capitalism. On the contrary, says Wallerstein, culture is the 'underside' which 'nourishes' the rest (1991c, p. 11 and pp. 158–62). While this appears to rescue the cultural realm from the epiphenomenalism of vulgar Marxism, apart from acknowledging the global reach of a dominant culture and the use of elemental, though obfuscatory, language like 'nourishes', this argument still has a strongly reductionist and functionalist feel to it (see Boyne, 1990). Because culture, or geoculture, is seen to stand as an ideological impediment to any radical transformation of the capitalist world-system, all the old nostrums seem to be firmly in place. But Wallerstein's position has undergone some changes during what he describes as the turbulent mid to late 1980s. The upshot is that, in a reified form, culture now appears as a more strategic zone for confronting the inequalities of the modern world-system, while still remaining marginal in theoretical terms.

The growing strategic importance of cultural phenomena can be traced to the fact that they have become the site of both intellectual and phenomenal struggles to deconstruct the false totality and the universalist pretensions of global liberalism. In other words, forms of cultural resistance to world-system domination appear as the (forlorn) hope of those concerned to oppose the integrative power of the global geoculture. As legitimate expressions of authentic though often suppressed identities, anti-systemic forces and counter-cultural phenomena provide evidence of the underlying cultural asymmetry of a world still ensnared by the ideology of liberalism.

But here too Wallerstein is ambivalent about the theoretical purchase of 'meaning' relative to material factors, and about the extent to which oppositional cultural identities afford a practical demonstration that people have the power to shape their own destinies. On the one hand he acknowledges that the tensions between the 'objective' and material aspects of the world-system (primarily economic and political), and the 'metaphysical presuppositions.' (motivations, culture) of various anti-systemic forces, offer considerable scope for increased conflict, which will, or rather may, work against the logic of the world capitalist system. On the other hand he damns with faint praise, seeing most anti-systemic groups and movements as little more than vehicles for 'sustaining political activity' (Wallerstein, 1991c, p. 12) or, in less studied terms, a form of whistling in the dark. In fact there is some similarity here with Habermas's discussion of crisis tendencies in what he calls 'late capitalism', but without the latter's voluntarism. During this stage of capitalist development, says Habermas (1972), the cultural realm becomes the locus of uncompromised forms of political and cultural activity, because the logic of capitalist development produces identity problems which cannot be contained by an economic system that is only geared to the production of goods to satisfy consumer needs, and which has destroyed many of the non-material contexts upon which people relied for their identity and security. As socially integrative media like religion, family or local traditions are gradually replaced by what Habermas calls steering media, which rely upon bureaucratic and market mechanisms to supply meaning and to secure compliance and identity, the locus of crisis potential is shifted from the economic realm to that of the cultural, as those areas of life come under pressure from the logic of capitalist expansion and state intervention.

For Wallerstein and for Habermas, the translation of identity problems into a politics with transformative potential is nonetheless highly problematic, leading them to search for new and uncorrupted forms of political activism and organization in areas like direct citizen action, ethnic consciousness, gender issues, and the 'rehearsal' for systemic transformation imputed to events across the Western world in 1968 and in Central and Eastern Europe throughout 1989 and 1990 (Habermas, 1984; Arrighi et al., 1989; Wallerstein, 1994).

Wallerstein's revisionism is voluntarism of a sort, but it is hardly incorporated into the theoretical account, and ambivalence remains its most obvious feature. Thus *culture* as an expression of the authentic lived experience or the collective memory of groups, social movements and civilizations does qualify as a locus of potential opposition in a world permeated with, though obviously not entirely conditioned by, the 'culture' of global liberalism. But the latter version of 'culture' remains an enduring problem for any scheme to transform the capitalist world-system through the self-conscious actions of human agents, because it persists as an ideological barrier to the formation and full mobilization of anti-systemic identities. Wallerstein sees that there is a good deal of cultural diversity, but for him this is just a datum rather than an indication of the transformative capacity of competing and antagonistic definitions or models of world order. Anyway, most such potential is cloaked in the shrouds of false consciousness, and vitiated by the extent to which actors accept the legitimacy or the inevitability of the capitalist world order, and are constrained and particularized in their opposition to it. In the sense used by Anthony Giddens, culture, or to be precise the global cultural system of liberalism, functions as a constraint on, rather than as an enabling factor for, anti-systemic forces.

To avoid a gaunt determinism, Wallerstein alludes to the emergence of 'new' and uncompromised cultural phenomena which are capable of challenging the ideology of liberalism, and which will contribute to the demise of the capitalist world-system by providing the basis for a growing cultural disorder, perhaps even laying the ground rules for a new sort of geoculture. At least some of these new forces are seen as capable of mobilization into world-wide anti-systemic movements. The unmasking of racism and sexism as fundamental premises of the old geocultural order, the rejection of the principles of a rationalist science, and the immanent anti-system logic of the collapse of state socialism, all release a disruptive energy which, at the very least, is intensely destabilizing for the capitalist world-system (Wallerstein, 1989; 1991a; 1991b, 1994).

New kinds of anti-systemic movements, some born of what Wallerstein calls the 'world revolution' of 1968, others galvanized by the rejection of usual politics expressed in the Days of May, have taken up the torch from older, compromised forms, mostly of the 'old left' variety (1994, p. 12; 1991a, p. 15). With suitable caution, Wallerstein hedges on the likelihood of all these anti-systemic forces achieving anything like a critical mass and developing a world-wide anti-systemic strategy. Curiously, he also depicts the current 'moment' in the playing out of the world-system, where human agency reappears as a variable in historical change, as one in which the usual system features of constants, cycles and trends are in suspension, and during which uncertainty rules.

In one respect this seems acceptable because, as the world turns, presumably so do the bases of social action. Yet in another sense it all seems rather threadbare, resembling nothing so much as an attempt to paper over the cracks in a theory by resorting to what Alvin Gouldner (1980) called 'paradigm normalization'. This is the practice of treating as anomalous those events and processes which are discommoding to a theory, or else trying to subsume them within its original premises. So, for Wallerstein, unusual circumstances suspend the normal operation of the system, allowing scope for the emergence of new 'disorderly' forces and challenges to the smooth functioning of the capitalist world order. The problem is that, unless critical mass is achieved and results in transformation during such a moment, the resumption of the routine operation of the system must be assumed. In the end, unwilling or unable to specify the tolerances of the world-system in the face of a rejuvenated and unified assault from anti-systemic elements and activist pressures, Wallerstein falls back on the tried, but not tested, formula that the system will collapse under the weight of its own internal contradictions. Uncertainty may be rife after 1989, but *that* certainty remains.

This is harsh, but is not meant to be dismissive. Wallerstein's recent work on the changing world-system is a sustained attempt to come to grips with the new realities of the post-Cold-War era. In fact, Wallersteinian world-system analysis is one of the few areas of social theory which might have 'predicted' the systemic transformation of state socialism in the 1990s. But the lessons of the 1980s, to which he refers in a work published in 1991 (Wallerstein, 1991a), are difficult to learn by way of a theoretical stance still strongly wedded to functionalist analysis and to offering the material facets of the world-system as dominant for explanatory purposes. The problem is that, for all the intellectual turmoil and apparent revisionism seen in his more recent work, the Wallersteinian concept of system dynamics relies on the effective reduction of culture, in the form of Western liberalism, to the 'needs' of global capitalism.

In true functionalist fashion, culture is treated as the realm of normative integration and thus secondary to the integrative power of market relations supported by the political-military power of core states. Chase-Dunn, more of a structural purist in this respect than Wallerstein, is prepared to relegate even the consensus-generating influence of normative factors to the margins of explanatory power, on the grounds that (1) in his estimation there is no world culture, and (2) exchange relations, the real 'glue' of the world-system, require only limited social agreements between buyers and sellers to reproduce the system (1989, chapter 5). Material exchanges in the form of money, commodities and market mechanisms dispense altogether with the need for normative integration, except at a very general level, since they integrate 'behind the backs' of participants (Mouzelis, 1993, p. 271). Although there is a strong tendency to reduce 'culture' to the promotion of a functional normative consensus, even in this respect, its contribution is limited. Apart from the sense that economic factors are insulated from other sorts of social relations, any *active* component of systemness is missing from this account. Wallerstein's position also relies on the idea that counter-cultures or 'alternative metaphysical presuppositions' are merely anti-systemic, and are thus contingent upon shifts in the dominant culture and the material infrastructure both to call them into being and to sustain or to destroy them. Because of this, his treatment of human agency in the possible transformation of the world-system moves between a gut determinism and a grudging voluntarism, with agency generally appearing as a contingent rather than as a constitutive element of world-systemness.

For all this, Wallerstein's recognition of cultural diversity, and of the cultural challenges posed by anti-systemic forces, hints at a more pluralistic definition of the world as a social system. The fact remains, however, that the treatment of culture is tied irrevocably to a functionalist analysis of the health or ill-health of the capitalist world-system. Because the world-system is already configured by the needs of historical capitalism, culture must be either system integrative or, in particularistic and local forms, anti-systemic – and even the latter may contribute to the maintenance of the world-system. In either case, short of the transformative 'critical mass' of opposition needed, the concept of culture in a world-systemic sense has no real significance beyond the degree to which it underpins the existing world-system of capitalism or, acting as a locus and resource for frail human effort, may hasten its supersession.

There are two related consequences for our understanding of the world as a social system. The first is that, in the obvious but critical sense, culture is reduced to structure, and human agency is left as a residual category, more often than not constrained by a dominant cultural systems of ideas. In this, Wallerstein practises what Margaret Archer (1988) calls the 'fallacy of downward conflation', treating culture as the means whereby societies are normatively integrated, thus perpetuating the still powerful 'myth of cultural integration'.

The second consequence in part follows from the first: seeing culture as functional for the maintenance of the world-system of capitalism leaves little room for the possibility that there might be other cultural definitions of the global order, other 'presuppositions' and identities, whose origins have little or nothing to do with the world-system of capitalism (Robertson, 1992). These may take that world-system as a point of reference, but equally they may not. Robertson argues for a multi-dimensional and pluralistic conception of the global system, in which a variety of cultural identities – organizational, local and national as well as international and transnational – are to be seen as constitutive of a world 'still in the process of crystallization' (1992, p. 68).

Now this is not so much a purely 'cultural' definition of the world-system, which in itself would be another form of reductionism, as an appeal both to recognize and to theorize the indeterminate and multi-dimensional character of globalization processes. Robertson's (1992, p. 61) account offers a useful antidote to the over-systematized and reductionist flavour of Wallerstein's argument. The developing focus of Robertson's work has been the overall processes of globalization, which are making the world into one place with systemic qualities, although in fact he prefers the expression 'global field' to 'global system'. The global 'field' is a socio-cultural system which is the result of the 'compression' of 'civilizational cultures, national societies, intra- and cross-national movements and organizations, sub-societies and ethnic groups, intra-societal groups, individuals and so on', such that they are 'constrained to identify' themselves in relation to the global human circumstance, but may not be subsumed by dominant, globalizing pressures (Robertson, 1992, chapters 3 and 4). In order to entertain such an argument, we must suspend the idea that a system has a given or 'core' identity, which resides in one part or element of the system as opposed to another, and maintenance of which 'explains' the continued viability of that system.

Unhappily, Robertson's notion of actors being 'constrained to identify' with the global condition does rather convey the sense of them bowing to circumstances beyond their control, although this is not his intention. My position is that the need to reunite structure and action, which, as Margaret Archer says, is indispensable to sociological explanation, should concentrate on the ways in which actors 'enact' structures and thereby reproduce them, but also on the ways in which individual identities and structures as contexts for action are transformed through the interruption of routine reproduction by more knowledgeable, more insecure, more demanding and reflexive agents.

Functionalist analysis

Most systems-theoretic and functionalist accounts of the constitution of social systems would find difficulty with this prescription. Functionalist approaches are concerned with factors which promote the survival of systems, and these factors, whether in the realms of production or socialization, are assessed in terms of the extent to which they contribute to, or detract from, functionally defined system 'needs' or necessary conditions of existence. In its most socially relevant form, that of Parsonian structural functionalism, the social system – a functional complex of institutions within which cultural values are made binding for social action – strives to achieve or to maintain a desired 'goal state' through the contribution of different 'pattern variables' or 'exigencies' to the maintenance of its overall properties. These 'exigencies' are 'goal attainment', 'adaptation', 'integration' and 'pattern maintenance' (Parsons, 1966; 1971; Smith, 1973), and the survival of the system requires that the 'learning capacity' of the system takes place within the empirically specifiable tolerances laid down in the goal states and goal values.

The key terms 'survival' and 'needs' are closely linked with the important systems concept of 'environment'. Following the lead of Ludwig von Bertalanffy (1968), biological and social systems are often characterized as 'open systems', meaning that the system exists in a state of continuous exchange with its environment, and survival becomes a matter of achieving an appropriate relationship or 'fit' with that environment. Like biological systems, social systems are seen to require adequate control processes (homeostatic processes) to regulate their exchanges with the environment. Without them, it would be very difficult for the system to attain a steady state (homeostasis) and to realize an enduring form. The system is described as open and in constant interaction with its environment, from which it is clearly demarcated, and it creates, but more typically re-creates, the conditions for its own survival by way of functional interdependence internally and through exchanges with or adaptation to the environment.

Now this sort of imagery, which may be suitable for the analysis of organisms in the natural world, breaks down when applied to social systems. Unlike the reproduction of organic life forms, social systems are socially constructed phenomena, 'made' or given identity through the actions of the individuals, groups and organizations which populate them. Because of this, the 'goal states' which figure prominently in functionalist analysis cannot be taken as givens, or as empirically obvious, but are the outcome of the creative activities of human agents, and therefore subject both to the intended and to the unintended consequences of human action.

Two obvious limitations of functionalist reasoning arise from this important insight into how social systems are 'made'. The first is that functionalist accounts rely upon a concept of 'system' that requires 'essential' structures and functions. Challenges to these throw doubts upon the continued viability of the system, but need not be fatal while the homeostatic mechanisms of the system are in good order. These 'essential' elements are held to function within empirically specifiable limits and to be reliable indicators of the viability of the system. But it is much harder to achieve such precision in the case of social systems than it is with organic ones. As a result, much functionalist analysis has taken refuge in both teleology and tautology, by specifying a necessary 'functional unity' wherein all parts of the system work for all the other parts, so that the system is neatly self-regulating, and by defining overriding system needs against which the functional contribution of parts and processes can be judged (see Smith, 1973 for commentary; and also Morgan, 1986).

The second limitation flows from the first. It is not only difficult to conceive of a social system as consisting of a set of processes which express a functional unity, and which work within easily specifiable tolerances, but it is equally difficult to see this putative unity clearly separated from its environment. Nevertheless, the imagery is pervasive: social systems are at one and the same time said to be separate from but in constant exchange with their environment, and either adapt to this environment (as in types of contingency theory) or survive in it through a process akin to 'natural selection', which has been the message of many studies of organizational ecology (Peters and Waterman, 1982; Burns and Stalker, 1961; Boulding, 1956).

Once the idea of social systems as socially constructed through the motives and interpretative actions of human beings is admitted, it is hard to sustain these lines of argument. In the first place, it is quite possible for members of a system to alter their goal values, and thus the goal states of the system. They may not be able to do so heedless of the structural and cultural properties of that system, but this is a long way short of 'essentialism', and a pertinent reminder that the identity of a social system, as well as its learning capacity, is not objectively determined by transcendental system 'needs', but subject to the interpretations and actions of the members of that system (Cohen, 1989; McCarthy, 1978; Sensat, 1979). In the same way, the idea that systems adapt to their environments, or that environments select appropriate systems for survival, has these systems and their members subject to forces operating in an external world, rather than constituted by active agents in the construction of that world. Finally, there is the tenet that systems, as reified actors, are constituted in a way which allows them to recognize and act upon their own needs. The objections to this sort of attribution are numerous, but for current purposes the most critical are those which deny either that systems can behave like agents, that is have volitions, or that they possess capacities which, *in the last instance*, completely negate the interventionist power of agency (see for example Giddens, 1984).

In my interpretation, what functionalists wrongly construe as system 'needs' are the outcomes of how agents interact in conditions where resources are almost always unequally distributed. As Wendt says, in the last analysis, 'agents and structures are produced and reproduced by what actors do. Systemic structures and processes may affect the contexts of interaction, but specific actions are rarely dictated by them' (1994, p. 390). Wallerstein's systems-theoretic approach to the constitution of the world-system encounters many of the problems with functionalist analysis identified above. Its inadequacy lies in the attempt to explain the phenomena of socialization and culture purely functionally, in terms of their contribution to systems maintenance, and in promulgating a form of essentialism in which the 'deep structures' of capitalism give identity to the system and self-evidently embody its 'needs'.

Voluntaristic and multi-dimensional models of the world as a social system

These points are made forcefully by Roland Robertson (1992), who sees the need for a systematic account of the analytically separate but interconnected logics of economics, politics and culture in the making of the world 'as single place', but suggests that aggressively non-functionalist approaches like Giddens's structuration theory and Margaret Archer's culture–agency problematic fail to fit the bill because of their excessive abstractionism. Robertson emphasizes the importance of addressing what he still chooses to call the 'concrete structuration' of the world as a place with systemic qualities, but in the event he too abjures the difficult task of specifying in detail the interrelationships between factors which have facilitated the shifts towards a single world and the more obviously abstract themes of agency, structure and culture (pp. 50–7). In its place is a rich tapestry woven from a permissive or 'voluntaristic' theory of globalization, which turns on the relationships between the universal and the particular as the main axis of the structuration of the world as a whole (p. 102). His argument is agnostic on the 'direction' in which the process of global compression is moving, on what sort of a global system is being produced, while acknowledging the increasing pace and intensity of globalizing pressures. Robertson attempts to steer a course between the gaunt foundationalism of world-system analysis, with its emphasis upon the constraints and totalizing effects of the world-system, and the rash of anti-foundationalist arguments which muster under the banners of poststructuralism and postmodernism, with their anti-categorical and anti-universalizing credos.

Robertson is at pains to emphasize the many tensions which appear in the world cultural space as a result of the interpenetration of universal and particular, of global and local. In systematic terms, each of the elements of the 'global human condition' – which Robertson defines as national societies, individual selves, the world system of societies and humankind – is under constraint from the other three, but the complexity of their interrelationships beggars any attempt to 'fundamentalize' the globalization process or to reduce it to just one dominant set of presuppositions. By the same token, the degree of global complexity and conflicts over the 'definition of the global situation' are seen as evidence of a globalization process which in principle could have proceeded along any one of a number of trajectories and which now shows ever more evidence of disorder and discord.

In fact, Robertson is at one with many other commentaries in identifying the main processes which have driven globalization in recent times: the dynamics of capitalism, the interstate system and the creation of a new international division of labour. But his argument is that these processes, although part of a 'totalizing' tendency, produce global complexity rather than uniformity, because one of their main effects is to 'relativize' or to 'challenge ... the stability of particular perspectives on and collective and individual participation in the overall globalization process' (p. 29). The idea of globalization as a process of relativization usefully clarifies the sense of actors simply being 'constrained' to identify with the global system. 'Constraint' here implies that, increasingly, actors expect to adopt a global 'mind-set' or demeanour, but that individual and collective attempts to make analytical and interpretative sense of the 'global human condition' may include efforts to deny the idea that the world is one, or even to recognize the world as a constraint altogether (p. 26).

Thus one of the paradoxes of a world relativized by the process of globalization is that it breeds a heightened self-consciousness or sense of difference, either as a direct result or as an unintended consequence of global compression. Life-worlds or identities are not just being eroded, willy-nilly, by the growing cultural 'oneness' of the world, and this crucial observation is taken up more fully in chapter 6. Particularistic identities of all kinds can be strengthened or even reinvented as cultures of resistance to the spread of global values. To a degree this is also Wallerstein's point, and in his capitalist world-system accounts for the vitality of the cultural sphere as a source of anti-systemic consciousness and action. But Robertson's argument is that these outcomes and the possible creation of what Stuart Hall calls 'hybrid identities', which are neither new nor traditional, neither local nor global, are all part of the contradictory and paradoxical processes of globalization (Hall, 1992, pp. 310–14). For Robertson, questions about the degree to which globalization implies homogenization as opposed to fragmentation, and universalization as opposed to particularization, are seen as crucial to the structuration of the global system.

At the same time, it is clear that Robertson too is cautious about the use of the term 'system', because although the world is held to exhibit systemic properties, the idea of the world is 'not exhausted by its systemic qualities' (1992, p. 13). It is thus only 'convenient' to speak of a global 'system', and more appropriately cautious to identify a global 'field', which avoids the sense that the systemic whole dominates the constituent parts. Perhaps understandably, he is anxious to distance himself from what Boris Frankel dismissively calls 'homogenizing' systems theory, conveniently summarized in Wallerstein's account of a capitalist world-system and consisting of a succession of hegemonic and core states presiding over the unfolding stages of world-system development (Frankel, 1983, p. 178).

Frankel's own revisionist Marxist critique of the simplified social reality of the world-system and modes of production analyses rejects the teleology of the former in favour of a theory of the *desynchronization* of key processes in contemporary capitalism. He identifies these processes as electoral, production, credit and food production – and says that they operate at local, national and supranational levels, producing crisis phenomena as the result of the interactions and tensions within and between them. The analysis is in some ways similar to Ilya Prigogine's (1984) work on disorderly systems or 'dissipated structures', although Frankel's interest lies in demonstrating the difficulties of producing systemic order from the wide variety of behaviours and interests seen in his decentralized system and desynchronized processes.

In one respect Frankel's (1983) argument is simply a restatement of the familiar complaint against Wallerstein, which is that he misconceives the true identity of capitalism, and reduces world-historical complexity to a one-dimensional, global mode of production. More tellingly, it is also a plea not to impart the undoubted growing inter-dependence between local subjects and global processes with the pro-perties of systemicity. World-historical change has produced, not system and order, but 'organized anarchy' (p. 179) which inhibits (Frankel says prevents) the possibility of the successful regulation and management of the 'capitalist world'. The very idea of a single world-system, let alone one socially integrated or coordinated in hierar-chical fashion, as prescribed in both utilitarian and structuralist versions of world-system analysis, is ruled out of court. Instead, the world is full of complexity, and in fact is so characteristically com-plex that the reproduction of social relations becomes a matter of contingency.

This is light years away from the symmetry of economistic world-system analysis. At the core of these objections is the sheer improbabi-lity of systemic order in face of decentralizing processes or competing definitions of global order, in other words in face of palpable dis-order, and the message is that systems-analytic approaches cannot capture the complexity and the indeterminacy of global conditions which are subject to ever-increasing flux and change. In chapter 8, I will examine the idea that disorder too must be understood as systemic and that treating with disorder as a property of social sys-tems requires not the debunking of the concept 'system', but its reworking. In the rest of this chapter I propose to examine a number of positions which self-consciously attempt to explore the organiza-tion of social relations either from outside a systems perspective or from within some modified systems framework, or else reject the usefulness of talking about social relations in an ordered sense at all. I then intend to offer a further critique and development of structura-tion theory and institutionalist analysis, as a means of grasping the complexities of global systemness.

Non-system metaphors for depicting the global condition

Global fields

The principal coordinating mechanisms in the world-system per-spectives of Wallerstein and Chase-Dunn are those of the market, which organizes exchanges between buyers and sellers, and the hierarchy of the international system of states, which reproduces inequalities in the notionally equal relationships between the parties to market exchanges. But market and hierarchy do not exhaust the range of mechanisms for social coordination. In a well-known paper published in 1984, Aristide Zolberg, as an aside to a wholesale rejection of the linking of 'world' with 'system', offers a less demanding heuristic device with which to depict the 'unruly process of the interpenetration' between a variety of social processes at the societal and the extrasocietal levels (pp. 284–5).

Drawing on the work of Pierre Bourdieu (1984), he likens these processes to the different forces and flows at work in a 'global field'. The main features of this field in its present condition are what he calls 'statist societies' (for others, just states, or nation-states). These societies are connected by way of an increasing variety of interactions and flows: some act as constraints upon globalizing or unifying tendencies and forces, like the particularizing force of nationality translated into immigration law and policy; others serve to intensify interpenetration or at least interaction, for example by exposing national cultures to the flows of an increasingly transnational communications industry. Statist societies, which in many respects sunder or fragment the world because of their very exclusiveness, have never existed in isolation and their widespread appearance across the world is also a constitutive feature of the identity of each. In other words, individual states are what they are because of their shared identity of 'statehood'.

In the name of theoretical abstinence, Zolberg forbears to specify the manner in which and the conditions under which global economic, political and cultural structures interact as 'interdependent determinants'; but, once again, his stress on the indeterminateness of globalization processes is a useful correction to holistic accounts of the world-system. However, references to the intensification of interaction, or to the interconnectedness within and between states and societies, or even to the 'intensification of patterns of interconnectedness' (Held, 1992, pp. 32–3), appear at worst as circumlocutions, and at best cautious travellers in the difficult realm which lies between the holism of functionalist systems analysis (and other meta-narratives) and the radical deconstructionism of those who oppose grand theories and meta-narratives.

Postmodernist social theory and globalization

The attractiveness of postmodernist ideas lies in their rejection of conventional ways of looking at social relations, particularly through their critique of the central sociological concept of society and their denial of modernist 'givens' like 'subject' and 'object' or 'author' and 'text' (McGrew, 1992; George, 1994, p. 192). They direct attention away from the national, the societal and the endogenous as the key focal points of social investigation and social explanation (Smart, 1993). Postmodernist writings mirror the disorderliness and the plurality which are characteristic of the processes of globalization. However, while postmodernist representations of social reality may echo the sense of globalization as a tortured and irresolute process, most postmodernist epistemologies do not address themselves directly to the global circumstance, being rather more exercised by the nature of social inquiry than by its objects (Parker, 1993).

It is difficult to convey the range and complexity of postmodernist thinking in a limited space but, in order to address its uses and limitations for my purposes, a brief excursion is necessary. The concept of *difference* has been most widely used by postmodernists, along with a profound scepticism for grounded categories and foundational truths. For authors like François Lyotard (1984) the world is a complex and irreducible 'plurality', and what is usually called 'the social' displays an almost infinite variety of 'discourses' or 'language games' (Jessop, 1990, p. 291; McLennan, 1992, p. 338; Derrida, 1976). In fact the social is coterminous with these discursive practices, making holistic concepts like 'society' largely empty of meaning (Laclau and Mouffe, 1987; Laclau, 1988). Instead, meaning and identity are derived solely from such discourses or narratives, whether of a social, a religious, a political or an entirely personal kind. Thus knowledge of the world and experience of it too are completely subjective, and the social is no more than the outcome of contingent relations or articulations between various discourses, none of which is inherently 'privileged' over any other, for there are no 'irreducible realities' (George, 1994, p. 222). For all this, in Laclau and Mouffe's attempt to ground a 'post-Marxist' discourse analysis, while the possibility of society is ruled out, they do admit the possibility of partial, 'totalizing' projects in which a discourse can achieve hegemony through a chain of (still) contingent connections. Even in such circumstances, the possibility of complete closure, and thus the achievement of full identity, is circumscribed by the open character of the social, and by the relativized and subjective quality of discourses.

It has to be said that there is a liberating quality about much of this sort of thinking when set against 'objective' treatments of the constitution of social life, and without doubt it affords a purchase on some of the features of a world frantically 'deconstructing' old identities and reconstructing others, but it also has a number of difficulties. First, the incredulity over meta-narratives presumably must extend to the analysis of globalization, although the stress on 'difference' is itself a useful antidote to the idea of globalization as a totalizing process. Second, as a normative concern, the post-modernist insistence on the 'irreducible heterogeneity of language games' and the plurality of voices (Lyotard, 1984) calls into question the whole Enlightenment project of universal political emancipation. I will return to this question in chapter 8. Third, as Jessop indicates, there is an unyielding psychologism at work in much of this litera-ture, which results from the 'obsessive desire to avoid reifying social structures and to insist on the discursive construction of reality' (1990, p. 298). This in turn produces a kind of methodological indi-vidualism which is even more abstract than that found in most strains of empiricist phenomenology and ethnomethodology. While the intensive pluralization of life-worlds, and the frantic making and remaking of identities, are indeed features of a globalized world, in arguments which 'deconstruct' the social it is *only* the discursive practices of individuals which are eligible for analysis, and the corol-lary for 'life-world', namely 'system', is neglected (Bhaskar, 1976; 1979).

Thus identity formation, which is so crucial to postmodernist analysis, takes place in an 'institutional vacuum' (Mouzelis, quoted in Jessop, 1990, p. 298) and the relations between agency and struc-ture are rendered conveniently unproblematic. Apart from being a highly abstract form of action theory, these positions give no clue as to how institutions both facilitate and inhibit action, and because of this they are only partial accounts of the constitution of social systems. Put another way, they 'tend to emphasize the psychic meaning of discourses, at the expense of social experience' (Jessop, 1990, p. 299) and thus fail to recognize that the complexity of social life can be glimpsed, but not fully understood, through the lens of individual sub-jectivity. The significance of postmodern views on the transformation of personal and collective identities is taken further in chapter 8.

Networks and flows

By contrast, network analysis (Hannerz, 1990; 1992a; Emirbayer and Goodwin, 1994) offers an altogether more systematic picture of the organization of global social relations, noting both the frames of meaning used by actors and the circumstances in and on which they act. In Jessop's (1990) terms, this involves recognizing both how an actor constructs identity from among available meanings, and the nature of the reflexive relationships between the actor and a notionally external world which is both natural and social. Writing more out of the traditions of macro-anthropology than action theory, Ulf Hannerz suggests treating what he calls the 'global ecumene' as a network of networks, where individuals and groups are drawn 'into a more globalized existence' (1992, p. 47; Craven and Wellman, 1974; Wellman and Berkovitz, 1988).

The advantages of network analysis for the study of globalization are obvious. In the first place, networks can be both intra- and inter-organizational and can cut across more conventional units of analysis to clarify linkages which exist between different personal and institutional domains. Further, and perhaps most appropriate to the global setting, the concept of networks allows social relationships to be examined without the constraint of place and the need for face-to-face encounters. Networks can include relationships which are symmetrical and reciprocal, like those between members of an 'intellectual community' which spans territorial boundaries and cultures, but the linkages can be more 'one-directional' depending on what Massey calls the 'power geometry' involved and how individuals use the various media at their disposal (1991, pp. 25–6). For example, the kind of linkage fashioned through the global availability of the cultural products of the American entertainments industry – game shows, television soaps   may look more like a form of cultural diffusion than network formation, but the actual power directionality of relationships which involve 'flows' of cultural products is contingent upon their reception and use by participants in particular locales.

Hannerz's immediate concern is with the cultural forms of globalization and with the ways in which local and global social relationships are articulated, and either reproduced or modified by sustained and 'fleeting encounters'. World-system analysis portrays the reconstruction or adaptation of local cultures in response to the impact of Western capitalism, and other areas of research, mainly from anthropology and cultural studies, emphasize the growing cultural homogenization of the world through the diffusion of popular cultures and the ideology of consumerism (Mattelhart, 1983). But the network perspective, no less concerned with the processes through which the world is becoming culturally integrated, draws attention to those increasingly widespread and diverse networks – of business men and women, of exchange students, of international pen-pals and of diasporas – whose relationships may either be long-distance or involve mixtures of presence and absence, of coming together and moving apart, or of 'brief encounters' on the telephone, which are all part of the routine and the more torrid flows of globalization. Now it might be argued that networks, like those policy networks which have established a transnational policy space in the European Union, are not 'networks of meaning' at all, although they may modify the behaviour of actors (Wendt, 1994). This is an important distinction, and I want to tackle it more fully in chapters 5 and 6; but whether or not policy networks in the European Union are contributing to the formation of a European consciousness must be treated first and foremost as an empirical question.

The strength of the network metaphor is that it captures the openness of social relationships which do not involve only economic or market exchanges, and are not just governed by administrative rules, the systematic use of power or the constraints of place. To that extent it shares some of the anti-categorical fervour seen in postmodernist writing. The network idea stresses complementarity and commitment, as well as accommodation between individuals and collective actors, in which the key 'entanglements' are those of reciprocity and trust (Powell, 1991, p. 272). However, just as market relations and administrative forms of rule also rely on reciprocity and trust, for example between consumers and producers in conditions of perfect information, or between public servants and citizen claimants, so networks are unlikely to be entirely pacific entities, from which conflict and power are completely absent.

For all this, the network metaphor points up many features of globalization which are not easily explainable in terms of markets or power relations. We can gain insights into a world becoming more integrated, but see that the processes of integration may be 'more pluralistic ... decentralized and mutable' than is often assumed (Marcus and Fischer, 1986, quoted in Hannerz, 1992a, p. 36). In place of or as well as the image of a world being made one either through a creeping process of cultural assimilation or diffusion, or through a more conflictual process in which cultural particularisms fight a rearguard action against the spread of market forces, network analysis portrays a looseness and a diversity which capture the inchoate character of globalization and afford a glimpse of the diverse contexts through which a more acute consciousness of the world is occurring for many people.

Because of this, examination of the ways in which networks are established and spread, as well as how they wither and perish, will throw light on the cultural patterns and flows in the global system, and I shall return to this question in chapter 6 (Hannerz, 1992a). For the moment it can be said that the idea of the global system as a network of networks is a plausible one, which affords some new and useful insights into the relations between agency and the structures of culture. Perspective, and even identity, result from the meaning which an individual appropriates from the different 'realities' with which that agent is in contact. These realities may be more or less formal structures (rules of various kinds) and can also include the perspectives of others, of which the agent has to make sense. Culture is better seen as a kind of enactment (Weick, 1979) in which individuals construct their everyday world of shared meanings and points of reference. Even this model may be too passive a conception of the ways in which individuals construct identities, which require the use of active verbs like 'appropriate' and 'interpret'. These describe more active and reflexive engagements between agents and the social institutions with which they have to deal.

From the network perspective, culture as a collective phenomenon is no more than a network of individual perspectives (Hannerz, 1992a). This may look like relying on the theoretical possibility of a cultural whole being created out of the random connection of individual discourses, but, unlike entirely subjectivist accounts, network analysis sees the organization of social relations as the interaction between agents and social phenomena that have a kind of 'objectivity' for the agent because they constitute more or less enduring contexts for action (Giddens, 1993; Meyer et al., 1987).

From a global perspective, it is clear that networks which involve the exchange of material resources, or the management of power relations, have often treated place as secondary to the global reach of the activity and the network. For example, for networks of commodity dealers on the world market, place has meaning only to the extent that local factors impinge upon the smooth functioning of the globalized market, through civil war, famine or change of regime. On the other hand much sociological analysis of culture has, for the most part, treated it as the property of particular territories. Hannerz suggests that culture treated as a collective phenomenon should be understood to belong to social relationships and their networks, and only derivatively to particular territories (1992a, p. 40). But this is too sweeping a claim which, in its most radical form, reduces locality to a space through which meanings flow, rather than viewing it as a possible context for identity formation. However, it has the signal virtue of admitting all relationships and all channels through which the production and reproduction of meaning occur as eligible for analysis, and making it easier to see how meanings are organized in the varied connections between the local and the far-away.

Autopoiesis

The construction of meaning and identity is a key factor in explaining the production and reproduction of social systems. If we think of culture as the medium through which people create and re-create the worlds in which they live, in other words as a process of 'enacting' and interpreting reality, this is a much more dynamic conception than one which depicts actors as living in a reality with objective, 'external' characteristics which impinge on their actions, often without mediation. The idea of an 'enacted' reality implies not just following rules, but invoking rules as a way of making sense of circumstances. It also collapses the conventional distinction between agent, system and environment, and modifies the way of looking at how systems change over time. Rather than assuming that a system adapts to an environment, or that the environment selects appropriate system configurations for survival, the understanding here is that processes of enactment and interpretation enable actors to intervene in creating and re-creating their identities (Morgan, 1986, p. 241). What were previously defined as separate realms are now better seen as a complex unified system of interactions.

The idea that systems enact their environments receives support from work which is conceived as part of the 'grand tradition' in social theory, and which is loosely functionalist but also consciously anti-Parsonian. This theory, or rather group of theories, is derived from pioneering work in physics and biology (Maturana and Varela, 1980) and to date has attracted only limited support in its application to social systems (Zeleny, 1981; Luhmann, 1982a; 1982b; Teubner, 1988). Functionalist approaches to social systems are predicated on the assumption that change originates in the environment. Usually the system is depicted as 'open' and in permanent interaction with its environment, transforming inputs of various kinds into outputs, always in ways appropriate for its survival.

Against this view is a novel formulation which argues that living systems are characterized by three main features: *autonomy*, *circularity* and, most important of all, *self-reference*. Such systems are capable of self-reproduction through a closed system of relations or, in the term coined by Maturana and Varela, by *autopoiesis*. Autopoietic systems try to achieve a form of closure in relation to their environments, which act as sources of disturbance and of potential change. The key point about autopoietic systems however is that such change as occurs from the system's *structural coupling* with its environment is governed by that system's understanding of its own identity – in other words, through self-referencing.

Thus changing is the result of the combined effect of the system's pre-existing identity, called by some its 'principles of organization', and the nature and degree of disturbance originating in the environment, which can include other autopoietic systems. Consequently the idea of change being caused by internal as opposed to external factors becomes redundant. Now, while autopoiesis is maintained by way of structural coupling, so that changes occur which are not system threatening, there is also the possibility of the complete destruction of the system when environmental disturbances are so great that the system cannot change sufficiently to meet them and still retain its identity. So, many of the difficulties which all kinds of systems experience in dealing with their environments are closely related to the sort of identity they have and are trying to maintain (Morgan, 1986, p. 240).

As a metaphor for grasping some of the complexities of the global system, the concept of autopoiesis has a number of advantages, not the least of which is that it emphasizes the endogenous sources of identity and change, those which stem from the self-referential processes which organize and reproduce environments (p. 268). But, perhaps more tellingly, it has a number of serious disadvantages. Still on the credit side, there is the commitment to the radical autonomy of the systems and subsystems which make up the autopoietic universe. No single, functionally dominant subsystem can determine development in a social universe which is so 'differentiated and polycentric'; no one coordinating mechanism has a handle on the diversity of interactions, organizations and institutions which populate the global stage (Jessop, 1990, p. 320). Pluralism rules, but the downside is that, in its most pristine form, so does a particularly extreme type of contingency, which stems from the notion of the social being no more than a series of self-closed systems, whose relations are entirely a product of happenstance. Autopoiesis is thus a 'quintessentially postmodern paradigm' (Zolo, 1990–1).

As Jessop points out, such a view is incompatible with the very idea of interdiscursivity, let alone that of functional interdependence. It is thus too committed to a view of social systems in which stability and change result from factors internal to those systems. In addition, the idea of system closure, or self-reference, sits a mite uneasily with the idea of a global 'systemness' constituted by the intersection of multiple social systems, which are not separate from, but 'embedded' in, many others. And the concept of 'self-referencing' presents further difficulties when used in the context of 'closed' systems, since the 'observation' or 'monitoring' of the self can take place only in a context which is supplied 'internally' rather than, for example, through the reflexive monitoring of the 'real world' by agents who recognize its 'objectivity'.

So, to be in any way persuasive as an organizing concept, self-closure must surely have limits when faced with the need for private discourses to be intelligible to the wider unity, and autonomy must be circumscribed where 'disjunctions in the evolution of independent subsystems threaten the survival of the whole' (Jessop, 1990, p. 320). There is of course a strongly functionalist quality to this line of objection, and it might be rejected on these grounds alone. Even in its own terms, however, autopoietic theory needs some mechanism to turn the chance 'coevolution' of mutually indifferent systems and the chance interactions of agents into the functional interdependence of parts of a social system.

Of course in practice there are obviously a variety of ways in which self-referentially autonomous systems can be connected or coupled. This would involve a process of reflexive monitoring and learning by subsystems, so that (in 'normal' circumstances) knowledge of the dynamics of other systems results in changes which still maintain the system's 'core' identity, with any modifications falling within the learning tolerances of the subsystems involved. In the global system, the radical autonomy of local systems is modified by the host of formal and informal networks – interdiscursive, economic, political, religious and so on – which cross the boundaries of localities. These networks may result in the fragmentation of local identities, but they can also serve to intensify homogenization in local (or internal) constructions of the (external) world. The outcomes might be intensified forms of local cultural resistance, or the transformation of local identities and local contexts.

At the heart of the autopoietic metaphor is the very postmodern idea of contingency and, in Niklas Luhmann's assault on the Parsonian tradition, this appears as a sort of 'contingency functionalism' (Fuchs, 1991). Whereas Parsons's structural functionalism emphasized stability, consensus and the 'unproblematic cultural "givenness" of social order', Luhmann stresses change, conflict and the unlikelihood of order (Fuchs, 1991, p. 455). In Luhmann's contingency functionalism there are apparently no essentials, only the dynamic self-reflection of autonomous subsystems, linked contingently with each other. Social order, including degrees of disorder, emerges as a result of (improbable) adjustments between the identities of autonomous units.

One of the difficulties, or rather one of the confusing aspects, of this revisionist version of general systems theory is the place within it of knowledgeable human agents. On the face of it, the idea that systems enact their environment would seem to support the argument that agents actively and self-referentially construct social reality, but the status of 'personal systems' (as Luhmann calls them) or agency within autopoietic theory remains problematic. Inevitably, different readings of Luhmann are possible. In one version he appears to reject the interactionist argument that agents actively construct social reality. The concept of system in use here is that criticized by Habermas (1970; 1971; 1973) in his defence of the autonomy of personal life-worlds struggling against colonization by the 'reified' instrumental systems of the state and the economy.

Against this view is a sense that Luhmann's concept of 'systemness' is much closer to the hermeneutic and normative traditions than many have assumed. Autopoietic theories clearly need some sort of 'phenomenological turn', as this would provide one way to deal with their central problematic, namely that, if social order is only the unlikely aggregate of several autopoietic subsystems, it has to explain not only the self-closure of such systems, but the structural coupling which produces and sustains a 'society effect' from among autonomous subsystems (Jessop, 1987; 1990, pp. 329–31). It is clear that subsystems can be connected by common structures, for example laws which regulate economic behaviour, or through policy networks which link individuals and roles in a more or less formal manner across space and time. Or they can be connected through the self-referential but interdiscursive activities of agents, which may take a variety of forms: direct communications between individuals occupying different roles in different subsystems, communications between organizations, and so on. Producers and consumers in a market relationship are an obvious example of communication across subsystems, but, less obviously, so is the work of the social worker who, in certain circumstances, operates across the boundaries of the health care, judicial and social welfare subsystems.

Put like this, relations between subsystems look less like blind 'coevolution' and more like functional interdependence. Indeed, Luhmann adopts a functionalist stance when he argues that autopoiesis is possible to the extent that each subsystem performs a necessary function for societal reproduction (for a critique, see Jessop, 1987; Zolo, 1990–1). More than this, he offers a further gloss on the possibility of social order, which relies heavily upon the singular integrative properties of the economic subsystem in capitalist formations, which are likely to make it dominant in relations with other subsystems or, in autopoietic terms, which enable it to exert a greater capacity for disturbance. Thus while the functional differentiation and complex social division of labour of modern societies make it very unlikely that any one functional subsystem will be able to occupy pole position in a hierarchy of subsystems, or to act as the primary means of integration, because it possesses a degree of organized complexity and flexibility the economic subsystem is likely to be more privileged then the others. Although this is not Luhmann's intention, it is only a very short walk from here to the reintroduction of the primacy of the economic, even if only in the last instance.

At the last, the whole issue of the 'coevolution' or the structural coupling of autonomous subsystems remains problematic. The reintroduction of an interactionist perspective ameliorates this problem by admitting, or appearing to admit, that the identity or goal states of subsystems are the product of the 'self-referential microconstruction' of social order, in other words of deliberation by knowledgeable agents possessing differential resources (Berger and Luckmann, 1966). The difficulties are not resolved, however, since a recognition of the importance of agency is only part of the issue. It is the relationships between social forces (actors) and systemic properties which reveal the 'systemness' of the social system, and the manner of their interconnectedness which offers a clue to the dynamics of change. It is to these issues that I now want to turn.

Systemness revisited

Let me recap briefly. Any real attempt to grasp the *systemness* of the global system has to ask the key question: 'how is such a system possible?' This is not just a matter of cataloguing the various manifestations of stability and change. Rather, it needs a way to understand just how the system is structured through the articulation of human agency with social structures and with the structures of culture (Archer, 1988). The views of social life and of the global condition canvassed earlier in this chapter and in chapter 2 either relegate agency to the rim of social explanation, as in Wallerstein's conception of a world-system in which actors are confronted by the realities of an objectified world economy, or else imbue structures with a plasticity to the point where they no longer have any substance independent of the constructed realities of autonomous agents. The latter positions often go beyond social constructionism or forms of 'constructivism' (Gusterson, 1993; Koslowski and Kratochwil, 1994;

Wendt, 1987) to embrace different styles of postmodernist thinking (Derrida, 1976; Foucault, 1972; Lyotard 1984).

I have criticized both system-centred and actor-centred theories of social life from a variety of perspectives, and the burden of the argument thus far is that, in Margaret Archer's words, 'action and structure presuppose one another, structural patterning is inextricably grounded in practical interaction. Simultaneously ... social practice is ineluctably shaped by the unacknowledged conditions of action' (1988, p. 59). Such practices produce both intended and unintended consequences, which in turn form the basis or context for further interaction. In saying this I do not want to suggest that social practice is shaped only by the 'unacknowledged conditions of action'. For example, in the international system of nation-states, the global institution of 'sovereignty' is completely 'visible' as a norm or script against which the behaviour of states can be judged and their legitimacy measured (Koslowski and Kratochwil, 1994, p. 222).

None of this is too startling when applied to the analysis of social systems in general, although there are no uncontested positions on how social systems are constituted. Used to analyse global systemness, however, even this broad prescription opens up conceptual possibilities denied in the one-sided 'systemic' accounts which have dominated discussion in this area until recently. Over the years there have been substantial attempts to reunite structure and action, whether from the perspectives of humanistic Marxism, or through revisionist strains of interactionism (Archer, 1988, pp. 59ff). Of late, these venerable themes have been given new life in the structurationist perspective, most closely identified with the work of Anthony Giddens but also with that of Pierre Bourdieu (1977; 1990) and in the writing of those sometimes designated as 'institutionalists' or even 'new institutionalists (for extended comment on 'new' institutionalism see Cammack, 1992).

Although Giddens and Bourdieu are writing out of rather different intellectual traditions, with Giddens strongly influenced by Goffman and the ethnomethodologists, and Bourdieu by ethnomethodologists like Marcel Mauss (1979a; 1979b), they share a concern to assign equal weight to action and to structure. The institutionalists on the other hand cleave to the idea that social action is highly structured by institutionalized rules, where the latter refer to the broad patterning of social structure around general, constitutive rules or norms. Institutions are 'cultural rules giving collective meaning and value to particular entities and activities, integrating them into larger schemes' (Meyer et al., 1987, p. 21). Thus the existence and characteristics of actors are seen as socially constructed, but remain highly problematic because 'action is the result of broad institutional scripts, or cultural accounts, rather than a matter of internally generated and autonomous rational choice, motivation and purpose' (p. 22). At first sight this view of action as 'scripted' is a far cry from the main burden of the structurationist perspective on the constitution of social life, and both are a long way from providing a handle on the constitution of the global system. In fact, a modified reading of both positions suggests the possibility of reconciliation, for while both have weaknesses as tools for empirical research, they offer clues for an improved reading of global systemness (but see Krasner, 1994; Wendt, 1994).

The core of the structurationist project is to unite structure and culture, to recognize that the constitution of social systems consists of a mutually constitutive 'duality' of agency and structure, wherein the 'creativity of actors in introducing cultural metamorphosis is mirrored by its opposite, the "ruttedness" of recursively produced actions, actions which are generated by drawing upon and thus reproducing cultural rules' (Archer, 1988). Thus what are conventionally known as structures or institutions are both 'the medium for and the outcome of the contingently accomplished activities of situated actors' (Giddens, 1984, p. 25). Actors reproduce systems through the routine operation of their interaction with institutional rules of one sort or another. Rules as social institutions consist of two broad types. Searle (1965) distinguishes *regulative* practices which prescribe and proscribe behaviour in defined circumstances, and *constitutive* rules which 'create and define new forms of behaviour'. As well as their effects on behaviour, as constitutive frameworks for action, rules also 'validate the ontological status of actors by providing the broad cultural frameworks for the sort of social arrangements that are possible' (Barrett, 1992). Social units, for example those actors in European policy networks, reinforce the constructed social and cultural reality by 'ritualizing, codifying and transmitting cultural products' (Barrett, 1992).

The key point here is that structure is not 'external' to individuals but instantiated in social practices, and thus both constrains and (critically) enables action. All social systems have structural properties, that is they possess social forms and institutions that pre-exist and outlast individual actors, and which 'codify' rules and provide resources. This is an important point, since it corrects the tendency to see structures or institutions simply as extensions of individual self-identities. Otherwise, there is the risk of turning the reflexive activity of *strategic monitoring* into little more than 'an interplay between action and meaning, in which actors continually discover who they are through a looking-glass process that allows for no level of reality external to the phenomenological situation itself' (Meyer et al., 1987, p. 23). At the same time, institutional rules only appear as structural constraints, where it can be shown that the individual agent is unable to change them, and even then they exercise no necessary dominion over human actors. Generally, structures are better understood as contexts which supply meaning and legitimacy for actors and their actions.

But while structures define both the rules (which consist of techniques, procedures and norms of greater or lesser generality) guiding action, and the resources (both authoritative and allocative) empowering action, agents do not just reproduce structures through routine patterns of behaviour. They also have the potential to transform structures and to change the world by engaging in reflexive action over time. Of course, change does not have to be transformative, that is, altering the constitutive rules of the system, since the reproduction of systemic structures allows for modest amounts of change, provided that this occurs without breaching any constitutive rules.

The power of individual actors to change rules is central to this formulation, but in a globalized world the scope for effective interventions by individuals may be limited because social relations are increasingly ordered without the benefit of intimate, face-to-face contacts. Agents confront not just local rules and resources in local contexts, but those operating at a very general level, including societal and world-wide institutional forms. The resources at their disposal may be of limited use, and in such circumstances it is difficult to see both how individuals might intervene to some effect, and what form their interventions might take. It is also hard to grasp how a system can be transformed simply through routine or practical orientations to rules and resources which are themselves the medium for and the outcome of action by agents (Mouzelis, 1993; Whittington, 1992).

These are legitimate concerns, but can be dealt with by acknowledging the part played by collective actors, like consumer groups, environmental organizations and transnational social movements, in both the maintenance and the transformation of social relations, where face-to-face action is not the norm. Individuals may be relatively powerless, despite what Giddens calls their 'habitual theorizing' over the conditions of everyday life, which allows them to adopt a more strategic orientation towards the rules affecting their lives (1993, p. 6). But as part of some collective, organized action they are engaged *consciously* in processes which bear upon rule maintenance or change, rather than being implicated in these things just by being there.

My concern here is not just to demonstrate that individuals in their everyday practices 'connect to' global outcomes, for example in the sense that what a person eats or drives is in some way linked to questions of global ecology (Giddens, 1993, p. 6), but to suggest a medium through which conscious agency can use the rules and resources 'supplied by' system structures to influence matters. Now Mouzelis (1989) says that such a recognition requires an analytical dualism or separation between agency and structure, mainly because the concept of duality of structure cannot handle either collective action, or forms of interaction which are not face-to-face. In other words the growing probability that agents have to 'confront' structures (rules and resources) in large-scale, rather than purely local, environments requires the micro-macro distinction. This seems to me to be less of a problem than implied, because it is possible to acknowledge the 'objectivity' of wider, even global, social and cultural contexts, and their importance in providing frameworks or 'memory traces' for action, and still see that social reality is 'made' or constructed through social interaction (Giddens, 1984, p. 17; see also Whittington, 1992, p. 704).

So the question is, under what conditions and what rules does interaction take place? Mouzelis suggests that the power of individual agency is likely to be confined to local and face-to-face situations; however, while this has a common-sense appeal about it, it fails to recognize that the scope for effective agency turns not on the spatial reach of the relationships or interactions involved, but on questions of power and on the ability of agents to appropriate rules and resources for purposes of social critique. This is the burden of Giddens's emphasis on the significance of 'institutional reflexivity', or the institutionalization of an investigative and calculative attitude towards the general conditions of system reproduction (1993, p. 6). The institutionalization of reflexivity through the various institutions of the Western cultural account requires that actors constitute social reality by legitimating frameworks for action which have meaning, or in Giddens's sense 'objectivity', for them. This is not a conflation of agency and structure (Callinicos, 1989; Clegg, 1989; Mouzelis, 1989; and, from an international relations perspective, Krasner, 1994), since these frameworks are more than projections of subjectivity on to the 'external' world; they subsist as scripts of great social and cultural power, which supply rules and resources and carry meaning, often regardless of the actuality of the situation as this is seen by individual actors. Alexander Wendt provides a useful illustration of this argument in his discussion of the 'structural context' which was the Cold War (1994, p. 389). Although he wishes to interpret the Cold War as a 'discursive structure' and an intersubjective phenomenon rather than just a material one, he notes that worlds which are 'defined intersubjectively' are not necessarily malleable, since 'intersubjective constructions confront actors as obdurate social facts. Sometimes structures cannot be changed in a given historical context' (p. 389).

The key point is whether and how agency uses available rules and resources, or structural properties, to reproduce itself and the contexts which supply meaning. The part played by agency in the reproduction and transformation of structure can now be seen in the ways in which social institutions, as frameworks for action, are initiated, legitimated and diffused by the practice of situated actors in transmitting cultural products both in their everyday practices and through more conscious or 'distanced' interventions, for example as members of transnational networks. Seen in this light, the institutionalization of reflexivity, so characteristic of modernity, must also be dealt with as a constructed cultural reality or framework, with its reproduction increasingly problematic given radically changing circumstances and the vitality of alternative world views. Given the weight attached to the concept, any modification or transformation will have important consequences for the demeanour of the modern global system.

My argument here is that the structurationist idea of disparate structural rules and resources providing both an enabling and a constraining framework for action is a fruitful approach to understanding the constitution of the global system. The scope for effective agency is enlarged because of the growing complexity and globalization of modern life, in which agents are faced not just by a dominant set of structural properties but by intersecting, overlapping and sometimes contradictory sets, where institutional scripts (national, local, employment, gender and so on) cross-cut. As a result of access to a wider range of structural rules and resources, individual agents and collective actors may reproduce a dominant rule, consciously choose the most appropriate rule in the context or defy prevailing rules altogether. Thus workers may be empowered by their status as shareholders in a privatized concern, rather than just be threatened as disposable factors of production; migrants can draw upon the rules about the universality of human rights and not rely upon those governing the relationships between foreign labour and domestic capital in national settings. Agents may even mobilize rules and resources for purposes other than those which have been culturally sanctioned, so that the use of female contraception appears not just as a means to prevent unwanted pregnancies, but as a symbol of women's liberation, when appropriated in a politics of sexuality.

Pluralism of 'external' rules is frequently matched by 'internal' ambiguity and tension, so that agents do not just 'enact' and thus vivify structural rules by routine engagement, but can also effect a critical distance from institutional orders. Nonetheless these orders persist as 'memory traces' or, as Meyer et al. (1987) would have it, as 'institutional scripts of which, in normal circumstances, the individual may be conscious in only limited cognitive and normative ways', but which function as frames of reference and meaning for agency. However, even in 'normal' circumstances, individuals do not so much act out these scripts as interpret them. Thus, while actors can and do choose between structural rules, and do instantiate structures through their routine behaviour, the social is not just a matter of continuous instantiation and negotiation by active agents; it is also a matter of the extent to which actors and action 'occur' in the context of institutionalized rules often, but by no means always, of great generality and scope (p. 22).

So rules both constitute actors and legitimate types of action; in other words, they 'define the ontological value of both actor and action (p. 24). Routine interactions like buying and selling labour, or providing hospitality for strangers, take place 'in the context of highly general historical rules legitimating and constructing the economy and polity and their participants' (p. 24). Such a view does not reinstate the primacy of structure over action, because it is clear that the boundaries and legitimacy of even highly general rules, like a belief in the rights of human beings, can be changed by the intervention of organized actors, such that rights defining the status of the individual can be extended to previously excluded groups of humans and, so it seems, to non-human animals too. As definitions of what constitute legitimate institutional rules expand or contract, so the range of acceptable actors and actions follows suit.

Where does this leave us in relation to the original attempt to understand how a social system is possible and can be changed? Actors and action are 'institutionally anchored', while institutional orders are also socially constructed. Actors and their actions are defined by broad institutional scripts in the sense that what they do, and how they perceive themselves, are set in the context of more or less chronic structures. At the same time actors can and sometimes do modify or transform the conditions of their existence, and this transformative capacity has been enhanced by the increasing complexity of a social universe in which local and global are increasingly interpenetrated, and local scripts are relativized by global forces. Systemness now appears less as a neat functional accommodation and more as a negotiated and contingent condition, where the sites of negotiation are the rules which constitute action and the identities of practitioners.

This portrayal of how a social system is possible and can be changed is analogous to the globalization of social life, described earlier as the contested and tortuous processes through which the world is being made into one place with systemic properties. These same processes have relativized the world by penetrating and dissolving the boundaries of previously 'closed' systems, usually of a communitarian or ethnic variety, creating inter-societal spaces and networks of relationships along the time–space edges of existence. The upshot will be not a homogenized and culturally anodyne 'world-system', but a global social system which displays elements of the institutionalized 'Western cultural account' and evidence of the vitality of other accounts, and of the power of agents both to imagine these and to enact them. The chapters which follow are an attempt to map these and other features of a globalized modernity, which may have slipped already into postmodernity, and thus to come to grips with global systemness.

4 The World Economy

World economy and global system

The character of global systemness can be seen most clearly in the development of the world economy over the last few decades, which has seen a transformation from 'organized' to 'disorganized' capitalism on a global scale (Lash and Urry, 1987) and the emergence of what Carnoy et al. (1993) call 'the new global information economy'. As such it affords a vantage point from which to view the 'economies of signs and space' which now are as characteristic of the global political economy as the production and movement of material goods (Lash and Urry, 1994).

Much recent discussion of the world economy has emphasized the complete 'globalization' of economic relations, so much so that there is sometimes an unquestioning certainty about the existence of a truly global economy. In part this arises from a reductionist treatment of the significance of broadly economic and technological factors relative to others, and in part because there has been a persuasive neatness about the transnationalization of production, trade and finance compared with evidence of resolute difference elsewhere (Hirst and Thompson, 1992; Campanella, 1902). There is also a casual assumption that changes in the organization of production and consumption have the power to transform meaning structures and identities in a more or less direct fashion. In short, the economic realm is said to display greater interdependence and homogeneity than the curmudgeonly and fragmented political sphere, and certainly more than the cultural realm with its still fragile evidence of global themes. The purpose of this chapter is to garner evidence for and against this claim, bearing in mind previous warnings on the need to treat globalization as an asymmetrical process, and to exercise some caution in assessing the power of 'diverse totalizing orders and impulsions' (Giddens, 1993, p. 8).

The asymmetrical nature of globalizing processes is very apparent in the 'turbulent' 1990s, when the multilateralist institutions most closely associated with global economic liberalization are being challenged by regional trading blocs and by forms of 'minilateralism' (Campanella, 1992; Ruggie, 1992). Even so, it is still right to see these tensions as the outcome of increasingly contested processes of globalization rather than as clear evidence of the *deglobalization* of the world economy. At all events, challenges to world economic integration are not new: indeed the very dynamism of the modern world economy turned on the classic antinomy between global interdependence and national autonomy. In chapter 2, I outlined Wallerstein's conception of a capitalist world economy which seeks to trace the emergence and functioning of a global political economy by connecting the processes of capital accumulation on a global scale with the geopolitical rivalries of nation-states. Further evidence of tensions in the global political economy are visible in the conflicts between the relatively ordered world of multilateral institutions like the General Agreement on Tariffs and Trade (GATT) and the other pillars of the international trading order of liberalism, namely the International Monetary Fund (IMF) and the World Bank, and the rational anarchy of the money markets, the high-rollers of 'casino capitalism' (Strange, 1988; 1986).

All these tensions suggest that growing interconnectedness and interdependence produce not stability but the greater vulnerability of actors under high-risk conditions. Many of the developments in the global economy in recent years, notably the shift to forms of more managed trade, and the appeal of different forms of protectionism, can be seen as a response to endemic uncertainty and rapid change. As a result, the global economy is located somewhere between a realist set, featuring the knock-about of national competition, and a postmodern space of flows – of goods, services, people, images and information. High-tech firms or industries now require economic units that are larger than most national states, but continue to demand the protection afforded by managed trade, or the comfortable reciprocities between trading blocs. Such developments do form part of what Robertson (1992) calls the 'trend to unicity', but reinforce the idea of global systemness as being fundamentally contested.

The idea of a global economy

The imagery of a *borderless world* (Ohmae, 1990) is in common use as a description of the global economy. Some accounts focus on the major growth in transnational microeconomic links among the 'triad' economies of Europe, the Americas and the Pacific Rim (Ruggie, 1993) and see the processes of globalization as the wave of a post-industrial future (Drucker, 1993). Generally these accounts adopt a strongly liberal stance and point to the obvious and growing irrelevance of states and of the very idea of *national* economies. On the other hand, realist interpretations of the international economy still insist that 'economic realities' are the province of the national company, and see the territorial state as the key instrument of international regulation and governance (Kapstein, 1991–2).

Between these lie a range of interpretations which recognize the transformative potential of cross-national production networks and global communication flows, but continue to believe that the nation-state is an important actor in global economic management and in both corporate and national success (Porter, 1990; Reich, 1992). Nor is this debate confined to the writings of international relations theorists and international economics. For some time now, students of strategic management have explored the phenomenon of the global company (Prahalad and Doz, 1987; Bartlett and Ghoshal, 1989; 1992; Bartlett et al., 1990). By and large this debate has been conducted over the extent to which recent developments – cheap and powerful computing and communications, the breaking down of barriers to foreign direct investment (FDI) and capital raising, along with the global spread of consumerist ideologies – have turned large companies into 'world players' independent of their national origins.

The conception of a global company differs from the older though still widely used concept of the multinational corporation (MNC) which dominated the pattern of international business activity from the 1950s to the 1970s. MNCs consisted of a dominant parent company and various foreign offspring, fighting competitors in overseas markets. By the 1990s, runs the argument, the multinational corporation had given way to the phenomenon of the global corporation. Firms now locate production wherever the costs are lowest and organize on the basis of overseas transplants or through mergers and acquisitions, but increasingly through more collaborative and equal ventures involving FDI. The latter arrangements may involve spreading investment risks in the exercise of high-cost and long-term research and development programmes, or piggy-backing in new and untried markets, or may just indicate a fear of flying in the competitive world of the internal market in Europe. In some fields it is not too fanciful to suggest that the idea of separate domestic and foreign markets has become altogether redundant.

At the same time, the picture painted is seldom one of the homogenization of products. There may be global or generic strategies but, except in the case of very specialized and high value-added products, or those which by dint of marketing or serendipity achieve the status of consumer icons, for example Coca-Cola, there are unlikely to be global customers (if by that is meant consumers with uniform demands and uniform tastes). So to some extent there is a powerful mythology at work here, or at the very least a confusion over the meaning of the term 'global business'. Let me recap: there is a definitional world of difference between the concept of a multinational corporation, which implies that a corporation may be very 'national' in key aspects of its functioning and governance, and that of a transnational corporation (TNC) or global corporation, which suggests that the company has broken free from or transcended the bounds of nationality. Undoubtedly MNCs are very visible and powerful actors in the world economy, although it is only partly true that they can conduct business without regard for the sensibilities of nation-states. As we shall see, a good deal of evidence supports the claim that national factors contribute significantly to corporate success (Porter, 1990; Carnoy et al., 1993).

Truly transnational actors, however, are still few and far between, and the ties that bind even the biggest corporations to particular nation-states remain strong. According to Yao-Su Hu (1992), only a very few companies, like Shell, Unilever, Nestlé, ABB and ICI, can be defined as real transnationals. This is because most very large corporations, like Du Pont or General Motors, have less than half of their operations and employees abroad, because 'foreigners' occupy only a very small proportion of senior management positions, and because they are subject to a legal and fiscal nationality which, in the last resort, is more significant than other jurisdictions within whose remit they fall. Even companies who meet these criteria, and who may have required their overseas outposts to embrace the local business culture or 'go native', still owe some debt of allegiance to the 'mother country' and are particularly sensitive to its politics and shifts in policy. They are also likely to be carrying around at least some cultural baggage which identifies them as 'foreign' and may well trade on this awareness of difference to their competitive advantage. The French hotel group Méridien, though hardly a world player, has carved useful market niches in overseas markets like the United States by trading on its very Frenchness. The burden of all this is that Japanese or Korean companies in the United States or Britain will remain Japanese or Korean in some fundamental sense; and, of course, the opposite is also true.

However, attention to the 'objective' or easily measurable factors of globalization may miss the point. If the global corporation is still more myth than reality, it is one which now exercises a powerful hold over the strategic vision as well as the management styles of large corporations with international connections and markets. Many such organizations are adopting a self-conscious 'global rationale' and at least the rhetoric of global management informs much of their discourse, playing a growing part in more formal schemes of management training and development as well as in marketing strategies. Managers in such organizations 'speak globally' in the sense that they have come to see the world as a putative operational whole (Wildish and Case, 1994, p. 7). This notional cultural change is in marked contrast to the received model of preparation for 'overseas' management, or even forms of cross-cultural training in which more or less sophisticated advice and schooling are offered to the novice 'expatriate' being groomed for extended periods overseas. Being a 'global manager' implies travel, but more critically it suggests that it is possible to be a 'world-wide' business without transferring staff from one country to another (p. 8).

Instead, a global mentality is instantiated through strategic networks of communication between managers as professionals, through interpersonal networks, as well as through different forms of functional integration. Thus for many writers on international management, it is the management style of an organization that is the key determinant of its taxonomic status as a global company, as opposed to the product or service which it produces or provides, or even where its key functions are located (Wildish and Case, 1994). In the new information economy, the importance of place, or of vertical integration as a means of creating an economy of scale, gives way to forms of strategic networking, where coordination or a 'single face' is achieved by independent companies working together. The 'globalness' of such alliances is not diminished by the rootedness of participants in particular locales. So the 'essence' of a global company may be best understood by looking at the way in which it is managed and how it identifies itself in relation to the changing competitive environments in which it is located.

Of course, in this respect the 'soft' side of the globalizing equation sometimes lags behind developments in the 'hard' indicators. The injunction to 'think globally and manage locally' has attained the status of lore, but the reality for many small to medium businesses is that local considerations and a parochial 'mindset' remain powerful constraints on the achievement of a global mentality. The completion of the internal market in Europe, widely bruited as a fundamental fracture line in the operating environment of businesses, evoked almost universal apathy or benign optimism among the owner-managers of small businesses throughout the Community member states (Axford et al., 1991). So, if it is true that organizations enact their environments in their own image (Morgan, 1986; Wendt, 1987), then many are reproducing an environment at odds with the exigencies of the contexts in which they are operating or will be operating.

A no-nonsense realist response to these sorts of arguments would point to the continuing power of states to intervene effectively in the organization of economic life and to shape or control aspects of the global cultural economy, even where these may be transmitted by the electronic impulses which carry them down wires or beam them through space. In swashbuckling style, Kapstein (1991–2) suggests that information satellites could be shot down by a government bent on interrupting communication flows which it deemed not in the national interest. This is good knock-about stuff but something of a limiting case, and one need not go quite this far to underscore the viability and continuing importance of national factors as the basis for corporate success. It is possible to accept the premise that markets and businesses are becoming more global and still argue, as Michael Porter (1990) does, that this makes nations more, rather than less, important. In brief, Porter's argument is that it is the national business environment which determines the competitive advantage of firms, and paradoxically the nurturing of difference, reflected in different national virtues or styles, itself becomes a means of overcoming the constraints imposed by an increasingly homogenized world.

Porter's analytical framework makes much of those domestic conditions – factors of production, the quality of home demand, the intensity of domestic competition, and the regimes under which business is conducted within a nation – which favour and promote or sustain competitiveness. His argument is that these factors become more significant as globalization proceeds and uncertainty deepens. The very appeal of the domestic sources of 'competitiveness' school of international economics and strategic management – not least their appeal to the protectionist Clinton administration in the United States – is a corollary of the faltering tide of liberal-economic discourse during the early 1990s and its partial replacement by regimes of managed trade and trading blocs. For the United States these developments have been attended by the clamorous rhetoric of national decline (Kennedy, 1993). But in the nature of uncertain times, none of these trends is clear cut. Thus the growth in the volume of cross-national, defensive joint ventures demonstrates that companies are aware of the threats and opportunities opened up by the liberalizing of markets, and also shows that the globalization of risk requires insurance which cannot be provided by national administrations, but is as yet unavailable through forms of international governance or regulation.

Against these views of the salience of country of origin is the argument, put most strongly by Kenichi Ohmae (1990), that the nationality of companies is irrelevant in what he terms a 'borderless world'. In the global economic space, big firms at least have to operate in many different markets and for competitive reasons they have to behave like locals wherever they find themselves. So although they may have a headquarters operation, or have most of their shares owned in one country, they have become multinational in terms of their identity, and may even have engineered or 'grown' a culture which is not tied to any one place. Nonetheless, the 'foreignness' of multinational firms, to use Michael Reich's (1992) term, remains an issue in the domestic politics of many countries which are the recipients of inward investment by such businesses, as well as a matter of concern to the stewards of national economies who see their own 'domestic' multinationals exporting jobs to locations with cheaper sources of labour supply (Carnoy et al., 1993).

At this stage of the argument we need not worry about who is right, Porter or Ohmae, because in a sense they both identify salient features of the world economy seen from the point of view of different actors – states and businesses. Moreover, both have the same view of the nation-state, which is that it is primarily a convenient supplier of intrastructural and cultural resources which may contribute to corporate performance. The tensions, or possible tensions, between national goals and national administrations and those of private multinational corporations do not enter these discussions (Carnoy et al., 1993).

But in other respects, the sort of world economic order painted by Ohmae, and implied by Porter too, is remarkably benign. In reality the borderless world, where the only effective global actors are global companies and in which production is globalized and consumption increasingly specialized, will continue to produce winners and losers and to exacerbate the differences between haves and have-nots (Kennedy, 1993, chapters 2 and 3). The prospects for a globalized post-capitalist nirvana based upon 'knowledge' work or 'reflexive accumulation' rather than labour in the traditional sense, or a post-scarcity world economy in which industrial and agricultural production has been revolutionized by robotics and biotechnology, still look slim given the pace of the technological revolution in the developed world and the population explosion in the periphery of the world economy (Drucker, 1993, pp. 60–109; Kennedy, 1993).

Generally speaking, debate about the borderless world has been innocent of any treatment of the world-historical legacies of imperialism and of global inequalities, preferring to concentrate upon the dynamic qualities of economies like the self-styled 'intelligent island' of Singapore, or the globe-compressing power of clever machines. Some of these issues are taken up later in this chapter, and the issue of the nation-state in the world economy is discussed in chapter 5.

Ideal types and global realities: cross-currents in the world economy

In a key article, Paul Hirst and Grahame Thompson ask, 'how can we characterize the present state of the world economy?' (1942, p. 357). In this section I will look at the global economy as an ideal type, drawing upon and elaborating the version found in Hirst and Thompson, before examining some of the main currents in the world economy. The idea of a global economy as this has developed in recent decades should be seen as part of a much longer-term trend towards the internationalization of economic relations. This has not been a linear and unbroken trend; indeed, it is probable that the international economy was more open to the flow of money, goods and people in the late nineteenth century than at any time during the last thirty years (Glyn and Sutcliffe, 1992). Arguably, there has been a secular trend in the internationalization of economic relations, making the trade and investment economies of nation-states more and more interdependent. Under both the British and American hegemonies, the ideal of a liberal, international trading economy was pursued for the most part as an article of faith and each major power acted as a guarantor of this open system, using mechanisms like the Gold Standard under the later years of British hegemony, and the

Bretton Woods agreement after the Second World War, to institutionalize a liberal world trading order.

But the most characteristic feature of the world economy up to the Second World War was that it was still a function of its constituent, national parts. The period between 1870 and 1913 was particularly integrationist, with large-scale migration between Europe and the New World, low or non-existent tariff barriers and low or uniform interest rates throughout the world. Yet during these forty years of quite intense economic globalization, nation-states flourished. Indeed, it could be said that the growing economic connectedness of the globe, for example in trade in manufactured goods or in financial markets, were further opportunities for aggressive nation-states to assert themselves, rather than clear evidence of a globalized economy in which states were marginalized. Even in the immediate aftermath of the Second World War, it was still valid to talk of national governments 'managing' an economy, both in terms of their ability to deploy a range of domestic policies to some effect, and in the sense of being voluntary partners in a world economy whose vagaries they could still control, or at least finesse.

By contrast the new, globalized international economy affords much less scope for national autonomy and a consequent loss of control for national policy-makers in key areas of economic management like control of interest rates or levels of public spending. The globalized economy thus problematizes the question of economic governance and the regulation of markets and systems of production which are no longer under the control of nation-states. In this economy, actors like firms, consumers, regions and states are, says Kenichi Ohmae (1993), subsumed into, or rearticulated with, a global nexus of skills, information, trade and investment, in which the traditional boundaries of economic flows become increasingly irrelevant because they no longer provide a map of 'real' flows of economic activity.

For example, those firms, localities or regions which have attracted foreign direct investment to their area, who have established permanent offices in Brussels, or who regularly lobby the central institutions of the European Union, have become active participants in a regional political economy. The creation of transnational policy networks goes some way to bypass resistant national governments, thereby marginalizing local political and policy discourses that are still exercised by the threats of 'foreign' intervention, or intent on using national means of protection for domestic markets. Obviously the actors in European networks have been 'constrained to identify' with the European Union and their behaviour has been modified accordingly. How far they have been 'Europeanized' in terms of their identities is another matter.

Nation-states, regions, cities and townships have all become bidders for the investment largesse of transnational corporations and investors (Kennedy, 1993). The growing interpenetration of the local and the global economies means that the conventional distinction between the specific and general business environment becomes less and less relevant to the actual flows of commodities, capital and people. Overall, then, there has been a significant deterritorialization of business activity, evident in the massive growth of cross-border transactions and collaborative ventures, in the creation of truly global markets in finance and telecommunications, and through the establishment of networks of professional epistemic communities – commodity brokers, bankers, management trainers and scientific research groups – who communicate through technical language, irrespective of national origins and culture (Haas, 1992; Featherstone, 1990; Appadurai, 1990).

As a variation on this theme, Ohmae (1993) portrays the region-state as an economic space which can be subnational, but consists more often of a cross-border region of some 5 to 20 million people. He mentions the special economic zones in China, Hong Kong and the Pearl River delta, California, or the whole of the Pacific north-west of North America. In his estimation these are now the 'natural' economic zones drawn 'by the deft hand of the market', not by political fiat (p. 78). The main linkages of such regions are, he says, not with their host nations but with the global economy. In a particularly sharp attack on what he sees as an outmoded form of economic governance, Ohmae depicts the nation-state as a dysfunctional unit for organizing human activity and managing economic endeavour, one that overlooks 'the true linkages and synergies that exist among often disparate populations' (p. 92). But if all this suggests a new division of labour, and a new sort of globalized economy, we should still be a little cautious about the idea of a 'borderless world'. What are the realities in the key areas of trade, production, finance and the soft technologies in communications and information? In other words, what sort of global economic integration are we talking about?

The globalization of trade

Trade, as *The Economist* has said, is the high ground of economic policy. Expanding trade, particularly in manufactured and semi-manufactured goods, among the rich nations of the Organization for Economic Cooperation and Development (OECD) has been, and in some respects continues to be, a clear indicator of the progress of global economic integration. Between 1950 and 1975, the volume of world trade expanded by as much as 500 per cent, largely as a result of tariff liberalization, against an increase in global output over the same period of some 220 per cent (*The Economist*, 22 September 1990; Jerome, 1992). By the early 1990s over 80 per cent of world trade was conducted between the 'Western' members of the OECD, with the newly market-oriented countries of the former Soviet bloc, the less developed countries (LDCs) and even the dynamic economies of the newly industrialized countries (NICs) accounting for only a small part of these overall transactions. The global trading economy is still largely confined to the richer nations, and the volume of intra-core trade continues the pattern of unequal exchange as a mechanism for the reproduction of global inequalites.

However, during the 1970s a number of NICs, notably Hong Kong, Taiwan and South Korea, achieved a rise in exports of manufactured products from 35 to 59 per cent of GNP, while throughout the Third World as a whole the volume of manufactured goods exported practically doubled (from 27 to 47 per cent) over the period between 1963 and 1981 (Carnoy et al., 1993, chapters 1 and 4). Even among the major trading economies of the 'triad' countries, the proportion of imports and exports relative to total GNP is only some 15–20 per cent. But since the mid 1970s, although the volume of global trade has continued to grow, it has done so at a slower rate than previously, and most noticeably in relation to global output. However, this should not detract from the important fact that world economic integration is being speeded up by the growth in trade, which in real terms has amounted to something like a fourteenfold increase in the flow of goods and services over the period between 1950 and 1992 (UNCTAD, 1993).

These figures also subsume another critical fact of global economic life, namely the drift from domestic sourcing of production to the widespread use of non-domestic outsourcing as a means of reducing costs (Drucker, 1993, pp. 84–6). In the most radical shift, outsourcing takes in not only material goods, but services and human skills as well. Yet another pointer to the globalizing of the world economy and the deterritorialization of business activity is the substantial growth of intrafirm transfers and of 'trade' between partners in collaborative ventures or strategic alliances in different parts of the globe. These developments, which have been gathering pace since the

1980s, form part of the drive to develop and sustain a liberal system of global trade. Attempts to codify such a system can be seen in GATT rules about local content and reciprocities, or in the establishment of an internal market in Europe.

Global markets in goods and increasingly in services now connect countries, regions, cities, organizations and individuals in a nexus going far beyond the notion of trade as the exchange of national products. In short, much of the world's economic progress since the Second World War can be understood in terms of the relative success of international trade and of the multilateral trade regimes, like the GATT, set up to facilitate it. The system set in train by the imperfect GATT agreements has been showing marked signs of stress for a number of years, and the setting up of a new international trading organization (ITO) as part of the Uruguay Round completed in 1994 is unlikely to alleviate this stress in the short to medium term (Campanella, 1992). In Europe, the free movement of goods, services, capital and people which was the goal of the completion of the internal market in 1993 is still, in the words of Germany's finance minister Herr Rexrodt in May 1994, 'hampered by too many legal stipulations and administrative provisions (The Economist, 21–27 May 1994). Among other inhibiting factors, bureaucratic inertia and the strength of national protectionist instincts are particularly culpable. I return to threats to the global trading order and to multilateralism as a means of regulating it below and in chapter 5.

The globalization of production

The staple of both classic dependency theory and 'economic' strains of world-system analysis is an international division of labour in which core countries produce manufactured goods for domestic consumption and export, while peripheral economies trade in primary products from the extractive industries and from agriculture. Although this understanding of the global division of labour goes some way to explaining the uneven development of the world economy, it cannot explain the rapid industrialization of some Third World countries, or their entry into world markets as producers and exporters of finished and high value-added products. If it is still useful to hold on to the concept of the 'periphery', it is also important to recognize considerable variation in the ways in which Third World countries are being integrated into the world economy. Variation occurs in the part played by different patterns of foreign direct investment (FDI) and by other forms of investment, notably portfolio investment, which has played a major part in the attractiveness of India to Western capital in recent years; in the shift of manufacturing capacity from the First to the Third World in a number of sectors; and in the differential advantage taken by NICs of the new technological revolutions (Castells, 1993; Castells and Laserna, 1989; Harris, 1986).

In fact, FDI flows to the periphery fell during the latter part of the 1980s as major sources of investment in Europe and Japan switched their focus to the opportunities available in core locations for both acquisitions and mergers. In the USA, Matsushita, Toshiba and C. Itoh invested $10 billion worth of new capital into an ailing entertainments industry, while Nestlé and Procter and Gamble looked for new investment possibilities in Japan. It is also true that, of late, long-term international investment flows have seen direct investments dwarfed by more arm's-length forms of cross-border capital movements, principally in the form of international bond and bank lending and in strains of portfolio investment (Frieden, 1991).

As part of the major restructuring of the world economy that took place in the wake of the oil crisis of the early 1970s, the reorganization of capitalist production has seen the movement of large areas of manufacturing capacity to parts of the Third World, mainly to the more dynamic NICs, but now also to parts of the former Soviet bloc (Purcell, 1989). For the most part this has involved moving production only, 'transplanting' workshops and assembly facilities, although sometimes key research and development functions have been relocated, usually between core states. This global shift was built on a number of factors: first, the efforts of multilateral institutions like the IMF, the World Bank and the OECD to facilitate and support foreign investment; second, much greater capital mobility and a spate of frenetic lending by banks and other financial institutions during the 1970s and 1980s, both to the Third World directly and to investors looking for quick profit in the periphery or in 'vulnerable' core states. Also important were the advances in transportation and communications (container freighting, wide-bodied jets, fibre-optic and satellite hook-ups) which have significantly reduced the organizational and technical costs previously associated with relocation of a company.

Challenges to the liberal trading order take a number of forms, including the setting up of trading blocs or systems of managed trade and a return to voluntary restraint agreements on the volume of key exports. These make relocation or some form of foreign cloning of productive capacity an attractive way for the global company to achieve a limited form of comparative advantage. However, the advantage to be gained from shifting production to relatively low-cost labour markets is likely to be very short term, unless allied to improvements in the technological facets of production and in management capabilities in the new locations. Thus the simple *maquiladora* model of development, in which companies from core states take advantage of the cost–price differentials in peripheral economies (as well as contributing to the competitiveness of export goods from those regions), is not likely to offer an attractive or viable long-term model for the development of proto-capitalist economies in Central and Eastern Europe and the former Soviet Union, although it remains an attractive proposition in the short term (Carnoy et al., 1993).

As a corollary to the export of jobs from the core to the periphery of the world economy, the 'long wave' of capitalist expansion in the West between 1945 and the mid 1970s was fed in part by the large-scale migration of people from the Third to the First World. Apart from the economic impact of such movements, their most obvious effect was to turn these core countries into 'world spaces' in Balibar's (1991) sense, and to place multiculturalism, racism and latterly the whole question of citizenship on the policy agenda of national governments and that of multilateral bodies like the EU. Newer sources of immigration, notably from parts of the old Soviet empire, present further challenges to the liberal tradition of rights and to the conception of citizenship as tied to nationality, with both in the gift of nation-states.

The globalization of finance

The change in money and capital markets since the 1970s is perhaps the most unequivocal indicator of the globalization of economic affairs. Capital mobility across national borders is a routine though occasionally dramatic feature of the world economy, and certainly not a historically unique phenomenon. But if not unique, recent trends are certainly impressive, with massive increases in international liquidity and financial flows occuring during the 1970s and 1980s and continuing unabated into the 1990s (Goldstein et al., 1991; Frieden, 1991). Today the daily volume of foreign exchange trading is many hundreds of times bigger than the volume of traded goods, and while it is true that financial liberalization has contributed to the growth of commerce, it is also true that financial flows are increasingly separate from trade in manufactures and services, leading some to suggest that they now form a separate global economy (Kennedy, 1993, p. 50).

The underlying logic of the unfettered market in the borderless world is seen more clearly in global financial transactions than anywhere else, and the reasons are not hard to find. Technological innovations in computer software have made communications between traders, widely separated by time and space, a routine and speedy affair. Decision-taking is sometimes even removed from human agency altogether, as computerized expert systems 'trade' across the time zones. Other, more immediate factors are also significant. These include: (1) the floating of currency exchange rates after the breakdown of the Bretton Woods system in the 1970s; (2) the deregulation of financial markets by national governments in the 1980s heyday of liberalization; (3) structural imbalances on balance of payment accounts in some of the bigger economies; and (4) the willingness of banks and other lending institutions to subvent growing debt in the Third World (Spero, 1991).

The relaxing of exchange controls encourages rapid movement in and out of currencies and exacerbates the divide between the 'real' economies of trade in manufactured goods and services and the 'casino' world of currency dealers and 'speculators'. This relaxation introduces much more liquidity into world trade and increases the volume of transnational capital investments: to that extent it is of a piece with the liberalization of the global trading system. At the same time, it produces much greater volatility and insecurity in the world economy, because the rationality of financial markets, which are geared to short-term profit considerations and very sensitive to variations in national policies, makes it more difficult for national governments to carry through measures like tax increases, interest rate changes or social welfare measures, and even to stick to exchange rates deemed to be out of line with what the markets will stand.

Thus the development of a globalized economy in financial markets has for many commentators a direct political consequence, namely the challenge to the nation-state as the prime mover in domestic politics and policy and as the major player in international affairs (Gourevitch, 1986; Cox, 1987). In a comment that was state of the art in 1990, John Freeman opined that, in the context of global finance, 'the nation-state has become at best immobilized and at worst obsolete' (p. 5). This is a highly contestable argument, even though it might occasion cynical agreement among national policy-makers in the United Kingdom and France in the wake of Britain's decision to leave the European exchange rate mechanism (ERM) in October 1992, and in the light of the effective collapse of the currency mechanism in July 1993, following energetic speculation on the pound and later on the French franc. It is a fine irony that the fixing of exchange rates in a world of mobile capital also implies forgoing national monetary autonomy in order to secure currency stability. Caught between speculators and markets on the one hand and international regimes on the other, nation-states may founder on the proverbial rock or the well-known hard place.

The effective demise of the ERM signalled the interruption of the Maastricht 'vision' of European integration, with its programme of full monetary and economic union and its infinitely more contested project of ever-closer political union. The fact that the ERM failed, or was severely mauled by those forces much less interested in currency stability than in the flexibility allowed by monetary autonomy subject only to the harsh disciplines of global market forces, might suggest that volatility is now endemic in the world financial system. In this scenario the ERM has simply gone the way of all attempts at regional or global financial governance: the Gold Standard, Bretton Woods and the European currency 'snake'. Recent evidence of more balanced trade on current accounts among big financial players like the United States, the United Kingdom, Germany and Japan (Hirst and Thompson, 1992) seems not to have provided that element of stability needed to defuse speculative activity and to cut down on exchange rate uncertainty. In this area too the seams of managed or organized capitalism look to have worn exceedingly thin.

The globalization of technology

The globalization of economic processes has been intensified by major advances in technology, notably the diffusion of the so-called 'soft' technologies in the fields of communication and information (Campanella, 1992). No area of life, at least in the advanced economies, remains untouched by the weight of these changes. I have already commented upon some of the factors correlated with the spread of new technologies, but it is worth reiterating that the enormous increase in the power of computers, in computer software and in related developments in communications technology have served to compress the world in many ways. Flows of money, goods and people are accelerated by the various technologies in use, particularly those from within the telecommunications sector. The revolutionizing effects of fibre-optic and satellite technology on the movement of information and images of various kinds bring the prospects of a global multi-media 'information super-highway' much closer, although the appearance of truly interactive television and multi-way video telephones is unlikely before the turn of the twenty-first century (*The Economist*, 26 February 1994).

For those actors – whether states, national governments, groups or individuals – concerned to defend both economic and cultural boundaries, the effects of the new technologies are already profoundly dislocating. Global opportunities require global players, and the multi-media revolution in the entertainments industries is already breaking down the traditional demarcations between print and visual media companies, forcing national governments to rethink their regulatory frameworks, including those pertaining to multi-media ownership. In the United Kingdom, which in the Broadcasting Act of 1990 agonized over the principle and merits of widespread ownership, recent consolidation in the ownership of regional companies in the independent television network reflects the growing awareness by media companies of the need to position themselves in the new race. On a grander scale, the trend towards international multi-media alliances cutting across different delivery systems is exemplified by Rupert Murdoch's News International conglomerate and in the 1994 merger of Viacom, the US cable company, and Blockbuster, the video shop chain, in order to purchase Paramount Films. However, the proposed takeover of TCI, a large cable TV operator, by Bell Atlantic in 1994 was shelved on the grounds that the 'unsettled regulatory climate' was unfavourable to such a move.

The products of the transglobal culture industry already circulate world-wide to mass audiences, while the niche market opportunities opened up by the new telecommunications media create demands which national governments are increasingly powerless to resist, even if they wish to. During 1993 and early 1994, the French government renewed its allegations of cultural imperialism carried by the Anglo-American entertainments industry (Nicholson-Lord, 1993). But it is not only the products of mass culture that worry the defenders of national identity and morality. More exotic forms of cultural fare, like soft-porn movies or electronic political bulletin boards, may also escape the control of national regulators in the free-for-all of the information super-highway.

This is not to argue for some kind of technological determinism. A reflexive relationship between actors and the properties of larger-scale social systems, including the structures (the hardware and software) of technological change, means that the forces of technology are not unmediated and do not flow only in one direction. Contrary to much pious discussion about the 'decline' in broadcasting standards, or jeremiads on the vegetative condition induced by a diet of

TV soaps, is the belief that new forms of broadcasting may actually increase more than limit the power and autonomy of agents. CNN, the American news channel, already convenes live video press conferences, and the Internet concept of multicasting will soon permit every viewer to transmit digitized pictures to every other viewer (*The Guardian*, 23 June 1994). Videotron, the London-based cable operator, is fast developing a system that allows viewers to communicate directly with broadcasters through set-top 'smart' boxes.

This is not all. The boost to localisms offered by access to thousands of channels world-wide, both terrestrial and non-terrestrial, may even confound the cultural centralism and elitism of national broadcasting traditions like the British, while the techniques of 'narrowcasting' will permit 'live' connections between anywhere in the world, provided that a video camera is linked to the global fibre-optical grid (Bowen, 1994). Thus the opportunities for what Lash and Urry call 'mobile subjects' to engage in both frivolous observation and serious reflection on the conditions of their existence will know no technological boundaries (1994, chapters 2 and 3). Of course, access to as well as control of the new, liberating technologies remains a critical issue. In the United States, concern about how much of the new 'communications highway' will reach 'have-nots' in the population has prompted the federal government to promise a relaxation in the rules restricting US telecommunications and television companies from carrying programmes down telephone wires, but only if these same organizations ensure the availability of their services at reasonable cost to a wide market. I will return to the question of the information economy later in the chapter.

This brief survey of trends in the world economy describes a complex web of actors, processes and institutions, and in general supports the claim that the world economy is being systematically globalized, but by a process which is neither homogenizing nor symmetrical. There are clear disjunctures between the older institutional identities of the nation-states, especially in their role as economic managers, and the pressures of global markets, seen clearly in the currency crisis of autumn 1992. These two institutional orders are the phenomenal and ideological forms of historically related but distinct global social institutions or cultural accounts: the world polity of sovereign nation-states and the culture of global market-driven capitalism. Disjunctions arise between national institutions and actors and those ordered at a global 'level', thus demonstrating that the world cultural economy 'moves' to different and competing 'logics', national and local as well as political, cultural and economic. The diffusion throughout the global system of social institutions like the nation-state, or of cultural scripts like consumerism, provides frameworks of meaning for actors. However, these meaning frameworks do not always produce global isomorphism, and may deepen the sense of difference. The trend to unicity therefore remains fundamentally contested.

Capitalism and post-capitalism: the global economy in the information age

The making of the modern global system involves a complex inter-weaving of historically specific discourses, of which the most significant are those of industrialism and capitalism. However, the value of these historical categories is now doubtful because of revolutionary changes in how and where goods are produced and consumed, in how work is organized and, most important of all, in the extent to which information and knowledge have replaced the conventional categories of labour and capital as sources of economic growth and success. Thus it is a matter of debate as to whether the global economy can be seen as 'capitalist', or whether it has been transformed into 'post-capitalist', or into a 'disorganized' variant in the sense identified by Offe (1985) and Lash and Urry (1987; 1994). Before taking this question up directly, it will be useful to explicate the two basic concepts.

Capitalism, as Dennis Wrong opines, is not a uniform entity but a complex of interdependent attributes (1992, pp. 153–4). Chief among these are the idea of price setting by free markets, and commodity production for profit, with the means to secure this in the relationships between privately owned capital and a free, though propertyless, class of wage labour. I have already noted Wallerstein's gloss on these precepts and his insistence on market exchanges as the defining characteristic of capitalism, which interpretation allows him to entertain the notion of a single, world mode of production in which there are quite different mechanisms for the extraction of surplus, some economic, others political.

Industrialism denotes the processes whereby raw materials of various sorts are converted into commodities by the use of machinery or other sources of inanimate power, and is a concept applicable to both capitalist and non-capitalist (socialist) systems of production. Moreover, discussion of industrialized systems of production should not be confined to technology and to the workplace, but needs to include many aspects of domestic life like transport systems, travel and communications (Giddens, 1990, p. 56).

My previous discussion of the world economy points to major changes in these key institutional clusters over the last fifty years or so. In brief, these involve the shift from what is often called 'organized capitalism', in which production, consumption, money and labour circulate nationally, to 'disorganized capitalism', in which these circuits become increasingly global in scope (Lash and Urry, 1987; 1994, pp. 322–3). This spatial shift has been accompanied by transformations in the design of production systems, in the organization and meaning of work, and by an 'explosion' of consumption in both mass and specialized markets. In the rest of this section, I will look at further evidence for the radical transformation of capitalism and industrialism in the creation of a global information and knowledge economy and at the new international division of labour which derives from it. Finally I will offer some preliminary thoughts on the integration of former command economies into the world market economy, before turning in the final section to the question of its governance.

The knowledge economy

The global economy remains a market economy, one that is being extended piecemeal to the former planned economies of state socialism. But as Drucker (1993, chapter 1) says, the substance of this globalized market economy has been radically altered over recent decades. If 'market' is an acceptable substitute for 'capitalist' then the economy is still capitalist but that epithet now disguises its most obvious characteristic, which is, in the clumsy neologism, that it has become 'informatized' or transformed by information and communications technology. To say this is not just to point to the impact of new technology upon systems of production, impressive as this is, but to see the informatization of the world economy as changing the 'conditions and possibilities for national policies ... facilitating ... the globalization of local social movements, and perhaps most critical of all ... changing the emphasis of production in advanced capitalist societies from material goods to information processing activities' (Carnoy, 1993, p. 105).

This transformation is seen most clearly in the transition to a 'service' economy in the core states, and in the preoccupation with the reproduction of meta-economic functions like education and health care as the basis for 'successful' economies. It is also apparent in the startling success of 'knowledge-based' industries on a global scale – those, like Microsoft, which have invested in the production and reproduction of knowledge to steal a competitive edge and become global. When Microsoft's market value overtook that of General Motors in January 1992, *The New York Times* was moved to comment that its only factory asset was the imagination of its workers (see Handy, 1994). What this means is that the traditional sources of comparative advantage – technology, labour, land and money – count for less when set against the 'new' factors of computer-driven scientific innovation, the transferable skills of 'knowledge workers', and core management competences (Peters, 1990; Castells, 1993; Drucker, 1993; Prahalad and Hamel, 1990). As Handy (1994) suggests, in the globalized economy, intelligence is the new form of property and the basis for wealth creation.

Earlier, I referred to the spatial shifts in production that are a feature of the globalized economy, to the networks of both large and small enterprises, and to those 'epistemic communities' found among managers and scientists which now subsist across national boundaries. In addition, significant changes in the organization of production and of the work process are well in train. These changes have been fully documented in terms which describe the growing 'flexibilities' of organizational form, and management systems, in the composition and structure of the workforce and in working practices, all characteristic of the transition from a 'Fordist' system of production to a 'post-Fordist' or 'flexible postmodern' regime (Harvey, 1989). At the heart of these changes, systems of standardized mass production have given way 'to flexible, customized production, and from vertically integrated, large-scale bureaucratic organizations to vertical disintegration, flatter organizational structures and both personal and strategic networking within and between economic units' (Castells, 1993, p. 18; see also Harvey, 1989; Lash and Urry, 1994).

In the West, such changes are often based upon the reheating of successful Japanese models of strategic management and organizational change. Systems of 'flexible specialization' (Harvey, 1989) stress adaptability to rapidly changing and even chaotic conditions (Pascale, 1986; Peters, 1987). The key elements vary considerably, especially in their take-up by Western companies, who have often rejected the holistic philosophies of their Japanese competitors in favour of a more piecemeal approach, or one more suited to the traditions and practices of national capitalisms and particular regimes of accumulation (Lash and Urry, 1994, chapter 4). They include the precepts of total quality management, or more recently of 'change re-engineering' with its born-again ethos; the disciplines of 'just-in-time' supply systems; 'outsourcing' of all but the core functions of an organization, including the widespread use of contract and part-time labour of various sorts; and the ideological transformation of the culture of industrial relations to an anodyne and individualized culture of human resources management (Clegg, 1992; Hammer and Champy, 1993; Coulson-Thomas, 1992). In addition to their wider, structural effects on the make-up of the workforce, 'flexibilities' of this sort also serve to 'hollow out' the workplace organization, in much the same way as can be seen in the conscious, though often defensive, hiving-off of the functions and responsibilities of the nation-state to a variety of non-state and suprastate organizations (Rhodes, 1994; Handy, 1994; Hammer and Champy, 1993).

In its most radical form, still only partially realized in most countries of the advanced West, the 'knowledge economy' deconstructs 'labour' as a major resource item and ideological totem (Drucker, 1993; Handy, 1994). This is mainly because labour is no longer a major competitive asset, a key factor of production. Many large organizations and some smaller ones now routinely 'export' unproductive but often costly forms of work and dispense with the people who perform it. As Handy (1994) points out, instead of a pool of surplus labour and skill being kept 'inside' the organization, they are imported as necessary, and the costs of unproductive time pass from the business to the workers, or to other organizations including, most controversially, the state and the mythologized 'community'. In their most pristine form, still hardly realized, postmodern business organizations are not just 'lean', in the cant 1980s expression, or 'flexible', or 'decentralized': they become 'organizationless', or *virtual* organizations, consisting of little more than shifting clusters of skills and project teams, held together by those relatively few 'core' workers who define the organizational identity and goals, and by the routine use of advanced communications technology (Clegg, 1992; Castells, 1989).

The Virgin Group of companies is often held up as an exemplar of an organizationless business form, being highly diversified and decentralized, and producing information and leisure services rather than commodities. In this they seem to epitomize Lash and Urry's idea of a global, post-capitalist economy based upon 'reflexive accumulation', in which knowledge and information are central to economic life, and consumption (especially of 'life-enhancing' services like tourism, or therapeutic services like counselling) is increasingly tailored to 'niche' markets. Here communications technology and automated productions systems reduce the gap between producers and consumers, to the extent that buyers of new motor cars will soon be able to 'design' their own vehicle through the installation of easy-to-use design 'menus' on showroom terminals (1994, pp. 60–1).

Like businesses, all national economies are vitally interested in maintaining and improving productivity, but where this has occurred it has always been accompanied by a fall in the percentage of workers employed directly in manufacturing. In the United States, total manufacturing production grew more than two and a half times between 1975 and 1990, but during the same period the percentage of the workforce employed in making things fell dramatically from 25 per cent of the total labour force in 1960 to 17 per cent in 1990 (Cohen, 1993). The same trends are apparent elsewhere in the leading economies, and look set to continue despite political concerns about the shrinking manufacturing base in many core countries. The reasons lie in the shift of employment into the service sector, and in the exporting of manufacturing jobs to developing economies, where the return on investment in giving a job to an unskilled worker is much greater than that which could be recouped by giving a similar job to an expensively educated worker in the core economy.

The point here is not that advanced economies cease to manufacture: on the contrary, manufacturing work now concentrates upon the high-tech production of high value-added goods, produced by a smaller number of 'knowledge' workers, educated to a high standard. Those less developed countries (LDCs) which looked to the core economies to provide 'exported' jobs for cheaper domestic labour, and to admit migrant workers to the metropole economy, will now find at least some of these sources drying up. Migrant populations already domiciled in core countries are likely to find themselves further marginalized economically and vilified politically, as pressures to create flexible workforces put more sections of the indigenous workforce at risk (Handy, 1994; Gray, 1994). This fate may also await some indigenous regional minorities and the uneducated underclass of core economies, thus creating new kinds of peripheries within the 'wild' urban zones of advanced economies (Lash and Urry, 1994, chapter 6).

Yet rather more sanguine and optimistic interpretations of these processes are also available, where the non-pathological image of the knowledge revolution is that of the 'learning culture' and where 'technologism' (Burke, 1970) does not degrade the quality of existence. In this idyll, fewer jobs, more flexibly organized, do not yield despair, but offer greater life chances and opportunities for 'reflexive learning' (Handy, 1994). In other respects too, the effects of information technology (IT) upon organizational authority structures may, and on some accounts do, enhance the capacities of individual workers and teams, or contribute to their 'empowerment', because IT constitutes a resource upon which agents can draw to reshape lines of authority and decision-making power, as well as use to contribute to their own sense of personal efficacy. Here they perform as competent organizational citizens, rather than as subordinates or wage slaves (Peters, 1990; Parker, 1994).

The zonal world economy?

All this depicts a world economy which increasingly defies description in conventional and familiar terms. Lash and Urry (1987; 1994) and Offe (1985) have spoken of 'disorganized capitalism', and this label seems appropriate to a period in which the basis of the global economy is a new division of labour that 'is based less on the location of natural resources, cheap and abundant labour, or even capital stock, and more on the capacity to create knowledge, and to apply it rapidly, via information processing and telecommunications, to a wide range of human activities in ever-broadening space and time' (Carnoy et al., 1993, p. 6). Because of these changes, many simple or even complex models and theories of the global economy are in need of revision.

In particular, centre–periphery models, or those which suggest a zonal configuration to the world economy, common to world-system and dependency theories, underestimate the complexity of the global economy, primarily because they cling to the conviction of a single, prime determinant of global development, rather than acknowledge what Appadurai has called the 'fundamental disjunctures' at work in the global cultural economy (1990, pp. 295–310). World-system and dependency arguments rely heavily upon the asymmetrical pattern of trade between core and peripheral societies to produce an uneven world-wide division of labour. Recent work suggests that these asymmetries still exist in terms of the flow of raw materials and processed goods passing between core and periphery, but that in other respects the model requires substantial revision (Carnoy et al., 1993; Caporaso, 1987). A number of critical factors are apparent.

First, as Carnoy and his colleagues argue, the structure and logic of the global information economy produces a new international division of labour (NIDL). This NIDL not only alters the balance of economic power between core states, including the erstwhile hegemon, the United States, but exacerbates trends towards economic multipolarity.

Second, at the same time a number of NICs have become world-competitive producers of high-tech (mainly electronic) goods, as a result of promotional activities by states, the application of 'post-modern' management techniques and the training of a technically proficient, though still low-wage, workforce. Such developments, principally in the Pacific Rim economies of Taiwan, South Korea, Singapore, Hong Kong, southern China and (in a different league) Japan, represent a qualitatively different phenomenon from that referred to by proponents of 'dependency reversal', wherein emerging specialization in low-wage, low-technology industries, like textile manufacture, serve to increase the volume of exports from Third to First World, and contribute to an increase in the upward mobility of peripheral and semi-peripheral countries in the world system.

Third, the experience of Pacific Rim economies confirms the message of the information economy, that making and sustaining the required technological leap, rather than relying on the short-term comparative advantage to be gained from cheap labour, hold the key to success in the globalized information economy. The division of labour now is one based upon the development and use of high-level as opposed to low-level technologies, and not just between developed and developing economies. It is still true that some multinational companies are attracted by the short-term cost advantages to be gained from producing in the squalid *maquiladora* zones of the world economy, like Brazil, and also true that some governments in the periphery are prepared to encourage direct investment by establishing unregulated zones for economic development. In Germany, in the autumn of 1993, a survey of 10,000 large and medium companies found that one in three planned to transfer production to Eastern Europe or Asia in the next three years because of lower labour costs and looser environmental standards (Nicholson-Lord, 1993). The longer-term projections on recipes for success argue that this will be a strategy with diminishing returns.

Fourth, elsewhere in the periphery a combination of factors has prevented or delayed critical transformations to higher levels of technology. Some of these, notably the debt burden of the 1980s, paradoxically, were a result of the liberalization of global capital markets. Brazil, Mexico and Venezuela, as well as Argentina and Nigeria, fell victim to the debt crisis, and as a consequence their full and successful integration into the global information economy remain in doubt, while the massive potential of India and China to use domestic demand as the basis for radical transformation also remains a source of speculation (Kennedy, 1993, chapter 9).

Neither the idea of a unified periphery, nor a crudely defined zonal model of the world economy, stands up in the face of this sort of complexity. As Cardoso, a scion of the school of structural dependency, argues, the Third World no longer exists (1993, pp. 149–59). It has been replaced by a more complex division of labour which turns on the ability of economies to produce goods and services related to information, and which, in addition to the categories outlined above, includes a tranche of entirely marginal countries, the 'rural economies and sprawling urban peripheries' of much of Africa and parts of Asia and Latin America (Castells, 1993, p. 37). In these countries of the putative Fourth World, exclusion from the economic mainstream either breeds or reinforces tendencies to political and cultural autarky. While this can be romanticized as a defence of local history and culture, as profoundly anti-systemic, or even as a conscious alternative to dominant models of modernization, in many cases it is quite often a further distortion of identities, as in the case of Cambodia under the tutelage of the Khmer Rouge, or Sudan under fundamentalist Islamic rule, and the consequences for already marginal populations are dire. These last areas will remain isolated from the main currents of the world economy, and their hope lies not in dependency reversal, or autonomous development, but in linkage to the world polity – to those currents of opinion, of moral consciousness and concern, which are also heightened by a globalized information and cultural order. It is of course a further irony that the attention on such peripheral areas has declined as their strategic importance has waned in the post-Cold-War era.

Just as the new information economy has major implications for the transformation of the Third World, so the end of state socialism removes the Second World as a global alternative to market capitalism and, in the case of the former Soviet Union, as a pillar of a strategic bipolarity. There has been a good deal of argument within world-system theory about the extent to which the former socialist economies were already integrated into the global division of labour, as players in the peripheral and semi-peripheral zones of the world economy (Zaslavsky, 1985; Arato, 1985; Luke, 1985), but the temptation now is to interpret the collapse of the command economies as a prelude to a fairly long-term, but inevitable, full integration into the world market economy. But the speed and manner of incorporation, as well as its effects across widely different regimes and civil societies, are still hard to predict. A variety of possible developments can be canvassed, some of which are already in train. These range from aid and investment in technology transfer and skills training from the West, exemplified in the EU-funded PHARE programme or the British Foreign Office's 'Know-How' fund, through FDI-fed transplanting of Western assembly plants, to schemes for exploitation of the resource-rich former Soviet heartlands.

In the more 'European' (Kumar, 1992) and apparently more stable countries of Central Europe – Poland, Hungary, the Czech Republic and Slovakia – systematic attempts at cross-border collaboration seem likely to speed up the process of transformation. Nonetheless, 'marketization' of Central and East European economies still requires a complete revision of the productive fabric of these regions, so that they can participate fully in the global information and consumer economy. The collapse of state socialism was a product of the confluence of a number of internal and external pressures, but was in no small measure founded on the inability of the planned economies to make the transition from old-style bureaucratic leviathans to the new age of organizational flexibility and production, driven by investment in 'knowledge' and not in things (Offe, 1991).

But the ideological and cultural legacies of communism have not disappeared with the crumbling of the Berlin Wall (Bryant and Mokrzycki, 1994). While it is conventional wisdom that the rediscovered 'Europeanness' of the Central European region-states predisposes them to move towards Western individualism rather than Eastern collectivism, even so it is best not to overestimate the commitment to the privatized and consumerist ideology of Western capitalism, a commitment which remains ambivalent and variable. In the former Soviet republics the distrust of the state, so apparent in Poland for example, is less obvious. Some writers suggest that the powerful legacy of the Asiatic state still pervades the temper and conduct of Russian government, but the stultifying effects of centralizing and bureaucratic tradition and the alleged absence of a strong civil society tradition seem less of an obstacle to the radical transformation of the Russian economy and civil society than the possibility of further fragmentation and descent into ethnic, religious and national chaos and the activities of a thriving criminal underclass in the black economy.

A regional global economy

In the period since 1945, the globalization of the world economy has proceeded in a secular though by no means linear fashion. In critical areas of trade, production and finance, the world is not only more interconnected but also more interdependent, although not for exclusively 'economic' reasons. The globalization of financial markets and their often volatile effects on national economic management seem, on the face of it, to have produced an increasingly integrated but still curiously anarchic structure, in which both nation-states and the institutions of liberal multilateralism are threatened and where market forces and the realist global ambitions of large corporations hold most sway.

These tensions are seen clearly in the pattern of interdependence as it has developed over the period, and they reflect a growing sense of vulnerability in conventional actors like nation-states. This growing vulnerability has two faces: that of adaptation to global pressures, and that of resistance. In fact both are at the root of one of the main features of the post-war global economy, namely the emergence of regional trading blocs within an integrating world economy. Potentially the most significant of these are the European Union (EU) after the completion of the single market, and the North American Free Trade Area (NAFTA) comprising the United States, Canada and Mexico, notable for its 'zone-spanning' composition. It is now commonplace to include Japan and the Pacific Rim as the third of the great trading blocs which will dominate the world economy into the twenty-first century, but, as Hirst and Thompson (1992) say, the Pacific Rim is in fact still a proto-trading bloc.

Proto-blocs, or groupings which have the potential to form blocs, can also be seen in other parts of the world, and their appearance further underlines the demise of the conception of a simple centre–periphery model. The development of trading blocs (or, in the case of the EU, a regional proto-polity) also reflects the fragility of the liberal trading order enshrined in the GATT and until recently given the imprimatur of America's economic hegemony. Both the European single market and NAFTA are essentially defensive responses to the threats and opportunities of globalization. In fact the EU in its 'relaunched' version, after the Single European Act (SEA) of 1986, represents a blend of optimism and pessimism. In one respect it is an optimistic adaptation to the new challenges of globalized markets, designed to achieve important economies of scale. At the same time it is also a defensive strategy, based on the recognition that the European economy was and is losing out to the more dynamic, expansionist and technologically efficient Japanese, and to the still massive economies of scale seen in the United States.

NAFTA too was born of a sense of growing weakness on the part of the Americans and a loss of faith in the liberalizing power of multilateralist institutions like the GATT, even though the United States remained a protagonist for the successful completion of the latest Uruguay Round of trade talks in 1994. Protectionism and the threat of trade wars between the 'triad' powers, about 'cultural copyrights' and agricultural subsidies, forced the idea of an open world trading order on to the defensive, and for the time being, there it remains.

The general form of the global economy going into the twenty-first century is one in which powerful regional actors are jockeying for position, and where both protectionism and defensive bilateralism seem on the increase. The experience of the Uruguay Round of the GATT encapsulates many of the tensions in the global political economy and shows the overlap between economic, political and cultural factors in its formation. The only clear winners from the freeing of world trade under GATT rules may be those 500 or so companies which control two-thirds of that trade (Nicholson-Lord, 1993). National governments remain more ambivalent, perhaps mistrustful of the optimistic forecasts provided by the OECD, the World Bank and the GATT itself, to the effect that a successful GATT will add $270 billion a year to world income by 2002. To some extent nation-states remain tied closely to domestic interests who feel threatened by the easing of the world's money economy and the freer movement of people and goods.

The Uruguay Round of GATT also provides a gloss on the clashes between global economic imperatives and national cultural institutions or local rules and traditions. Under the new agreements, any rule or institution that might hinder another nation's goods or services from entering freely will be counted as a tariff under a principle known as 'tariffication'. Under GATT rules, it must then be reduced. The scope and scale of possible 'hindrance' is enormous, but the point to carry forward to subsequent chapters is that these 'hindrances' are not just economic factors but extend to ways of life, to cultural diversity. The French fought a particularly bitter campaign over the maintenance of government subsidies to its film industry, a form of national protectionism anathema to the global players in Hollywood (Johnstone, 1994). But American trade negotiators were not just unhappy with a national defence of high culture; they also consider the Japanese practice of encouraging small shops in pedestrianized streets (*hokoosha tengoku*, 'pedestrian heavens') to be a restraint of trade because it interferes with the prospects of US developers and traders opening up large, out-of-town shopping facilities in Japan. Slight as they may seem in the broad warp of the world economy, these examples show the contested nature of the global cultural economy and highlight the positions of quite different stakeholders within it. The next chapter considers the position of national stakeholders and national identities.

5 States and the Global System

The state of the state

The narratives of the nation, the nation-state and the international system of nation-states are central to the making of the modern world. Yet the concept of the *state* often remains shadowy in many areas of social theory, although not in realist accounts of international relations. Skowronek (1982, p. 3) has spoken of the 'grand historical irony' of American politics, which has produced a political culture in many respects at odds with a developed sense or understanding of the state, at least in the senses handed down from Weber (1978) or Durkheim (1962; see also Katznelson, 1992). Indeed, most 'pluralist' attempts to trace the relations between political forms and social relations have treated the state as at most contextualizing, and often irrelevant to the real processes of social life and to the exercise of power. The equally 'societalist' interpretations of Marxist functionalists depict the state either as a repugnant instrument of class domination or, in the more arcane forms of structuralism and post-structuralism, as a social relation, scarcely there at all (Nordlinger, 1981; Dunleavy and O'Leary, 1987; Jessop, 1982; 1990).

In so far as the state is thematized in societalist accounts, it is largely in terms of its degree of 'autonomy' from social forces, most often from social class; here autonomy implies independent goal formulation, and power that is not ultimately dependent upon building coalitions between more or less powerful groups. Practically all such discussions have examined the relations between states and civil societies 'within' territorially bounded units, and until recently they have taken the historically atypical and relatively stateless forms of Anglo-American societies as exemplars of such relations, even where a growing wealth of historical evidence indicates that the more differentiated, centralized and institutionalized 'European' version, typified if at all in the French state, is closer to the historical norm (Badie and Birnbaum, 1983).

Exceptions to the notional rule, which arise from the fact that there are different sorts of state and many apparent variations on the predicted relationships, are dealt with as aberrations of one sort or another. Thus the phenomenon of 'totalitarian' states in 'actually existing socialism' (Bahro, 1981) is seen as some kind of evolutionary blip or stems from the innate backwardness of such societies; while from within the Marxist *oeuvre*, the historically anomalous and autonomous 'Caliban state' identified by Hal Draper is only possible during exceptional and crisis-ridden times (referred to in Gouldner, 1980; Axford and Deacon, 1982). To be sure, more recent developments within academic Marxism have 'rediscovered' the question of state autonomy and the need to treat politics seriously, but often as part of an ingenious attempt at theoretical boundary maintenance and consisting of a frequently sterile debate on the value of incremental adjustments to varieties of more or less vulgar Marxism (Axford and Deacon, 1984).

Despite the avowed need for 'paradigm reorientation' (Evans et al., 1985) and the claim by Ira Katznelson (1981) that Marxism is capable of a 'creative synthesis' between Lenin and Weber, the promise of new horizons produced little more than a hedging of bets on the necessary direction of class domination and its reflection in political and ideological forms, including those now increasingly ordered on a global scale (Held and McGrew, 1993, p. 281). In Eurocommunist and poststructuralist conceptions of the state, some of the obfuscations about 'relative autonomy' are set aside in favour of interpretations which look remarkably pluralist, and the state becomes fragmented, no more than a site for societal struggles whose outcome depends on the contingent ordering of key resources by non-state actors (Jessop, 1990; Miliband, 1985).

Attempts to specify the actual conditions under which states might act autonomously have been rare: indeed, in most cases even the notion of the state acting autonomously, except of course in 'exceptional' circumstances, is too radical a proposition to take on board (but see Skocpol, 1980; Gowa, 1984). More historically sensitive accounts of the origins of states and the modern state system almost let Weber out of the closet through portentous remarks on the subjectivity and the anthropomorphized 'self-interested' behaviour of the state as a reified collective actor. These do come closer to Eric Nordlinger's (1981) concern to deal with the question of autonomy as an empirical one, not foreclosed by *a priori* assumptions about the relationships between political power and class power (Mann, 1986; Trimberger, 1978; Evans et al., 1985; Giddens, 1985). At least some of these accounts manage to break through the cordon sanitaire around the sanctity of social class as an explanatory variable, but on the whole a theoretical breakthrough is abjured in favour of paradigm maintenance.

The obsession with the implied domination of societal power over state institutions and functions extends to discussion of Second and Third World states. Here too there has been an unreflective and ahistorical willingness to transfer the model of the class state in Anglo-American capitalism to quite different conditions existing elsewhere, especially in the Third World. Former socialist states escaped this fate only because of their allegedly unique genealogy in an 'Asiatic' mode of production, wherein social classes were subsumed by an all-embracing 'state class', the only allocator and distributor of values (Anderson, 1974). By contrast, peripheral states have been examined mainly through the lens of dependency theories, or world-system variants, in which state structures and state personnel function as elements in the peripheralization of colonial and post-colonial economies.

A rather different gloss on the functions of 'strong' states in the periphery, one which modifies the reliance on material factors, emerges from research on the exposure of states to currents in 'world culture' (Ramirez, 1987; Appelbaum and Henderson, 1992). Dependency theory, and theories of unequal exchange and power in the centre–periphery hierarchy, have no difficulty in cataloguing the negative effects of capitalism on autonomous forms of economic development, 'but neglect the reliance of non-core societies on both capitalist culture and the world-wide culture of the nation-state for their nationalist mobilization, for their sense of political identity and for their legitimacy' (Ramirez, 1987, p. 321). Accounts of the incorporation of peripheral or non-core states into the global system must of course deal with their location in the world economy, but at the same time must note the extent to which the culture of the world polity has legitimated aggressive state- and nation-building by providing models of national development. The linking of new states to the larger world-cultural frame of reference has operated as a spur to the adoption of various 'cultural products' of the global system –

constitutions, liberal education, population policy and, increasingly, environmental policies of various kinds – often regardless of the local contexts in which they are being applied. The pressure to adopt these cultural products in different contexts sometimes produces local (or even civilizational) resistance.

So the universalization of what Meyer et al. (1987) call the 'Western cultural account' has radically modified the expectation about models of national development, to the extent that quite different regimes produce policy outputs, and also justifications for these, that are very similar. At the same time the continuing power of local meaning structures, and the reflexive nature of identity construction, point up the ways in which global cultural products are 'indigenized' by a variety of situated actors. Once again, apparent global isomorphism hides a diversity of political identities and aspirations.

The spread of the nation-state as part of the cultural framework of the global system is best understood from a modified structurationist-institutionalist perspective. From this perspective, the identity of states is a product of their own 'local' history and culture and of the 'compelling links' which they have to the global cultural system. This is a considerable departure both from globally sensitive accounts of the behaviour of states and the state system in the relatively ordered world-system of capitalism, and also from the state-centred realist tradition or variants of it in the form of the 'competition state' (Reich, 1992). All forms of international relations theory deal with the world beyond the nation-state, but realism is as unconcerned theoretically with the significance of endogenous forces on state action and identity as many societalist accounts have been with the world in which the nation-state is embedded (Wendt, 1994). More than this, realists have emptied the concept *state* of anything which might suggest that the behaviour of states is a product of human intervention, or inter-subjectivity. Instead it is a 'reality' inscribed within an anarchic state of nature, and its behaviour is grounded in the unalterable logic of an international system which reproduces itself through the survival strategies of sovereign states, which are all 'egoistic actors' (Gusterson, 1993, p. 289; Wendt, 1994, p. 386). Rarely is there a suggestion that what states do and what they 'are' results from the conscious decisions and interactions of individuals and collectivities.

The argument to be pursued here is that it is the reflexive involvement of actors with institutional frameworks which both reproduces the institution as a constructed reality, and secures or transforms the identity of actors. Where the identity of the actor blurs or is at odds with the wider network of meanings within which it is embedded, there is room for the transformation of that identity and for the transformation of the institutional context. At the same time there is room for multiple identities, and these need not be contradictory or pathological. The whole debate about European unity centres on the compatibility of the egoistic identities of nation-states and the collective identity of a supraterritorial European Union. Proponents of one strand of 'integration theory' see ruin in the visions of the other, but rarely is there a sense that actors engaging with European rules may be fashioning and refashioning identities which are neither local nor 'communitarian' in the accepted sense of that term. I return to this point later in the chapter.

Another form of realism is found in the writings of the 'competetiveness' school of international economics and strategic management (Porter, 1990; Reich, 1992). Here states enhance the profitability of capital and labour by fostering a supportive environment for business activity, and this is seen as their primary function, embracing the reproduction of an efficient and flexible workforce and the political conditions necessary for accumulation (Reich, 1992). Politics is important, but still as the handmaiden of economics. Of course Porter and Reich would blanch at the suggestion that their view of politics is reductionist. Rather, they would argue that tasks undertaken by states to enhance their economies and to deal with the growing interdependence and pressures of the global information economy are no more than prudent measures to protect and promote the national interest, and are not, *pace* vulgar Marxism, evidence of the subordination of the state to the institutions of capital.

Let me summarize the argument so far. In Marxist and neo-Marxist positions, the state is treated as an actor whose autonomy and performance are in some way subordinated to the interests of a dominant class, and this holds for all class-divided societies. In the more 'eclectic' accounts of liberal institutionalism, the vogue is to explain the putative 'decline' of the state as the largely unmediated outcome of complex global pressures (Held and McGrew, 1993). To some extent this line of argument does locate the discussion of the state more firmly in the context of global interdependence, but ironically, at the expense of a needed dose of sociological realism, where that implies taking note of the still substantial freedom enjoyed by national states in their dealings with extranational actors and forces (Dessler, 1989). By contrast, realism proper remains wedded to the centrality of the nation-state as a global actor, but treats the identity and motivations of state actors as entirely unproblematic. As Held and McGrew suggest, the palpable need is thus for a transcendence of both the endogenous framework where state actions are ordered by societal forces and to meet functional imperatives, and exogenous frameworks wherein state autonomy and sovereignty are ever more compromised by the interdependence of the global system (1993, p. 282).

The state as subject and context

Which prescription is not without difficulties. Let me begin by looking at the defining features of states in general and of the modern nation-state in particular. These go beyond the 'legitimate domination over a spatial extension' (Giddens, 1981, p. 45) since this conception applies to all systems of rule, including those not defined on a territorial basis at all (Ruggie, 1993, p. 149). Rather, the main characteristic of the modern system of rule called the nation-state is that of the territorial organization of political life under a single, legitimate authority which enjoys an imputed monopoly of the means of violence. Such a 'sovereign' entity is differentiated from civil society by virtue of its monopoly of legitimate coercion, the extent of its allocative and distributive powers, and its stewardship of the public realm (Ruggie, 1993). There may be degrees of 'stateness', in the sense that state apparatuses can be more or less centralized or else look more like a polity, which is a much looser network of public and private actors. There may even be variability in terms of a state's capacity to act authoritatively, to mobilize those rules and resources theoretically at its disposal.

These features of 'stateness' (Nettl, 1968) define a phenomenon which, in the well-known phrase, is 'real in its consequences' and which cannot be treated simply as a social relation or an abstraction, even though it is helpful to describe the state as a more fragmented 'institutional ensemble' than is possible in realist accounts (Held and McGrew, 1993, p. 280; Jessop, 1990, chapter 11). Actions by state functionaries have symbolic and material effects regardless of the relative power of state and societal interests; alliances between states make up the strategic map of the world; and wars between states kill people. All of which suggests that it is useful to treat the state as an organizational actor, perhaps even in realist terms, since this focuses attention upon the actions of the state *as a state* and not just as the agent, facilitator or interlocutor for other social forces. Indeed, this is the burden of the 'organizational-realist' approach espoused by Theda Skocpol, with its mission to 'bring the state back in' to social theory (Skocpol, 1977; 1978; Evans et al., 1985).

Well and good, but an organizational-realist approach to the analysis of states sees them, courtesy of realism, as purposive actors rationally selecting means as a part of goal-seeking strategies. The content of action, as Meyer points out, is then explained by the properties and resources of actors and by their contingent preferences. While attention to the historical and genetic peculiarities of individual state formation restricts the realist tendency to impute 'given' preferences to states, these are still basically explanations that rely upon rationalist conceptions of self-interest (see for example Moravcsik, 1991). In such interpretations of state action wider environmental factors are entertained, but for the most part as a context in which action takes place rather than as providing a means to action, a set of rules through which action is made, or 'materials which are appropriated and instantiated (reproduced and transformed) through action' (Dessler, 1989, pp. 441–52). Actor and system are either separated in a kind of analytical dualism, or reduced to a series of interactions between more or less resourceful actors and environmental conditions which only 'channel' action through a set of constraints.

The argument to be used here follows the lines set out in chapters 1 and 3, namely that the behaviour of states reflects the socially constructed character of the entities and processes under discussion. In particular, this means that while it is important to deal with states as subjects having constructed identities, rather than actors whose ontology is given, it must be noted that their actions are situated within sets of institutional rules which not only regulate activity in the sense suggested by Giddens, but also constitute meaning structures which legitimate some actions and proscribe others. Of course, actors do not engage with these sets of rules *tabula rasa*, without identity, or without reflection: but it is through the reflexive engagement of active agents with cultural rules that structure and identity are reproduced and transformed (Dessler, 1989; Wendt, 1987; Bhaskar, 1979).

Using this kind of reasoning, much of the obvious uniformity of behaviour across states with quite different genealogies which would be otherwise inexplicable, or the result of serendipity, becomes clearer. Thus the adoption of standard policies and dogmas in areas like population control, and the justification for their use, reflects global system influence upon national policies, where there exists a prior set of rules or assumptions which are seen as legitimate. Nation-states adopt such policies as a measure of the extensiveness of their links to the world polity, or as a measure of their desire to effect such links (Ramirez, 1987; Barrett, 1992). Their own profiles of appropriate national development are thus influenced by meaning structures of global scope. I want to stress that I am not saying that rules alone can explain these outcomes, any more than can purely action-centred theories, but I am asserting that practice both reaffirms and transforms the conditions for action, at the same time as actors are invested with meanings that are supplied by those conditions, whether these are material structures or rules governing behaviour (Dessler, 1989, p. 453).

One objection to looking at the behaviour of states as ordered or given meaning by global institutions would be the realist claim that there are no rules governing the interaction of states in the international system, only a rational desire to survive under conditions of anarchy. Even with a dispensation for neo-realist rule-governed behaviours in international regimes, this claim underestimates the extent to which all social action, including self-help, depends on the pre-existence of rules which have meaning for actors (Dessler, 1989, p. 458). A structurationist view of the anarchic international system treats 'anarchy', or the state of nature itself, as a social construction which has achieved the status of a global institution, with war, strategic deterrence or balance of power politics all taken to be cultural products of that system which are reproduced and transformed through the practice (Gusterson, 1993; Koslowski and Kratochwil, 1994).

Alexander Wendt's analysis of global power politics as a social construction makes the point directly (1987; 1992; 1994). In realist accounts of the international system, the identity of that system is unproblematic because its fundamental features – anarchy and the rational strategies of survival under conditions of anarchy – are taken for granted. The making and transformation of identities are therefore bracketed as an issue. But a *constructivist* (Wendt's term) view of international relations, on the contrary, maintains that identities are not given but made. Thus power politics and strategies of self-help do not follow either logically or causally from anarchy. There is, he says, 'no logic of anarchy apart from the practices that create and instantiate one structure of identities and interests rather than another': in other words, 'anarchy is what states make of it' (1992, pp. 395–6). Dryzek et al. are more formal when they say that 'operant structures and individuated state actors both have ontological status': subject and system, part and whole, are taken as mutually constitutive rather than ordered as independent and dependent variables (Dryzek et al., 1989, pp. 502–3; see also Foucault, 1990). But the message is the same: structures do not stand outside actors impinging on their behaviours, but help to codify interests through the part they play in defining what actors collectively 'know' and thus what they 'are'.

By the same token, the social definition of a legitimate actor is grounded in this collective understanding. An actor's identity, and certainly the expression of its interests, cannot be separated from the social contexts in which the actor is situated and the operant meanings which legitimate and/or outlaw certain types of behaviour. As Wendt says, 'in the last resort, agents and structures are produced or reproduced by what actors do' (1994, p. 390). This intersubjective conception of social reality does not detract from the sense in which actors experience institutions as 'real', or objective. Indeed, the more stable or persistent the institutional scripts with which actors engage, the more 'natural' and immutable they seem (Krasner, 1988; Giddens, 1993). Institutions are generated through complex processes which involve the networking of ideas by actors and their legitimation over time as conventional forms and norms. Global institutions like sovereignty are reproduced through the practices of individual agents and collective actors like the nation-state itself, and diffused globally through the spread of the nation-state as an authoritative actor in the ontology and epistemology of world politics.

It follows then that the institution of sovereignty retains its power as a constitutive feature of the constructed social reality of states only so long as these actors continue to practise it, that is, to treat it as a universal framework for action. On Krasner's (1988) reasoning, statehood, or sovereignty as the badge of statehood, remains a global social institution because it continues to provide just such a framework for action. The identity of states as legitimate actors in world politics is still closely bound up with the institution of sovereignty. Because of this, sovereignty as an institution and the nation-state as an actor are hardly 'up for grabs' (Krasner, 1988). All the same, such a view may seriously understate the extent to which newer cultural scripts are having greater salience for a growing number and variety of actors, constraining them to adopt different behaviours and new identities. Developments in the process of European unity offer just such an illustration, and I will return to this below. On a related matter, John Ruggie (1993), writing about the 'embedded liberalism' of post-war free trade, is at pains to point out that the establishment of free trade regimes has not only altered the behaviour of states by applying external constraints, but altered states' perceptions of their identity and interests as economic actors.

Of course it speaks volumes for the continuing power of institutional paradigms like the nation-state that the development of supra- or non-territorial forms of governance, for example the European Union and the GATT, or the role of non-governmental organizations (NGOs) in formulating policy on global poverty and sustainable growth, are still discussed in the language of governance exemplified by the modern state (Ruggie, 1993; Axford, 1994). It is only a partial exaggeration to say that the very idea of politics is still constrained by what goes on within and between nation-states, although, as I will show in chapters 6, 7 and 8, the shoots of a supraterritorial and a postmodern politics are visible.

The state in the discourses of modernity and globalization

The persistence of the nation-state form, and its enduring appeal to nationalist and separatist political forces in this consciously 'interdependent' world, should not come as a surprise. As John Ruggie (1993, p. 139) observes, the world of states 'exists on a deeper and more extended temporal plane' than many of the 'globalizing' forces implicated in its putative decline. Through its links with the most powerful myth of political identity in the modern world, the narrative of nation, the state occupies a privileged place in the institutional dimensions of modernity and, as a 'system' of states, still offers a convenient shorthand for a world political system (Heller and Feher, 1988). The modern world is still a world of states, and routine interactions between nation-states in the form of embassies, treaties and immigration policies instantiate and normalize the idea of territoriality and the orderliness of world politics.

But the state is also the formal expression of national identity, of the claim to be legitimate as an international actor, while being different culturally. Arnason (1990) talks of nations as 'cultural totalities', and in Anderson's (1983) phrase they are 'imagined communities' which enjoy complex and ambiguous relationships with substate actors, with other states and with global forces. In their struggle to impose unity on the often divergent orders or life-worlds of traditional societies and localities, modern states have behaved as both context-destructive and context-generative forces, limiting the ability of local contexts to reproduce local subjects (a theme I will take up in chapter 6) as well as providing new contexts for identity formation. At the same time they have fostered interconnections and interdependencies between parts of the world, through military alliances or trade and through humanitarian multilateralism. Ironically, these connections present a challenge to the context-generative capacities of nation-states, since they introduce alternative sources of meaning for substate actors accustomed to make use of statist scripts.

Globalization is often closely associated with a notional 'crisis of the territorial nation-state' (McGrew, 1992, p. 87). Indeed, Held and McGrew speak of major and growing disjunctures between the formal and conventional authority claimed by the nation-state and the ways in which international, regional and global power structures condition the actual practices of states (1993, pp. 265–76). In their view, these power structures are international regimes and organizations, the increasingly dominant logic of the world economy, the constraints of international law and the declining security capabilities of nation-states. In addition there are the disjunctures between the state and subnational forces and actors which may have aspirations and claims that cannot be accommodated by weakened states. Held and McGrew are also rightly critical of the tendency to see global forces operating unmediated upon nation-states, and this shows a proper caution. At the same time they are reluctant to specify even a fairly abstract explanatory account of the relationships between states and globalizing processes. I want to pursue this line further before addressing the question of the 'decline' of the state directly.

As a feature of what Friedman calls the 'global social reality' (1993, p. 208), nation-states replicate both global structures and themselves as collective subjects, through practice. It is important to see states as both subjects and contexts in order to grasp the reflexiveness and intersubjectivity of the processes which are making the global system. The persistence of the state as both a subject and a global institution depends on the reproduction of the contexts in which states and other actors are participating (Dryzek et al., 1989). This is because the structures within which action takes place have great influence upon any subject's experience of reality and thus on its sense of identity. Individual subjects are linked to broader cultural scripts like that of sovereignty, or 'international anarchy', or 'free trade', in ways which tie their identity to the conditions and meanings prevailing there.

Having said this, I do want to reject the view that the identity of state actors is solely a product of their links to wider contexts. It is also necessary to conceive of states as 'imagined communities' which are built from 'below' as well as from 'above', and which have their own genealogy. Of course any treatment of the 'decline' of the state must deal with the ways in which global processes are limiting the power of the state as an actor and diminishing its status as a context for the identities of non-state and substate actors. In its most extreme form the declinist argument echoes Ohmae's position, outlined in chapter 4, in which the territorial state is more and more unreflective of real political and cultural flows and networks. More specifically, three aspects of decline are often mentioned, and together they add up to the putative transformation of conventional political architecture and the organization of political space (Ramirez, 1987; Cerny, 1990). These aspects are: changes in the doctrine of state sovereignty; the autonomy of the nation-state in key areas of policy-making and implementation; and its status as a focus for and expression of national identity. In what follows I will examine them by considering the alleged 'decline' of the nation-state in terms of its definitional sovereign status; explore the related but analytically separate issue of its decisional autonomy, drawing on ideas introduced in chapter 4 about the interconnectedness of markets and the space-devouring power of new technologies; and open a discussion on the state as a meaning structure or locus of identity for citizens and other political actors.

The decline of the state and territoriality

To reiterate the argument so far. The state in the modern global system is both actor and social institution. Actors employ cultural understandings to create and reproduce identities or self-definitions, and through their actions they reproduce structure and system. In turn self-definitions are organized around institutional rules of varying degrees of generality and power. But the persistence of these rules, and thus of an actor's self-definition under them, cannot be taken for granted. Changes in the character of rules or cultural scripts – for example the extent to which global media networks undermine national systems of information control, or national definitions of appropriate values – can cause disorder and redefinition at the local level (Friedman, 1993). This is because the opportunity for actors to corroborate their own identity and to re-enact the properties of the system are disrupted, because the identity of the larger system of meaning on which they depended for their own internal order itself has changed.

Now, actors who consciously try to re-enact the world as it was either are marginalized (as in the case of some business corporations clinging to outdated technologies), or try to achieve some degree of autarky through attempts at self-closure which are mostly unsuccessful (nation-states like Cambodia, Iran or North Korea), or are rearticulated with the new realities, having redefined themselves on the way. None of this should be read as some kind of simple functional accommodation to systemic constraints, or as a form of suprasystem dominance. For one thing, as Friedman indicates, the transformation of conditions of existence at the level of the global system can create 'space' for the forging of new identities in regions and localities, as well as make things difficult for existing identities (1993, p. 208). So global communication processes, or regional policy processes like those emergent in the European Union, can have a galvanizing effect on the formation of new identities among substate and non-state actors, by constraining ethnic groups, lobbyists, fundamentalist religious movements and other social and cultural forces to come to terms with changed conditions.

The phenomenon of transnational labour migration shows the ambiguities in these sorts of processes. Obviously, it can be read as part of the globalization of economic relations examined in chapter 4. At the same time, migration makes it more difficult for nation-states to maintain definitions of citizenship based upon rules and cultures which connect the status of citizenship to strict and exclusive definitions of nationality. The processes of economic migration have turned many metropolitan countries into multicultural world spaces (Balibar, 1991; Soysal, 1995) and exacerbated the tensions between the demands of particular national or racial and ethnic identities and the realities of qualified market societies, whose legitimacy and connection to the world polity owe much to those universalistic value systems which are the legacy of global liberalism and individualism (Axford, 1987). A resolution to the attitudinal and policy ambivalence often produced by these conjunctures can take a number of forms, including the adoption of 'colour blind' or universalist definitions of citizenship, attempts to establish a thoroughgoing multiculturalism, or regression to some form of ethnic or racial exclusivism. But the point is that because of the compelling links they have to the world polity, it would be difficult for national decision-makers to dissociate themselves completely from global cultural scripts, where these continue to exercise identity-securing power and confer legitimacy. Attempts to do so may produce legitimation deficits both among domestic populations and in the international community.

In Western Europe these factors, along with the processes of integration, have produced a politics of immigration in which the claims of immigrants to rights in any one country are increasingly a matter of concern at the Community level. Changes in the labour-market requirements of advanced economies coupled with the new phenomenon of east–west migration in Europe have hardened public opinion in many Western European countries against immigration, but these trends have deepened official and popular ambivalence about the place of migrants within national societies, rather than the opposite. So while official responses to perceived threats from 'economic' refugees have been to tighten immigration controls and those governing the treatment of asylum seekers, something like a politics of citizenship has emerged both within particular countries and across Europe (Salt, 1991). To the extent that this politics is about the implied naturalness of the exclusive link between citizenship and nationality, it is one more pressure on the ideology of the nation-state (Baldwin-Edwards and Schain, 1994).

My point is that the power of particular ideologies and institutions to secure identities in the face of rapid change must not be taken for granted, and of course this has always been true. For example, the medieval world was one of local and personal allegiances, or 'parcelized sovereignties' in Perry Anderson's (1974) phrase. That world was destroyed by the encompassing structures of modernity, which integrated the world politically around the 'identity space' of the nation-state. In the present era of rapid, global changing, it may be that the world is becoming 'medieval' again, as 'infranationalism', or the breakdown of the nation-state into smaller units, contends both with the ideology of the unified state and with the forces of multilateralism and supranationalism for the shape of the global system going into the twenty-first century (Stone, 1994). In this contest, the survival of the institution of nation-state sovereignty is of great significance, despite the fact that some authors choose to start from the assumption that sovereign statehood is 'defunct' (Scholte, 1994).

Sovereignty

The central attribute of 'modernity in international politics' has been that peculiar and historically unique configuration of territorial space, the nation-state (Ruggie, 1993, p. 168; Walker, 1993). Conventionally, the key attribute of statehood is that of sovereignty; and, although there are other forms of international governance (Strang, 1991), sovereign states are the 'distinctive signature of the modern political world, being territorially disjoint, mutually exclusive, functionally similar' (Ruggie, 1993, p. 151). The idea of sovereignty as applied to modern states implies two main things: (1) the right of a 'sovereign' authority to impose the law through use of force internally; and (2) the authority to carry war to the enemies of the state, and in less martial guise to act to protect and promote the national interest (Held, 1992, pp. 22–3).

It is important to note that the concept of sovereignty does not carry with it the clear expectation that sovereign actors have the capacities to carry out these functions of rule, but affirms that they are recognized as having the right so to do without undue let or hindrance from other state actors. Sovereignty is not a measure of the capacity of a state, or not only this, but is a form of signification and, in the sense conveyed by Alexander Wendt, an intersubjective system structure or interaction context (1994, p. 389). The doctrine of 'recognition' is central to the idea of sovereignty used in this way, in effect defining 'rigid spatial boundaries between the rights of the self and the other' (p. 388). Corporate security is thus secured by institutionalizing the self-interest of individual actors. At the same time and for the system to work, these actors must reproduce the institution. Let me illustrate what I mean. The capacity of a national government to ensure the compliance of groups of citizens or sojourners within its borders may be in doubt where separatist organizations like the Basque ETA directly confront the authority and power of the Spanish government, or where the power of the Shining Path guerrillas in Peru establishes virtual 'no-go' areas for government jurisdiction. But, provided that the government is recognized as the legitimate state authority, this may not be so disabling as to affect the legitimacy of the state in international affairs.

For the most part, the succession of rulers also does not raise problems of international legitimacy, except in special circumstances, such as occurred in Haiti in 1991, where a military regime usurped the power of an elected president. But a government challenged by oppositional forces who question its very legitimacy, one immobilized by powerful sectional interests or by a lack of popular consent, may actually compromise the standing of the state as a recognized entity in the international community, and possibly in international law. While other factors are often relevant, like the strategic position of the territory involved, 'internal' lack of legitimacy may well invite intervention from outside. Newly independent states are especially vulnerable to internal opposition and even annexation, because they are scarcely legitimated in international discourse and lack many of the accoutrements of established rule. In the name of non-interventionism and through expediency, the international community seldom acts directly in such cases, but, as will be shown, there is some limited evidence that this code is changing. Other factors too compromise the legal myth of sovereignty. The ability of a state to 'deploy' various resources in its own interests is often a function of its economic strength, and here the inequalities in the global hierarchy of states militate against the equality implied in the principle of sovereignty.

But there are other roots to the concept of sovereignty, like those derived from theories of majoritarian democracy and popular sovereignty. These alternative sources of meaning can limit the force of the idea of sovereignty as the doctrine of territorial integrity (Held, 1991, p. 229). Theories of constitutional rule are attempts to delineate the proper boundaries and intersection of the principles of state and popular sovereignty (Walker, 1993). But where constitutionalism fails and the rights of citizens are violated, or the conditions of governance are so despoiled as to make life for 'ordinary people' very difficult, recent practice suggests that the 'new' post-Cold-War order sanctions violation of the principle of state sovereignty (where that means non-intervention in the affairs of an independent state) in the name of 'humanity', 'human rights' or 'just war'.

The operation of 'aggressive multilateralism' in areas like northern Iraq, Somalia, Bosnia and Haiti is still riddled with many ambiguities, not least over the role of multilateral organizations like the United Nations. But, as Adam Roberts points out, the extent of the change in attitudes towards the organizing rules of the international community may be judged from a statement by the Secretary-General of the United Nations (UN), Dr Boutros-Boutros Ghali, in June 1992, to the effect that consent for UN peacekeeping or humanitarian actions may not be the fundamental barrier it once constituted, where civil war, famine or other humanitarian considerations are stronger than respect for the sovereignty of nations (quoted in Roberts, 1993, p. 434).

As a tocsin for the institution of state sovereignty this sounds a powerful warning, but applied outside the context of weak or peripheral states it loses some of its force, and even applied to hard cases within this category it may be just hortatory, meeting some domestic need for the smack of strong leadership, or appeasing a powerful domestic constituency. In the case of the death threat by Ayatollah Khomeini against the British author, Salman Rushdie, the idea of any sort of direct intervention in Iranian domestic affairs is too remote to contemplate. Even though the world turns very quickly these days, mounting an operation to mediate in the civil war in Georgia or to broker conflicts in the Ukraine or in Chechenia also appears entirely fanciful, given the sensitivity to Russian interests and the logistics of long-term intervention. But let me be quite clear about this point: these caveats apart, what may be different in the current climate is the degree of apparent consensus on the principle of humanitarian interventions.

Of course, a consensus on principles is far short of policy delivery, and individual countries will cavil at the likely efficacy of multilateral ventures, as well as the costs, as they slide into long-term military commitments. In Bosnia, such vacillation has produced a policy of drift and timid pragmatism interspersed with a thin bellicosity. Nonetheless, it is still important to look at the extent to which the institution of sovereignty is both reinforced and undermined by multilateral interventions. For example, while the Gulf War of 1991 was fought on the principle of defending the national sovereignty of Kuwait, as Pieterse says, it is the Kurdish question and the establishment of 'safe havens' in northern Iraq which 'expose(s) the ordered contingency of that principle' (1993, p. 229). By the same token, the reluctance to act in defence of the Marsh Arabs in the south-east of Iraq also demonstrates the difficult calculus involved in a trade-off between the principles of intervention and non-intervention, when mixed with a good dose of pragmatism. Inevitably, this issue raises crucial questions about the functions of international organizations as institutions of governance, notably with respect to the United Nations, and this is taken up in chapter 7. But the immediate point is how this confusing evidence bears on the demise of the institution of state sovereignty.

With admirable clarity, Krasner (1988) points to the continued vitality of the nation-state form as a focus for political aspiration, to the relative incoherence of alternative forms of governance and international regulation, and to the willingness of other states to reciprocate in the etiquette of sovereignty. Reciprocal sovereignty still constitutes the basis of the international order, and nation-states, regardless or pretty well regardless of their capacities, have been empowered because of their status as constitutive parts of a recognized order, or as Ruggie would have it, because of the power of the idea of sovereignty as a 'social episteme' (1993, p. 163), where that refers to the mental equipment that people draw upon in imagining and symbolizing forms of political community (p. 157). This equipment includes ideas about the organization of space, and the symbols that connect place to identity, as well as more formal political doctrines.

The persistence of sovereignty as a global episteme cannot be explained solely by reference to material factors, since taken alone these would seem to predict an even greater degree of global inequality, brought about by the lack of respect for the territorial integrity of less powerful or resourceful state actors and the globalizing of economic relations. Neither can it be imputed to the philosophical realism of rational actors, or the 'realist' strategies of state elites, found in some of the organizational-realist accounts from historical sociology (Skocpol, 1985; Mann, 1986). As Held says, the effective power which sovereignty bestows is, in considerable measure, connected to the economic resources a state can deploy (1992, pp. 201–4), but the persistence and power of an institution reflects not just the preferences of the units themselves but the willingness and ability of actors to reproduce it (Keohane, 1984; Krasner, 1988; Wendt, 1994). Thus any perceived erosion in the institution of sovereignty would require proof of its inability to anchor identities and affect behaviour. Of course the same would be true of all structures as contexts for action.

The 'unbundling' of the concepts of territoriality and sovereignty does intimate a transformation of world politics (Ruggie, 1993). Yet it may be too facile to depict the sovereign nation-state as crumbling between the pressures of 'supranationality and transnationality and tribalism' (Drucker, 1993). Challenges to the complete individuation of the 'territorial space' that is the modern state may signal terminal decline, but also can be seen as a kind of transformative practice in a dynamic global cultural economy (Agnew, 1994, p. 76). In practice, of course, the concept of the sovereign state has never meant complete individuation. Agreements over the constitution of international society also require attention to the governance of those 'global commons' – seaways, transborder waterways, the Antarctic continent and, of late, outer space – which could not be conveniently divided up as the province of one territorial unit or another (Vogler, 1992). Deconstruction of the principle of absolute sovereignty, 'unbundling' as Ruggie says, is apparent in the construction of a systematic 'extraterritoriality' in the form of functional regimes, for example the Climate Conference of 1992, the various agreements on the extraterritorial integrity of Antarctica, tariff and trade agreements like the GATT, as well as various regional common markets. Individual state actors fashion an identity within the epistemic confines of these regimes or institutions, thereby 'attentuating the paradox of absolute individuation' and constituting the flow or part of the flow of international society (Ruggie, 1993, p. 165; Dryzek et al., 1989).

The behavioural autonomy of states

Sovereignty is a global social institution which legitimates the idea of territorial integrity. In discussions about the decline of the nation-state it is often confused with the power of state elites to take decisions in the national interest and to secure and maintain the loyalty of citizens – their behavioural power. I am talking here about both the decisional autonomy of the nation-state and its function as the keeper of national identity. Take first of all the idea of national defence policy, and what *The Economist* (22 December 1990) calls the 'meat and potatoes' of the nation-state diet, namely the power to wage war. Few countries in the world are capable of sustaining high levels of defence expenditure without incurring unacceptable levels of national debt; but, leaving aside the resource implications, 'national' defence and security are generally things of the past for those nations firmly linked to supraterritorial forms of collective security and the ideologies of multilateralism that sustain them.

During the Cold War the concept of collective security became rooted in alliance structures like the North Atlantic Treaty Organization (NATO) and the Warsaw Pact, but in the precarious 'new world order' after the collapse of state socialism, collective decision-making about security issues is still much in evidence. However, the need to legitimate interventions even against 'rogue' states like Iraq and Haiti is a powerful constraint upon action. The conflict between America and Saddam Hussein, which resulted in the Gulf War of 1991 and further rumblings in 1994, saw the United States involved in a Byzantine exercise of alliance-building under the auspices of the United Nations, to create a coalition which would have legitimacy across otherwise disparate national and regional interests. In the Bosnian conflict, the preferences of national decision-makers for either intervention or disengagement are influenced by domestic public opinions, but also by the need to be seen as in step with collective actors like the UN, NATO or the European Union.

Because of the significance of economic and technological factors in the compression of the world, let me return to the paradigm case of the power of the state relative to global forces, namely the relations between nation-states and multinational and transnational corporations. There is an immanent tension between the ends of the nation-state and those of transnational businesses, and the undoubted resources of the latter make the question of how they can be harnessed to the goal of national development a crucial one for state elites (Carnoy et al., 1993). The policy choices for nation-states which are either the notional 'home' of TNCs and MNCs, or the recipients of direct investment, do reflect the facts of global economic life, especially with regard to the deregulation of cross-border enterprises and cross-border flows of capital, information and people.

In this regard it is clear that the internationalization of markets has put limits on the managerial powers of individual states. The marketization of the global economy has proceeded under the auspices of neo-liberal policies practised by world institutions like the IMF, the World Bank and the OECD. Keynesian policies aimed at stabilizing the effects of economic activity – complete with counter-cyclical programmes of job creation, national monetarist solutions to currency and exchange instability, fiscal regimes aimed at redistributing wealth, or government-led economic expansion – have become much less tenable since the failure of the French socialist 'experiment' of the early 1980s to buck the pressures of the international capital markets. For all this, forms of international Keynesianism are still mooted as possible solutions to the global recession of the mid 1990s, although the more interventionist slant of 'Clintonomics' in the United States received a buffet following Republican successes in the mid-term elections to the Congress in November 1994. Apart from this consideration, such a prospect will turn on the willingness and the ability of the United States to underwrite world economic expansion when it is so troubled by budget deficits and chronic urban crisis, and so preoccupied with forms of national protectionism. In other respects, neo-liberalism as the global geoculture is under pressure from national publics still wedded to high-profile welfare statism, from the now globalized ecology movement, and from citizenry rather unhappy at being cast as consumers and not as citizens.

But in general there does seem to be a systematic loosening of the power of the nation-state over the organization of economic life. We should not overstate this, since the continuing importance of national and regional factors in providing necessary supply-side conditions for greater competitiveness is also very strong. While it is possible to interpret this in some crudely instrumentalist fashion, such that MNCs and global companies merely 'use' the space provided by national jurisdictions in the same way that they might use any other 'resource', in reality it does point to more of a reflexive and synergistic relationship between these units of the global system than is often assumed. Thus the answer to the question, 'do nation-states still matter in terms of economic management?', is not, as Carnoy et al. say, a 'resounding yes' (1993, p. 88) but a more cautious affirmative.

One further area merits attention before we turn to the questions of governance and politics beyond the nation-state, and that is the idea of *national identity*, increasingly thematized as a problem area in world politics. The myth of development of the modern nation-state as a 'pacified social space' (Elias, 1978) prescribed the idea of a national identity or a common culture expressed through language, myth and the meaning attached to a particular territorial space. Where culture is seen as an attribute of territorially bounded social units, the various symbols of national identity – dress, language, flag, heroic myths and so on – have become the primary means of designating 'us' as opposed to 'them'. Moreover, the symbols of national (cultural) difference are sometimes linked with the ideologies and folklore of racial difference. Thus opposition to black immigration to the United Kingdom has often been expressed through a rejection of the cultural practices of migrants.

The locus and the guarantor of the 'imagined community' of national identity, in Anderson's phrase, has been the nation-state. This function goes beyond providing security, or material well-being, to the provision and maintenance of shared meanings, and even to providing collective definitions of society. Of course in practice the idea of an overarching cultural unity or national identity has been possible only by recognizing in both law and custom that most nation-states are really multinational or multi-ethnic units, or else are becoming multicultural in composition. In Australia today there are 141 officially recognized 'cultures', an acknowledgement that (white) Australian identity is being remade through the processes of immigration and integration.

Throughout this book I have argued that the reproduction of identity is often problematic because all identities are reconstituted through action, and that the context in which action takes place must itself be reproduced in order to be remembered. Such an argument can be applied to the nation-state as a context for identity formation. Apparent signs of decay are all around, challenging the claim of the territorial state to express a natural or even a crafted unity. In the former Soviet Union, itself a monumental attempt to unite nationalities, the 'unanticipated flourishing of ethnic minorities inside national minorities', referred to by Bauman (1990, p. 167), has widened the gap between nation, ethnie and state, and the conflict in Chechenia is a bloody reminder of the consequences. In Quebec, set in the post-industrial economy of the North American Free Trade Area, linguistic nationalists demand separation from Anglophone Canada, although not from the economic space created by cross-border networks of trade and capital flows on which a 'free Quebec' will rely for economic survival.

Territoriality remains the basis for much conflict in the globalized world. The twist in what might otherwise appear as an intensification of 'modern' politics is that the site of struggle is now often the territory and the identity space of the modern nation-state. In many areas this conflict may not be amenable to the positive-sum politics of interest-group bargaining, or capable of being sanitized in some form of official ethnic pluralism. Ethnic cleansing or partition are the more likely outcomes where, as Vincent Cable suggests, the politics of ethnic identity are articulated in demands for territorial sovereignty (1994, p. 47). Indeed, the ethnic basis of what is often called the 'new politics of identity' mocks the modern ideal of an inclusive national identity. 'Americans are those who wish to be', says Eric Hobsbawm (1990), but voluntarism as a model for identity formation and as the moral basis for nation-building and citizenship would receive short shrift on the streets of Sarajevo, in Rwanda, in some Boer farms on the High Veldt and among militant Israeli settlers in the Gaza Strip.

The phenomenon of infranationalism, or the breakdown of the nation-state, seems more likely to produce smaller units – in a partitioned Bosnia, in Abkhazia, in Macedonia, even in northern Italy or Belgium – which are distinguished and held together by their striving for ethnic, linguistic or religious sameness and, in varying degrees, by their fear of outsiders. Alternative suppositions or imaginings, which include federalist structures or forms of consociational democracy (Lijphart, 1968) reached through a process of elite accommodation and power-sharing, for example between Croats and Muslims in Bosnia, or between whites, Zulus and Khosa, are possible but seem less likely, or likely to be less enduring, in a world where visceral difference is replacing blander universalisms. In Italy, which made a state before it made a nation, the corruption and paralysis of national politics and government have bred demands for systematic reform, which, until the elections of 1994 and the formation of a successful short-lived 'freedom coalition' under Silvio Berlusconi, included a full-blooded call from the Northern League for the separation of the old kingdom of Lombardy from the Rome-dominated south of the country. The collapse of communism in Europe as the precursor for the spread of human rights, democracy and the market economy may not be a pipe-dream, but the fragmentation in the East is being accompanied by what Meštrović (1994) calls the 'Balkanization of the West', a tendency which threatens to fragment the Western world into smaller and more hostile units. In his interpretation, postcommunism in the East meets postmodernism in the West on the physical and psychological territory of the modern state, which may not be able to stand the strain. But if all this suggests that the nation-state is being unmade 'from below', what about 'from above'?

Beyond the nation-state

The answer is undeniably confused and I want to use the question of European unity as a means of addressing some of the issues involved. The nation-state was created by an act of will which transformed the 'aggregate of the inhabitants of a country under the direction of a single government into a community of affect' (Hirst and Thompson, 1992) and still serves as a powerful expression of political and cultural identity. In Hobsbawm's (1990) estimation, nationality is a mere parvenu in the list of more elemental attachments like the family, or ethnic, religious and local ties, but this is to underestimate the strong sense of 'belonging' to a country, or being the citizen of a state. The relocation of decisional authority from the nation-state to a growing complex of international and regional institutions still leaves most citizens unmoved, or bemused and cynical, over the antics of politicians and interest groups, even where their lives are directly touched by such changes. So the institutions of the nation-state remain the implicit and often the explicit focus of both demands and supports from citizens.

However, some strands of theorizing on the shape of Europe's 'would-be polity' in the form of the European Union have sought to trace the 'undoing' of the nation-state in the reorientation of various national actors to new centres of decision-making at the European level, thereby undermining the exclusivity of national identity (Lindberg and Scheingold, 1970; Haas, 1961). This 'neofunctionalist') representation of European integration predicted the 'Europeanization' of actor and interest group activity as a major factor in the creation of a viable European polity. This was not just a matter of changing behaviour, but of the redefinition of identities and interests. But the danger for this romanticized version of how a political community could be formed, and for the 'transactionalist' theories of writers like Karl Deutsch (1953; 1957), was that the 'spillover' from pragmatic accommodations by actors to shifts in the locus of decision-making, or to the growing intensity of routine communications across borders, would not lead to the emergence of a psychological community of identity based on European rather than national institutions. Both voluntarism and determinism informed these arguments, with 'spillover' supplying the evolutionary logic of an integration process still reliant on the motivations of actors to make it tick.

Such grand theorizing came under criticism during the prolonged stagnation of Community institutional development from the early 1970s to the mid 1980s. Of late it has achieved something of a comeback by seeming to provide a purchase on the conscious shift from the 'negative' integration of the Single European Act to the 'positive' integration of the Maastricht Treaty on European Union (Hix, 1994). However, it is not necessary to embrace crass neo-functionalism to see the significance of a more determinedly European orientation on the part of various national and subnational actors. In its most instrumental form, this spatial shift of emphasis simply reflects the extent to which changes in the EU following the passing of the Single European Act have made Brussels and Strasbourg more obvious outlets for much lobbying activity previously conducted through national systems of interest representation (Mazey and Richardson, 1993). In other words, what we see is a modification in their behaviour, but not necessarily a change in their identity. In so far as they conceptualize the issue at all, actors may be genuinely ambivalent about the Europeanization of their activities and about the extent of their 'Europeanness'.

An example may help to clarify this point. The response of traditionally insular British trade unions to the 'relaunch' of European integration in the Single European Act can be seen in part as a strategic, even an opportunist reaction to the decline in trade union fortunes under successive Conservative governments. But it is also a response which fundamentally 'Europeanizes' trade union identities (Rosamond, 1993). This is not the result of some neat neo-functionalist logic, but the outcome of practices in which agents are consciously choosing to enact, or being forced to come to terms with, a different institutional script. New rules, for example on public procurement or regional policy, which Searle (1965) distinguishes as *regulative* rules, prescribe empirical patterns of behaviour, but they may also function as *constitutive* frameworks for action and identity formation (Axford, 1994). Very little work on the European policy process, on interest group intermediation or on policy networks in the EU deals with the constitutive aspect of rules which, in Searle's terms, create and define new forms of practice and new kinds of identity, although there is a burgeoning literature on interest groups and the EU, some of it sensitive to the ways in which transnational networks affect interests and identity (for example Greenwood et al., 1992; Kohler-Koch, 1994; Boyce, 1994).

Overall, the development of the institutional and policy framework of the EU seems to widen the scope for participation by interests representing local, regional, ethnic and corporate constituencies, and at the same time also enlarges the scope for conflict. Thus the policy networks created do not mirror the neater and more consensual world of 'insiders' and 'outsiders' found in certain national systems of interest mediation (Grant, 1987; Marsh and Rhodes, 1992; Boyce, 1994). But these developments do not make national systems of interest representation obsolete, so much as contribute to a redefinition of national group–government relations. More and more groups are focusing on Brussels and there are an increasing number of 'Eurogroups' – transnational federations like the Committee of Common Market Automobile Constructors (CLCA) – which have achieved varying degees of 'private-interest government' in their relationships with European institutions (Greenwood and Ronit, 1994). Rules get institutionalized when key stakeholders in the policy process coordinate their activities and establish networks of communication. They also begin to define themselves in relation to the new contexts, which in turn are legitimated through routine and chronic practice.

To that extent it might be said that the EU has already achieved epistemic status for many actors (Ruggie, 1993). Kohler-Koch, for example, has hinted at the transformative capacities of European-oriented interest groups and trans-European political networks (1994, p. 179; also see Benington and Harvey, 1994), but it is clear that a reading of the internal market in Europe as a new sort of episteme, one in which 'the sovereign importance of place gives way to the sovereign importance of movement' (Ruggie, 1993, p. 173), has still to steer clear of any neo-functionalist 'logic'.

With suitable caution Ruggie himself says that the non-territorial form of the EU as an emergent space of signs and flows need not present any challenge to the integrity of the existing system of rule, the one based upon the centrality of member states in the decision-making process. But one need not be a whole-hearted supporter of neo-functionalism to see that Ruggie's idea of the EU as a 'non-territorial region' (1993, p. 173), complete with flows of capital, goods, people and electronic images, must contribute to the 'hollowing out' of the nation-state (Rhodes, 1994) as a place where policy is made and value is allocated. But I want to stress that this process is not just a matter of elements of control having passed to Brussels, allowing groups, localities and regions to bypass national centres of decision-making, but one that involves a restructuration in the identities of the various units of the European system. Furthermore, the outcomes may not even be conventionally 'European' in the sense of instantiating a Brussels-dominated superstate, or some federal version of territorial rule.

Let me take this point a little further. Throughout its history the EU and its predecessors have been handicapped by their ambiguous political status, in which patently state-like activity in various policy areas was not matched by the popular legitimacy which undergirds most democratic national states (see the contributions in Story, 1993). The sort of European polity which emerged under these conditions reflected the relative statelessness of the EU, and more closely resembled the American system of 'disjointed pluralism' – organized over three levels, regions, states and Brussels itself – than it did the neo-corporatist versions of interest-group representation found within many of the member states (Schmitter and Streeck, 1991b, p. 159; 1991a). But while the formation of transnational coalitions or networks of interests mediated by technocrats and consultants in the Brussels 'quasi-state' was clearly in line with Jean Monnet's conception of a European space driven by the rationality of 'linkage' politics (Featherstone, 1994), the very success of this bloodless model of politics and government has only served to emphasize the gap between the Community and the rootedness of a fully developed, legitimated polity. As a system of governance and a form of civil society, the EU is only a simulacrum of national traditions of democratic, territorial rule. Indeed its major weakness as a context for identity formation is precisely that it lacks the crafted authenticity of the nation-state and the assumed 'naturalness' of national identity.

The revival of interest in questions of democracy, accountability and identity since the fall of communism have also surfaced in the debates on the process of European unity, which until recently had been notable as an almost pristine model of elite autonomy (Bachrach, 1967). The reaction of voting publics in Denmark and France in the referendums on the Maastricht Treaty on European Union (TEU) was much more critical of the overtly elitist and technocratic process of decision-making than is conveyed in anodyne notions like 'democratic deficit' (Lodge, 1993), which centres on incremental changes in the personnel and practices of European institutions (Middlemass, 1993). Such grumbling reaffirmations of the existence and power of low politics are difficult to accommodate in the Community setting. For all its state-like attributes, the EU is not a state, and it is in the context of the nation-state that issues of democratic accountability and citizenship rights have been addressed. The translation of these questions to the Community level introduces problems for the relatively immature political system of the EU. Although a kind of social citizenship has been handed down through Community legislation, or mooted in pronouncements on the rights of employees or old people, more robust 'bottom-up' expressions of citizenship require the props of a functioning democracy, and therein lies the Community's 'catch-22'. To institute a European citizenship would not only be an audacious and at this stage unthinkable step, but would also be meaningless unless tied to the creation of a European state, or – wild imagining – redefined as an attribute of people in general (in a sociological rather than a juridical sense) and not of the denizens of territorially bounded jurisdictions in particular (Meehan, 1993).

The debate on European unity has traded in familiar antinomies, where more or less *intergovernmentalist* positions (forms of realism, concern for national interests) vie with divers *integrationist* ones (neo-functionalism, forms of federalism). But these one-or-other approaches to European unity may hide messier truths and more complex visions of European 'unity'. This complexity has a number of strands, one of which is the standard claim that European integration is undoing the nation-state. An apparently straightforward demonstration of this is a provision in the Maastricht Treaty that the member states of the Union will not run up massive budget deficits, and will heed the advice of the Community on managing their economies. But while this clearly limits the autonomy of member states, it in no way undermines the claim made by Alan Milward (1992) that European integration has salvaged the nation-state in Europe from its post-war weakness. What it does show, however, is that things have changed a lot in the meantime. For one thing, post-1992 Europe is ever more clamorous on the status and claims of localities and regions versus those of the state. Indeed the EU has gone so far as to institutionalize sub-national demands in Maastricht's Committee of the Regions, and in the direct representation of cities and regions at the level of the EU.

So far, so conventional: globalizing and regionalizing forces have the power to succour localities, even where this involves diminishing their reliance on the nation-state. But this is only one half of the equation. On the other hand, cultural products and cultural communities are already established across borders in Europe and across the world: what are their effects on the nation-state? Again, we must be cautious. In many cases these networks or cultural communities ought to be understood as forms of 'third culture' (Featherstone, 1990). Third cultures – of specialists, Euromanagers, transnational professional associations, agreed professional standards and so on – afford opportunities for new allegiances and identities, but without the concomitant destruction of old ones, because of their relative insulation from mainstream national, local or even Community cultures and because of their location in the hyperspace (Jameson,

1961) or cyberspace of European flows. Perhaps this is the burden of Ruggie's point about the co-existence of a Europe of flows and places, which creates not a standard integrationist's Europe but a postmodern political economy.

In some measure, the completion of the internal market augurs just such a Europe, although it also requires that member states play a more developed role in regulating the flows of goods, services, capital and people. On my reading, the single market process is neither state-centric nor communitarian in the accepted sense of that term (see also Wallace, 1993). The 1992 doctrine of 'mutual recognition' both limits the ability of national administrations to intervene in attempts by their citizens to take advantage of the internal market, and carries the liberal ideology of deregulation further by reducing the need for Community regulation, insisting only on the compatibility of national standards rather than on the elimination of differences between them. So, in principle, the need for extensive national and Community systems of regulation and policy accommodation is eliminated. The putative outcome is not only what Schmitter and Streeck call a 'formal devaluation of the vast political resources which have come to be organized in and around the nation-state' (1991b, p. 149) but a redefinition of a European polity as a space created and re-created by networks of interaction – cultural, educational, commercial and scientific – rather than a space to be governed or regulated in the conventional sense of these terms. In a further twist, Maastricht's concept of subsidiarity also carries a potentially lethal charge for communitarian principles and nation-states, by suggesting, or appearing to suggest, that the Community should act only in those areas that cannot be properly dealt with at the national level *or below*.

In practice, most treatments of European unity have been unable to dispense with the mythology and imagery of place, which is rather strange because Europe has never been 'a' place or possessed 'an' identity, save in the imaginary of a European 'civilization'. In Balibar's (1991) phrase it is now a 'world space' caught between the messy and increasingly confused authenticity of the local, the ethnic or the national, and the hyperspace of the global. Recent developments in the EU and in the world economy include greater freedom of movement for businesses, money and goods, as well as for people, ideas and symbols. The globalization of many areas of economic life is unlikely to be matched by the creation of a world political system that is beyond the nation-state. But the future of the nation-state looks precariously balanced between the potentially bloody excesses of infranationalism, or micronationalism, and the emotionally challenged arena of supranational rule through bureaucrats and regulatory regimes.

Though widely canvassed, this picture may be too stark. More prosaically, the nation-state does find itself strongly challenged as an effective instrument of policy-making and delivery in an increasing number of areas, but is still vital as the expression of a national identity, and of attachments to history, place and culture. Newer and older imaginings and identities constitute challenges to this paradigm status, which itself is still young in world-historical terms. Clearly, one of the major issues going into the twenty-first century will be the appropriate size and definition of units of government, and the continuing relevance and legitimacy of concepts like territoriality. My cautionary note about nation-states as expressive as well as instrumental institutions, and as being about meaning as much as materiality, provides an appropriate and timely reminder of the need to address the cultural make-up of the global system and those structures and flows which help secure and change identities.

6 Culture and the Global System

Introduction: national identity revisited

In chapter 5, I suggested that the nation-state has functioned both as a context in which local actors define their identities, and as a subject that also needs contextualization in relation to global scripts like 'sovereignty'. The nation-state is *the* modern form of collective political identity and has tried to nationalize individual and local identities through the granting of citizenship rights, in rules on nationality, and through various symbols of nationhood, like ceremonials, flags, the celebration of historical figures and the observance of national holidays. It has also tried to immunize or incorporate local and more visceral identities, which may have had prior claims on the allegiance of its subjects or citizens.

The subjugation and nationalization of the space occupied by the nation-state, and the creation and maintenance of a national identity, were difficult for many states and remain so for some whose boundaries do not correspond to a distinctive and homogeneous ethnic community, or which have become multicultural through migration or conquest (Smart, 1993, p. 143). For all this, the nation-state has become a meaningful institution or cultural script for its people by selling the apparent naturalness or 'isomorphism of people, territory and legitimate sovereignty' (Collins, 1990; Balibar, 1991). In some cases this required a greater use of coercion and violence than in others, but everywhere it involved ruptures in what Appadurai calls the self-reproduction or the context-generative capacity of localities (1993, pp. 5–10). In other words, through the more or less systematic and sometimes draconian employment of the 'techniques and artefacts of nationhood' – the building of roads, schools, hospitals and prisons, the provision of social welfare policies, conscription and public bureaucracies – the nation-state has modified the ability of localities to reproduce local subjects: such is the process of modernization (Appadurai, 1993, pp. 5–10).

In the more extreme examples of constructing 'nationness', local history and local culture are either obliterated or else reinvented and rendered safe as exotic or quaint variations of a standard national identity. The meaningfulness of place or locality is thus reduced from a primordial attachment to a more manageable sentimentality, exemplified in the idea of the 'heritage' culture, which transforms history into a consumer experience, usually without the warts (Robins, 1991). For all this, locality remains a potential source of conflict for the nation-state, challenging its control and its claim to express a cultural unity. At a time when nation-states are able to utilize forms of electronic communication to elaborate and sustain the sense of a national 'imagined community', locals and aboriginals, both authentic and born again, are reappearing everywhere (Robins, 1994, p. 97). I will return to the question of locality and of locals later in the chapter.

But the modernizing process of nation-state intervention in localities, usually called nation-building, is itself affected by global forces. Global electronic media, world markets and transnational institutions of governance complicate the relationships between territory and identity (Friedman, 1990), making it increasingly difficult for local subjects to reproduce identity by reference to purely local cultural scripts. The nation-state faces challenges to its power as a context-generative script from these same forces. One possible effect of globalizing processes may be to increase the scope for subjectivity and difference, opening up the taken-for-grantedness of both local and national scripts. By the same token, globalizing forces also run up against forms of cultural resistance which, though often 'local' in scope, sometimes take the form of fundamentalist opposition to the defiling of civilizational scripts, as well as nationalist mobilization in defence of a threatened cultural heritage.

One of the themes I want to address in this chapter concerns the extent to which culture as the realm of meaning and identity formation may be seen as a property of networks of interaction – spatial and transterritorial or global – rather than just an attribute of place (Hannerz, 1990). As I will show, the idea of global cultures as meaningful contexts for identity formation is at odds with the more reified concept of culture found in positivist and functionalist sociology and with the treatment of the 'authentic' sources of culture found in some accounts of nationalism and ethnic identities (Smith, 1990). Let us look first of all at the very idea of culture.

The meaning of culture: culture as meaning

Roland Robertson has pointed out the problematic status of 'culture' in sociological explanations of action or of stability and change, and noted the dependent status of cultural 'variables' in explanations of social structure (1992, chapter 2). For the most part the uses within sociology generally, and in subdisciplines like organizational studies or management theory, have been positivist (Bate, 1994). In much of this discourse, which is either broadly or explicitly functionalist, the assumption is that culture functions as a general value system for society or, more colloquially, as a kind of social cement that both holds the collectivity together by providing shared meanings and serves to delineate insiders from outsiders, through embodying and exemplifying the 'reality of a particular past' (Wallerstein, 1991b, p. 190).

Methodological individualism also needs the apparent explanatory power of socialization processes to ensure that some kind of social order is produced from the preferences of rational individuals. Meyer et al. (1987) have commented on the inadequacy of accounts of the socialized underpinnings of complex social institutions like the market economy, as well as on the infinitely regressive form of argument which suggests that apparent failures in socialization are themselves to be explained by the availability of alternative and more compelling 'cultures' or subcultures and *their* processes of socialization. The same obsession with functionality is found in neo-Marxist analysis, where culture is used as a means of rounding out excessively instrumental or reductionist positions by allowing for some kind of semi-autonomous ideological dynamic to soften harsh material realities. Even those arguments which display a more developed or unequivocal 'cultural turn', for example the cultural 'hegemony' strain developed from the works of Gramsci, often end up in obfuscation over degrees of allowable autonomy, or in the morass surrounding the 'cultural contradictions of capitalism' (Harvey, 1989). In the field of organizational studies, some Marxian interpretations of culture, which otherwise have a marked ethnographic feel about them, nonetheless still treat with culture as the surface appearance of a more corrosive and elemental dialectic involving the playing out of interests in the workplace, or in the home (Collinson, 1992).

Thus culture appears either as the convenient outcome of the choices of individual actors, or as just functional because it provides ideological protection for dominant societal interests. Attempts to define and thus to reify culture as a causal factor or intervening variable in explanations of systemic stability or organizational performance (Chapman, 1992; Ogbonna, 1993) ignore the fact that what is usually reified as culture should be understood as the contextual expression of interpretative practices by agents (Kunda, 1992). In other words, cultures do not exist outside their making; they are constituted in action (MacDonald, 1993, p. 6; Schlesinger, 1991, p. 300). The sociology here is that of Berger and Luckmann and of Garfinkel (1984), the anthropology that of Clifford Geertz and the psychology that of Karl Weick, but this powerfully phenomenological and interpretative turn in cultural analysis has to be set alongside the idea that reality construction takes place in the context of more or less powerful cultural scripts, or cultural structures in the sense conveyed by Giddens and by Archer. Here Clifford Geertz offers the useful caution that 'culture is not a power, something to which social behaviours, institutions, or processes can be causally attributed; it is a context, something within which they can be intelligibly – that is, thickly – described' (1973, p. 14).

There are of course numerous 'modes of interconnection' between agents and the structures of culture; and, as I have argued, it is not uncommon for agents to experience cultural rules as objective, because of their longevity and because they have been successfully institutionalized to become part of the intersubjective understanding of the conditions for action (Giddens, 1993). In other words, there is an 'interpretative enactment' of cultural rules by situated actors in which, as Meyer et al. say, these rules have both an 'ontological aspect, assigning reality to actors and action, and a significatory aspect, endowing actor and action with meaning and legitimacy' (1987, p. 21). Although often presented as natural, culture is itself the product of social practice in the sense that institutional scripts, or cultural rules, require enactment to give them force. Thus the units of the global system – nation-states, nations, diasporic networks, ethnic groups, transnational non-governmental organizations, even individuals – are themselves 'socially constructed elements of the wider system' (Friedman, 1993, p. 208). Actors are connected to institutions through processes which either consolidate their identity and that of the wider system, or serve to modify them. This is why the cultural realm has such fascination, even for those shriven by Marxism, since it appears rife with possibilities for disorder and transformation.

The idea of global cultures

Culture is then better seen as an interpretative framework or context, as a source of identity, or a means, Lash and Urry say, of 'telling people who they are' (1994, p. 129). Applied to a global context, this usage requires evidence of the ways in which local subjects are constituted through global relations (Friedman, 1993, p. 4). However, exactly what is meant by 'global culture' is still a matter of some dispute, despite the growing fascination with the idea (Featherstone, 1990).

'Is there a global culture?' asks Featherstone (1990, p. 1), while Immanuel Wallerstein, with a different agenda in mind, queries 'can there be a such a thing as world culture?' (1991b, p. 184). On the face of it these may seem strange questions given the apparent weight of evidence available. As Featherstone points out, even in the absence of the cultural homogeneity and integration which might be afforded by a world state, it would seem that global cultures exist, carried through networks which are not tied to any particular jurisdiction or national cultural milieu. It is also clear that not all global phenomena are world-integrative, even if they are world-wide: witness the deconstructive effects of ethno-nationalism. By contrast, the spread of universal or cosmopolitan cultures – through consumerist ideologies, global marketing strategies and, most significantly, through the potential of 'telecomedia' to change the way in which people live and think – presages a global future in which meaning and identities are not tied to place or limited in chronological time.

The sort of products available through global flows can be highly individuated, ranging from digital newspapers to interactive television drama, and they are 'localized' largely through the tailoring of products and services to fit market niches. Locality as visceral identity is replaced by locality as part of a map of variable tastes. 'Glocal' consumer products and cultures, for example the concept of the Ford Mondeo as a 'world car', rely on the ability of designers and marketeers to produce a standard overall design with sufficient flexibility to allow for local variation on the common denominators of taste. In this version the characteristics of global culture are that it is 'universal, timeless and technical' (Smith, 1990, p. 7). Previous 'universal' cultures – here Smith mentions the Greek and Roman cultures of the ancient world, and the Islamic and Christian cultures of the Middle Ages – were diffused from particular places and were heavy with history. By contrast, the putative global culture of today is 'bereft of roots' and 'situated in panoramic space' (p. 7). Because of these qualities, runs his argument, it is thin and inauthentic, and whole identities cannot be rooted in such poor soil.

Maybe so, but this argument seems to miss the key point about the significance of global culture or, more to the point, global processes, which is that they are likely to produce ambivalence rather than coherence of identity, or to spawn multiple identities: local, national or European; gay, black or Cherokee. Thus do they serve to 'weaken the seams of old orders' (Friedman, 1993, p. 212). Moreover, the claim that global culture is inauthentic when set against the 'real' identity space of the nation-state, and the 'culturally thicker' identities of localities and communities of affect, would not of itself negate the potential force of global processes in the destruction of these identities, especially where it can be seen that globalization does contribute to the creation of a vertiginous, rootless and, in Smith's sense, 'cultureless' space. In fact the normative burden of Smith's argument is precisely that global cultures encourage agents to 'forget history' in the sense written of by Ardener (1989) and to construct identities that are stripped of previous meanings in a world now dominated by Baudrillardian 'hypertechnology' (Baudrillard, 1983). Although Smith does not draw this parallel, similar kinds of argument are made about the 'presentism' that informs postmodernist constructions of social life.

Leaving aside normative judgements for the moment, it must be an empirical matter as to what sort of institutions and processes help to anchor and to change identities, not one that can be argued *a priori* (Schlesinger, 1991). Consequently, I want to oppose the idea that a contextless and 'free wheeling cosmopolitanism' is turning national and local cultures into shallow and homogenized cultural spaces (Smith, 1990). This rather simplistic interpretation of the effects of global cultures and cultural products fails to see beyond their 'mediatized' forms to the ways in which the 'signs and flows' of the global cultural economy are providing opportunities for the creation of those 'third cultures' which were mentioned in chapter 5 (Featherstone, 1990, p. 1). It is highly unlikely that these flows and signs, whether in mass communications or in tourism, will produce 'a' global culture, given the diversity in their reception and use by local audiences. However, because they permit forms of social interaction not tied to place or limited in time, it is proper to see them as contexts or frames of reference within which new identities may be formed, and new understandings of the world fashioned.

Furthermore, we do not have to dismiss the identity-generative power of global cultures to see that local cultures caught up in the processes of globalization can and do resist transformation, or otherwise retain their vitality. There is a wealth of evidence, not all of it anecdotal, to dispute the claim that the world is being homogenized culturally, and some of this will be examined later in the chapter (Harvey, 1989; Pred and Watts, 1992). Likewise the argument that cultural identities are increasingly negotiable in these confused times rings hollow in the face of the robustness of social and cultural forms and 'codes and practices which resist and play back systemicity' (Featherstone, 1990, p. 2). Of course it is sometimes tempting to treat these forms romantically, as the residues of more palpable 'communities' which once existed, but we should be wary of both nostalgia and colourful metaphors for the apocalypse. Pred and Watts (1992) describe the present global condition as a 'totality of fragments', and this is a useful encapsulation of a world connected but not unified economically and culturally, and in which the globalization of production and consumption has yet to produce globalized meaning. It is entirely appropriate that Pred and Watts's description can be read either in approbation of these developments, or as a lament.

Global culture and the hegemony of modernity

Underlying the claim that global culture is 'inauthentic', or even a contradiction in terms, is the idea that it cannot provide meaning or a secure cultural identity. In other words, global culture is said not to have the same totalizing effects as national cultures, or traditional and local cultures. In part this claim reflects the ambivalence many people feel about modernity and globalization as instruments in the destruction of traditional lifestyles. We like the ring of universalism and cosmopolitanism, where these offer the vision of a more benign world, but also see in them the ideological baggage of cultural imperialism, a transfer or imposition of mass culture from a Western cultural 'core' to other parts of the world. So the attraction of cultural resistance – almost in any form – for people like Immanuel Wallerstein is that it is a subversive strain in a modern world still entrapped by the 'geoculture' of the modern world-system.

Consequently, the particular features of the counter-cultural movement or group in question (the Shining Path guerrillas in Peru, the Khmer Rouge in Cambodia, the GIA in Algeria) are less important than their potential to disable, although it is true that approbation rarely extends to 'regressive' forms of ethno-nationalism seen in Bosnia, for example. Be that as it may, cultural resistance on the part of threatened minorities or indigenous peoples must be seen as part of what Friedman calls the 'dehegemonization' of the global cultural economy (1993, pp. 210–16; 1994). Nor is this simply a revolt of the 'have-nots', despite the tendency to dwell on those 'new communities of interest and belief' like homosexuals and indigenous peoples who are often marginal in political terms (Carter et al., 1993, p. ix). While these are important players in the game of cultural resistance, what might be called 'official' opposition to the dominance of the Western cultural account has come also from within the walls, from organizations like the United Nations agency UNESCO, or from clerics and churches influenced by the teachings of liberation theology.

Arguments predicting the end of Western cultural hegemony paint a picture of the global system quite at odds with the Fukuyama thesis, one in which the 'end of History' appears as the crisis of liberalism and liberal democracy and not their apotheosis. But it is wise to be careful about reading too much into recent events, for, depending upon how they are read, they provide ample but conflicting evidence of the fraying of dominant cultural scripts, and the exhaustion of any real systemic alternatives to Western liberalism. My point is that fragmentation and homogenization are both apparent in the global system, and neither is an imposter; and just as it is possible to underestimate the forces of cultural resistance and systemic transformation, so it is easy to overstate the degree of entropy in the Western cultural account as a global geoculture.

Nonetheless, it is now commonplace to portray the decline of the western Enlightenment tradition and its dominant cultural myths – those of the nation-state, universalized individualism and a belief in progress and justice – and to point to the power of 'new' political and cultural forces to explode the boundaries of political if not economic liberalism. These phenomena (the blossoming of ethnic identities, demands for the territorial rights of native peoples or the appeal of redemptive politics of a fundamentalist persuasion) are highly visible aspects of global cultural politics today, and their very fecundity presents powerful challenges to established scripts. But while noting this, we must not lose sight of the fact that the institutions of the Western cultural account still embody and confer powerful cultural legitimacy, and express a purpose and solidity which is enhanced by the diffusion and transfer of cultural products like education systems, high technology and mass entertainment. I will now examine the extent to which an allegedly attenuated globalized Western modernity is both underwritten and eroded by the spread of consumer culture and the informatized economy.

Meaning and materiality

The globalization of the Western cultural account is often seen in terms of the degree to which the more familiar products of its consumer culture – McDonald's, Coca-Cola, game shows, MTV – are the vehicles of global cultural homogenization. But while these products are consumed around the world, as were the products of earlier hegemonic cultures, their reception is 'localized' and made sense of through local world views and cultural practices. They have also served as a visible and convenient focus of cultural resistance in many localities. For example, in France the relative artistic merits of the motion-picture version of *Germinal* versus those of *Robocop* have been thematized as a defence of indigenous national culture versus the shallowness and meretriciousness of Americanized global cultures.

Now in one sense this can be seen as no more than a frisson of elite nostalgia, and a concern hardly shared by many French people, who have already made their accommodations with Hollywood culture and find themselves no less French as a result. However, elite responses of this sort express a more fundamental truth, which is that culture lies at the heart of the nationalist project and that nationalist elites will always try to make polity and culture completely aligned with each other (Collins, 1990, pp. 199–213). The hard lesson to be learned from globalization is that it is increasingly difficult to make and sustain this alignment, to rely upon the continued ability of local subjects to know who they are just by dint of local or even national cultural scripts. But though it seems difficult to object to this analysis, a number of points need to be made in order to underscore the complexity of the relationships involved and the plurality of outcomes that are still possible.

First, take the question of global communications and the new information order. Where these are concerned there has been an intensive denationalization of the communications industry, especially in the fast-developing world of multi-media technology, where would-be global players like News International, Viacom, Deutsche Telekom and Bertelsmann are buying into national companies and markets in order to position themselves to take advantage of technological breakthroughs and changes in national regulatory regimes (Bowen, 1994). The result may well be to broaden the gap between the purveyors of global cultural products in entertainment and popular culture and the defenders of national cultural integrity. At the same time, innovations in fibre-optic technology and the successful conclusion to the search for a 'killer application' in computer software will enable interactive television to be tailored to the viewing preferences and other consumer wants of individual subscribers wherever they are. At the very least such developments are likely to weaken the mediation of individual tastes by national cultural institutions. Even 'national champion' status, or the very idea of being a 'national' company, becomes more confused and difficult to sustain in this fluid cultural economy. Early in 1994, the Nissan Car Company in the UK ran a television advertisement, which indicated that it was the largest exporter of cars from the UK. The voice-over was accompanied by the strains of 'Rule Britannia'.

Second, cultural products and cultural communities are already constituted across borders as well as within them (Schlesinger, 1991). For the most part these do not obliterate aspects of national culture because of the protection afforded to the latter by language differences, and also because they constitute what Mike Featherstone (1990) calls 'third cultures' which, through their relative insulation from mainstream national or local cultures, afford opportunities for new allegiances, but without the concomitant destruction of old ones. In this concept lies an important vision of the global system, and a handle on what is meant by global cultures and on how they might subsist. In many ways the idea of 'third cultures' echoes Hannerz's idea of the global ecumene, a cultural space not configured by territory but constituted through despatialized agencies of communication. The ecumene consists of networks of specialists, managerial elites, transnational professional associations, agreed professional standards, e-mail addicts, video conferencing groups (Hannerz, 1989; 1992a; Ramirez, 1987) and perhaps the networks *manqués* constituted by viewers of CNN in hotel rooms around the world. Who knows, it may even take in fans of 'Oprah' across the globe.

Now it may be valid to suggest that these features of a 'nationless culture' sit a mite uneasily with the idea of a national culture (de Swann, 1989) but it is also misguided to argue that they do not qualify as 'real' culture, even if we were to disqualify the more frivolous examples. As I have argued, just how identities are formed and re-formed is a matter for empirical observation and not stipulation, although it is wise to be cautious about the identity-generative and -degenerative effects of 'global' cultures in the absence of an appreciable body of research into this question. But as John Thompson (1993) has pointed out in a paper about Habermas's conception of the public sphere, there is a tendency to interpret the cultural products of the global media as trivial, though still damaging to local cultures which it is felt can be sustained only through face-to-face interaction between agents. Spatially mediated communication of any sort, says Thompson, is often interpreted as 'a historical fall from grace' rather than an indication of the extent to which culture has become despatialized and non-dialogical (p. 187). The extent to which local identities, perhaps all identities, are now relativized by the symbolic products of global entertainment cultures and the material products of the global consumer economy, sits as one side of the equation whose other part is the degree to which local cultures 'indigenize' global scripts, or in other ways seek to resist them.

Global culture and postmodernity

Thompson's (1993) discussion of Habermas's concept of the public sphere conveys the modernist slant of much thinking about culture, which is ambivalent and guilty about its own universalist pretensions. Modernity destroys traditional cultures and replaces them with cultures built on reflexivity, but while traditional cultures are still viewed either with a certain amount of nostalgia as the residues of authentic communities or, more romantic still, as the home of atavistic and savage identities, postmodern transformations are generally anathema. Such at any rate is the claim of Frederick Jameson (1991) in his critique of the cultural *hyperspaces* of postmodernity, which draws upon a Marxist cultural problematic to examine the creation of what he calls the 'postmodern hyperspace'. Jameson has very little truck with the authentic–inauthentic divide referred to above; in the postmodern hyperspace what you see is what you get, there are no deeper meanings. For Jameson, hyperspace is the space – physical or discursive as well as epistemological – in which 'the truth of experience no longer coincides with the place in which it takes place' (p. 44). Instead there are economic and cultural flows and communication networks in which individuals are caught up and in which, through processes of aesthetic invention and reinvention, they are able to establish new self-identities of a more or less ephemeral nature (Lash and Urry, 1994).

The cultural politics of postmodernity is thus much more fluid than that dominated by the grand narratives of earlier phases of capitalism, principally the narrative of social class, which bred a one-dimensional politics of 'left' versus 'right'. Because of changes in the character of capitalist societies and the collapse of the state-socialist alternative there is greater room for the expression of previously non-thematized interests, notably feminism and the environmental movement, but also ethnic identities and forms of communitarianism. Jameson laments these changes, not because he objects to the formation of new identities and interests, but because he sees in them one more twist in the successful restructuration of capitalist hegemony and not its transcendence. But his pessimism over the demise of modernist narratives contrasts sharply with what Kenneth Thompson (1992, pp. 240–3) calls the 'constructive postmodernism' of writers like Dick Hebdige (1989).

In a significant contribution to the sociology of these 'new times', Hebdige (1989) also deconstructs the narrative of social class, but sees in the fragments a new politics and a more complex social and cultural division of labour, based on the shifting wants and aspirations of groups that form around any number of themes, issues and desires. In these new milieux identities are constructed from popular culture, from the mass media and in the fall-out from the once 'real' politics of class, which is replaced by a 'lifestyle' politics fed on aspiration marketing. Significantly, the changes are seen as generally emancipatory, offering new imaginaries and providing new possibilities for agents to realize their potential and to upset the course of usual politics. To be sure, restructuring in this way is unlikely to produce the pristine public realm of the bourgeois imagination (Habermas, 1994), but the point is that there are quite different ways of looking at these 'new realities' (Drucker, 1989).

One of these is to embrace the flows of cultural change and resistance as 'normal' aspects of the reflexive structuring and restructuring of life by knowledgeable agents; the other is to invoke comforting myths to frighten away demons. The latter practice can lead to both pathological and fundamentalist forms of identity politics which, as Parekh says, become obsessed with difference and the threat of 'otherness' (1994, p. 503). Some appeals are to a recent and modern past, to the myths of a 'golden age' of liberal-democratic politics and rational discourse. In an attack on the excesses of American presidential campaigns, Kathleen Hall-Jamieson (1992) inveighs against the power of the visual electronic campaign to 'reconfigure reality' (Axford, 1993). The viewer-elector is seen as mesmerized by a combination of powerful imagery and half-truths, in campaign advertisements and news bulletins often broadcast without the necessary contextualizing of the story. The problem is that Hall-Jamieson also fails to contextualize her own analysis. In part this is just a matter of a little liberal paranoia at the bad taste of tabloid campaigning and a willingness to see the 'decline' in standards as the outcome of a cynical use of medium and technology by politicians and of either bad faith or inefficiency on the part of media professionals. But an alternative interpretation, one more attuned to the cultural currents in American (and British or Italian) politics, would suggest a redrawing of the map of voting allegiance and of political culture to include the pull of aspiration marketing, the lure of visceral appeals and the importance of image as the most visible element in a growing aestheticization of politics. With the demise of the grander narratives of American politics, these features may not be aberrations from the liberal-democratic norm, but may be evidence of new contours in American political culture not amenable to remedial action seeking to refurbish a *particular* form of publicness that no longer exists (Adatto, 1990; Keane, 1991).

So, as a general rule the aim must be to identify the sites at which and the forms in which meaning and identity are instantiated and negotiated (Schlesinger, 1991). In this respect, the significance of the cultural frames of reference being provided by the global system, through processes like the rapidly developing world communications order, must be critical areas of attention. As Ien Ang says, 'every identity must define and position itself in relation to the cultural frames affirmed by the world system' (1990, p. 248). How far this is true, I will now examine by looking at the relations between local and global and at the problems involved in reproducing local subjects and local contexts in a rapidly globalizing world (Appadurai, 1993).

The local and the global

To reiterate, the main objection to the idea of global culture is that spatialized communities are the 'containers' of real culture, of meaning and identity, not the 'virtual' communities created by forms of electronic communication, and the networks built around flows of goods and services. An examination of the links between local and global is important because it allows us to address the assumed coincidence between culture and place (Carter et al., 1993). Once again it is wise to be cautious about the flow of influence in these relations, since it would be very easy to slip into the assumption that, because global flows constrain local production and consumption, they must also modify local cultures and identities.

Identities can be formed and reproduced around any number of institutions and cultural scripts, including social class, ethnicity, race, gender and religion. The local–global antinomy does not stand apart from these, although it may subsume them, given the extent to which the modern world and modern collective identities have been reproduced largely through the 'identity space' of the nation-state. National cultures and styles particularize many social movements which lay claim to universality, giving them a peculiarly local gloss, and this is true of the women's movement, for example, which shows the clear imprint of different national political styles and agendas. Of course, the relationship between territory and culture does not exhaust the range of possibilities for identity formation and reproduction. The vitality of diasporas shows that, even in the absence of face-to-face or localized encounters, trans-societal communities of affect can subsist, although they are often sustained by the myths of particular places and the promise of a return to them, or through a common language. Such communities, as expressions of what Dominic Anderson calls 'long-distance nationalism' (cited in Howell, 1993), have been given a fillip by the world-compressing power of electronic communications that have reinforced emotional ties perhaps worn thin or emptied of meaning by years of physical separation. Big business too has been quick to see the potential: in the United Kingdom, British Telecom ran a series of television advertisements in 1994 that played on the value of telecommunications as a means of bridging distance and time, but also as a way of reinforcing family and community ties.

The ideas of locality and of identities rooted in place carry with them a fundamental or an elemental quality which bespeaks depth and wholeness or, in the sense used above, 'authenticity' (Rorty, 1992; Bellah et al., 1985). The use of the term 'fundamental' here is both deliberate and appropriate, despite the fact that much current usage emphasizes the extreme or rabid demeanour of fundamentalists and the exclusiveness of fundamentalist ideology, as seen in the public statements of the Islamic Salvation Front (FIS) or the paramilitary Groupe Islamique Arme (GIA) in Algeria, who rail against foreigners as 'corrupters of the earth'. By contrast, in much Western anthropological writing on 'primitive' societies it is their fundamental or natural quality of 'otherness' which commands attention and respect, and their exotic innocence which is so attractive to the educated middle classes of occidental societies.

Nor are these yearnings confined to the treatment of the exotic and the far-away. The celebration of locality and rural landscapes in motion pictures like *A River Runs Through It* or *Field of Dreams*, and the corner-store traditions reinvented in Garrison Keillor's *Lake Wobegon Days* (1986), tap a deeply nostalgic and sentimental vein worlds away from the cultural hyperspaces of the postmodern imagination. This is true even when the images of the places we have lost are carried through the very media which are dissolving the psychological boundaries of the local imaginary, or eroding 'traditional spaces within a culture' (Rabinow, 1993). It is also very noticeable that these representations of local spaces and traditional imaginings invoke largely rural settings and imagery. Urban and especially metropolitan spaces are rarely the focus of nostalgia, except to detail the destruction of community as a result of the modernist excesses of planners, architects and politicians. This is hardly surprising: cities, certainly big cities, have become 'world spaces' – multicultural, ghettoized, violent, constantly in flux through the movement of peoples and the flows of communication. 'Global cities' like Rio or New York, London or Calcutta, have ceased to be *places* and have become spaces of flows, the haunts of strangers, maybe even 'ungovernable' as Lash and Urry say (1994, chapter 6; Sassen, 1992). Detroit as an urban nightmare, complete with high murder rates, abandoned tracts in the commercial district, endemic drug dependency among the black population and large-scale 'white flight', may be a safer bet for the shape of the future than the urban dream of Seattle, where only lovers are sleepless.

Only rarely are these global spaces traversed or settled by true cosmopolitans, competent transcultural travellers or connoisseurs and lovers of 'otherness' (Hannerz, 1990). Instead, the city as 'hyperspace' is home to shifting populations of locals, tourists, expatriates, business personnel, refugees and migrant workers. As Hannerz has argued, we should not mistake all this movement for cosmopolitanism, or confuse the creation of 'world spaces' with the growth of global cultures. For many sojourners in another land, culture is what they buy in gift shops and a sense of place is reduced to an appreciation of landscape at most (Urry, 1990). While there may be an increasing number of travellers in the global hyperspace – tourists, military personnel, business men and women, 'visiting friends and relatives' (VFRs) – they often take their 'home' with them (MacCannell, 1992).

But we should not weep too much. Nostalgia for the rural idyll and the local community is often an affectation on the part of those already skilled in negotiating the global hyperspace. For others who are less well-off, less educated and less mobile, exposure to other cultures and to global cultures can broaden experience and liberate from the stifling ties of place. While familiarity with cultural hyperspaces may breed contempt for their shallowness, or generate nostalgia for a more authentic way of life, it also equips at least some travellers with the necessary skills to subsist and to prosper in these milieux, to establish identities and structures of meaning appropriate to them. Thus when Appadurai (1990) points to the various 'scapes' which produce disjunctions in the global system, he is doing no more than indicate the opportunities for agents to create and re-create meaning in almost any circumstance, without loss of identity. The idea that locality represents a privileged frame of reference against which identity is produced and reproduced should not obscure this fact. If there is a lesson here it is, as Hannerz (1992a) says, that the constitution of global culture lies in the 'interconnectedness of various local cultures as well as [in] the development of cultures without anchorage in any one territory'.

This is an important observation, which emphasizes that the choice faced by local subjects and local cultures is neither cultural annihilation nor a forlorn and romantic quest for cultural autarky, even if political interests sometimes choose to present it in this way, but a more complex and messy 'organization of diversity' (Hannerz, 1992a; Schou, 1992; Morley, 1992). Much of the debate on the effects of globalizing forces has portrayed either a slow or a fast diffusion of Western cultural values, consumer patterns and technologies to all parts of the world, depending on the 'power geometry' involved (Massey, 1991). But as Stuart Hall writes, even if this is true, the outcome is often an uneasy mix in which national and other local identities are (1) eroded through cultural homogenization, (2) reinforced in the heat of cultural resistance to globalization or (3) replaced by 'hybrid' cultures, the result of the interpenetration of the local and the global (1992, p. 300). Significantly, these outcomes are not mutually exclusive and, where they overlap, the result does not have to be schizoid cultures and confused or pathological identities. I will take up this latter issue in chapter 8.

Such complexity of outcomes can be illustrated with respect to two processes which modify the interpretation of global cultures as one-way flows. The first is the concept of *indigenization*, which has appeared in a good deal of anthropological writing on globalization (Robertson, 1992); the second, perhaps more contentious, is that of *reciprocity* (Howell, 1993). Indigenization refers to the adaptation of 'alien' practices to local circumstances (Robertson, 1992, p. 171) such that the specificity or the idiosyncrasies of the local mediate or dispel the homogenizing power of global forces. In practice this suggests that while there may well be a largely one-directional flow of Western capitalist values and products to parts of the periphery, from America to the rest of the world, or from more powerful to less powerful countries, the force of that flow is vitiated and the global 'meaning' inscribed in the product or value is given a local gloss through complex processes of reception and appropriation.

For instance, the Islamic banking movement which came into

existence some twenty years ago has to pay close attention both to the requirements of Islamic economic thought and to the wider prescriptions and proscriptions of Islamic law (*shari'ah*) as well as looking to survive and prosper in increasingly competitive and global financial markets. The theory of Islamic banking prescribes that economic considerations should be subordinated to moral and ethical norms in a way scarcely countenanced in conventional economic theory (Sen, 1991). Because interest is seen as a source of social injustice, Islamic bankers do not conduct interest-based transactions. Although there are several different forms and degrees of orthodoxy in Islamic banking, all are supposed to operate under constraint of the same principles. Strict conformity to the requirements of the *Shari'ah* obviously inhibits the ability of Islamic banks to invest or to place surplus funds in the international money markets or with other (non-Islamic) banks.

In the same way, profitability (*halal* profit), though permitted and encouraged, is not the only criterion used in evaluating the success of Islamic banks, where social goals and responsibilities take precedence. This 'localization' of an increasingly globalized institution is not just an example of sophisticated market nicheing, but a systematic attempt to retain identity and the holistic quality of Islamic 'lifestyles'. As an exercise in commercial realism, the Islamic banking system is still on trial; but in an interesting spin-off to the processes described here, a number of Western banks have recently established Islamic desks which follow local practices, and a number of 'true' Islamic banks, for example in Jordan, now operate outside the protection afforded by a full Islamic banking system of the sort being constructed in Iran and Pakistan (Abdel-Haq, 1993). Yet the whole idea of 'Islamic banking' is only possible in a financial world already completely penetrated by the global script of financial markets. These same globalizing forces have drawn attention to what it means to be a follower of Islam in a system devoted to the secular pursuit of wealth creation.

On a different tack, attempts to transpose 'Western' models of management and organizational design and learning to firms in the transitional economies of Central and Eastern Europe and the former Soviet Union display much of the enthusiasm and naïveté of early theories of modernization. This stems from a rather mechanical-normative interpretation of how organizational cultures are made and changed as much as from an ideological interpretation of the processes of cultural diffusion (Peters and Waterman, 1982; Deal and Kennedy, 1988). A more sensitive interpretation of the processes at work would stress the extent to which agents in these firms are coming to terms with new cultural scripts, like those on permanence of employment, in the process of enacting organizational culture. These new scripts may have transformative potential, but the 'logic' of change that they embody is mediated by the force of 'old fictions' and old myths. In a manner reminiscent of Solzhenitsyn's story *For the Good of the Cause*, employees make everyday life tolerable and meaningful by working 'around' or 'in spite of' the new system, interpreting current realities through the lens of 'old fictions'. This is not just a matter of straightforward resistance to cultural change, although it is often reported as such, but a reminder that identities and cultures have to be made through practice, and cannot be imposed wholesale.

The schemes for educating managers and workers in former state-socialist enterprises are fraught with problems because they often treat agents as the objects of change and not as active participants reflexively involved in it (Antal and Merkens, 1993). The complete transformation of identities would require an interruption or a cessation in the ability of local scripts to act as meaning structures for local subjects. In practice, where markedly different views of reality meet each other, each comes to the encounter with its own salient cultural baggage, and makes sense of the 'other' in its own terms (Howell, 1991).

Friedman's (1993) account of the *sape* phenomenon offers a further example of the complexity of global–local interaction. Young men from the Congo and Zaire somehow acquire designer clothing, sojourn in Paris and then return home to parade their status as sophisticated consumers with cosmopolitan tastes. In Friedman's view this phenomenon is an obvious example of globalization, where this refers to the consumption of globalized commodities, or the willingness to 'buy into' a globally sanctioned version of high fashion. But it is not a sell-out of native culture in the crude sense of black Africans becoming thoroughly 'Westernized', or even a process which produces a 'hybrid' identity in the sense suggested by Hall (1992). Instead, the individuals involved are 'engaged in a specific practice of the accumulation of life-force' that 'assimilates the Western good to the particular expression of a process that is entirely African' (Friedman, 1993, p. 2). The Western artefact is encompassed by the local practice of *la sape*, but at the same time the *particular* form of the phenomenon is only imaginable when set in a global context. Much the same thing can be said of the millenarian cargo cults of Melanesia which, unless seen as the outcome of agents actively engaged in social practice, are liable to be interpreted either as the hybridized products of an unhealthy exposure to Western commercialism, or as some bizarre form of cultural resistance (Worsley, 1970).

Similarly, the adoption of black youth fashions and musical forms (hip-hop and rap) by some young, white, middle-class males and females in America, to become 'wiggers', does not ethnicize whites, although where it is politicized in opposition to racism it may be more than a passing 'style' revolt. More interesting to the present discussion is the phenomenon of young whites adopting the cultural products of a racially defined minority, whose 'native' culture is already transformed through its exposure to the dominant culture that they (the whites, that is) are choosing to reject (Usborne, 1993).

It is possible to take this line of reasoning further. The idea of cultural reciprocity (Howell, 1993; Hannerz, 1992b) also underlines the complexity of global–local interactions. Recent work in social anthropology has challenged the assumption that the flow of influence, power and cultural products in the global system is all in one direction, that is from core to periphery. Although there continues to be unequal cultural exchange (Hall, 1992, p. 305) there are greater areas of reciprocity than over-romanticized views of the 'corrupted innocence' of the non-Western world might suggest. Hall points to the relativizing of both core and periphery under the impact of globalizing forces and prefers an interpretation of the relationships between local and global in which local identities may be confirmed and even intensified by global processes. Howell (1993) cites the instance of the islanders of South Ryukyus, Japan, who adopted the Coca-Cola bottle as a convenient and cheap representation of the torso of a pregnant woman for use in religious ceremonies, and not as an icon of Western culture. Friedman (1993) also points to the production and marketing of cloth of 'tribal' design by European (not African) textile companies as confirming how global production and consumption relations support local differences.

The contacts between local and global, the West and the rest, produce ambivalent identities; and the prosaic truth is that national and local identities often incorporate 'foreign' concepts into their culture, stripped of their origins and their local meanings, in order to fill perceived needs or gaps in local knowledge (Howell, 1993). The translation of the Japanese work ethic into Western systems of production has seen it reduced to a range of disparate techniques; New Age religions purporting to 'Easternize' spirituality are often a potpourri of quite different (and, in their local contexts, incompatible) traditions, sieved through sophisticated marketing techniques; and multiculturalism becomes a kind of designer chic, apparent even in such 'genesis environments' (Stark, 1992) as the new South Africa. Here 'Afritude' means going ethnic in casual dress, the purchase of native art, or perhaps achieving some fluency in one or more ethnic languages (Silber, 1994).

Many national societies and all metropolitan ones have become multicultural through large-scale labour migration, mostly from the periphery to the core of the world economy. This movement has not produced cultural uniformity and in fact the opposite is common, with the increasing celebration of otherness sanctioned in official discourse and public policy in receiving societies. The proximity of 'alien' cultures to 'dominant' national ones need not produce cultural homogeneity because when one culture 'borrows' from another, what often happens is a decontextualization of the borrowed culture: witness the 'wigger' phenomenon and, *pace* Hall (1992), the deracination of Chinese and Indian restaurants in the United Kingdom to become part of mainstream 'British' culture.

As Howell (1993) says, the appropriation of an alien cultural tradition involves the take-up of the novel or exotic but then its gradual 'conventionalization' and sometimes its rejection. These processes are not confined to the Western appropriation of non-Western 'cultural knowledge' but, with due variation introduced by the inequalities of power involved, are integral to the way in which new cultural scripts become institutionalized. Overall, the process seems as likely to sustain diversity as it is to produce uniformity. However, it would not do to underestimate the problems facing the reproduction of locality in a globalizing world. According to Appadurai (1993), three critical forces bear upon local reproduction: the nation-state and nationalism, diasporic flows and electronic communication. The starkest message of those who see globalization as swamping difference is that, increasingly, people 'want Sony, not soil' (Ohmae, 1993) and that ties of 'blood and belonging' (Ignatieff, 1994) will count for less and less in a world networked by fibre optics and hooked on television soaps.

Nationalism, ethnicity and the global system

Yet in a world which has become 'deterritorialized, diasporic and transnational' (Appadurai, 1993) nationalism remains a potent force and national identity still a symbolic boundary to be defended, even though the articulating and cohering principle of the nation is rarely a single identity or a single consciousness (Donald, 1988) for all that its apologists in speech and song prescribe and 'imagine' such a unity. Nationalism is the ideology of the nation as an imagined collective identity (Arnason, 1990, p. 209; Hobsbawm and Ranger, 1983) and the nation-state is its organized form. The interrelationships between nationalism, nation and nation-state are extremely complex histori-cally but, following Gellner (1993), I want to underline the idea that nationalism is the link between the concept of the nation as an imagined community and the concept of state as its corporeal expres-sion. As Arnason has persuasively argued, nationalism defines and often justifies the use of power as a defence of culture (1990, p. 217). National culture provides a source of meaning for subjects and citizens by anchoring the modern 'subject' through foundational myths, the invention and reinvention of tradition, and appeals to the timeless 'natural' character of the nation (Hall, 1992; Rabinow, 1993).

Nationalism as a political force and as an ideology is an essentially modern phenomenon (Smith, 1990; Arnason, 1990). But as Anthony Smith (1990) points out, the idea of the nation combines both pre-modern and modern elements, building tensions and contradictions into the definition of nationhood and into the character of nationalist ideologies and movements. For Smith the tension lies between the identity of the nation as a primordial attachment, which he terms the 'ethnie' (ethnic identity), and the 'civic' traditions associated with Enlightenment modernity. National identities are often a fusion of the ethnic and civic strains rather than being purely modern. The consequences of this foundational tension should not be underesti-mated. Although many nation-states manage to tame and incor-porate certain of the myths and memories of the ethnie in their invention of nationhood, there often remain spaces and identities which attenuate the 'techniques of nationhood' and which constitute sources of unease or conflict for the nation-state (Appadurai, 1993, p. 12).

Nationalist and nationalizing projects have been repeatedly challenged in their attempts to control and amorphize the identity and experience of localities, indigenous peoples, subnationalisms and regional identities. Of course many nation-states have successfully built a national identity, but the 'integrative revolution' is often more incomplete than conventional theories of nation-building suggest (Lipset and Rokkan, 1968; Geertz, 1963). Many of the nation-states of the modern world have been built around what Smith calls 'domi-nant ethnic cores' which had common values, myths and symbols that facilitated attempts to establish a national identity: among these the British, the French and (more contentiously) the Russian come to mind. However, in the American case the invention of a nation did not draw upon the imagined world of a shared past, but granted immigrants citizenship almost as compensation for the loss of a past which was culturally richer but in which they were often impoverished, subordinated or repressed. Like Topsy, Americanness just 'grow'd' around the sheer newness of the political community set up after the Revolution and around the shared challenges of the 'frontier'. But it was always liable to be held hostage by its very willingness to accommodate 'hyphenated identities' and by the very success with which it seemed to have separated the political burden of ethnicity from its expression in cuisine, in dress and even in religion. American politics has always had a strong ethnic component, but as part of a culturally sanctioned and institutionalized political pluralism. Challenges to the validity of this cultural script have arisen because of the systematic contradiction between the political message of individualism in the liberal society and the fact that, historically, Americans were only too willing to discriminate between people on grounds of race or culture. In the case of Native Americans, forcible inclusion and near-genocide were justified in nineteenth-century pamphlets and in some official statements on the grounds that their very history and traditions made them unfit for the rigours of a modernizing frontier society (Rogin, 1971).

The civic component of nation-building, the modern element, has as its most obvious feature the granting of citizenship as a token of membership in a statist society. But even here it is clear that the implied universality of citizenship rights and duties has battled almost everywhere with more particularistic traditions associating citizenship with nationality, and the latter with more or less exclusivist criteria for 'belonging' to a particular territory and culture (Axford, 1987). The British case, although not typical, is instructive on the tensions that result. In Britain the question of the rights of citizens in general and black citizens in particular has been subsumed in a debate over allowable categories of immigration. At root this debate has been about the extension of citizenship rights to people whose identity and culture are not thought to be 'authentically' British. But the political charge attached to the issue of citizenship has been defused by treating immigration control as no more than a managerial solution to the 'potential' problem of numbers of immigrants and as a convenient means of establishing citizenship status by restricting both entry to and settlement in the UK to those who can demonstrate some 'close connection' through blood or marriage.

Now the point here is not to rehearse the crisis management

techniques of the British state but to suggest that, apart from the official response to the 'problem' of immigration, the politics of race in Britain (and perhaps elsewhere) reflects two quite different traditions. The first, which is highly particularistic, permits appeals to and use of racial imagery and stereotypes that appear to result from differences of colour and culture which are 'natural' to human society. In turn these allow recourse to ideologies which can be represented as dissociated from or anterior to the universalist claims of liberalism and individualism, that is, to modernity itself. At the same time, an unambiguous understanding of race and even racism as natural in origin encounters the essentially universalistic norms of the Western cultural account, too radical violation of which would in all probability produce some kind of legitimation deficit (Axford, 1987; Habermas, 1972). Even in the British case, where there has been a reluctance to admit universal principles in law and which has always been held up as a model of stability and cultural homogeneity (Almond and Verba, 1963), these tensions have resulted in a growing thematization of the politics of identity, despite the largely successful attempts by the state to immunize the politics of race as an electoral issue and the willingness of the major political parties to shy away from extending the ideals of pluralism to ethnic and racial demands (Brier and Axford, 1975). The large-scale movements of people around the world, whether as free labour or refugees of one sort or another, can only serve to increase these tensions and confrontations.

The new politics of identity

For many nations the recognition of cultural diversity is fraught with difficulties, and the bringing together of diverse identities to fashion an approximation of national unity requires sustained efforts to ensure that locals and other identities 'forget' their origins and their distinctiveness, or else are encouraged to uncouple the links between cultural identity and political aspiration (Ardener, 1989). There are different ways of achieving these aims, which range from a reliance on the effects of modernizing processes like urbanization and industrialization to dissolve local tradition, through attempts by a dominant culture to eliminate cultural difference and political resistance (like the language in Wales or Tibet), to policies which institutionalize multiculturalism in educational provision or in terms of ethnic quotas for political representation (the former Soviet Union or Canada and many federal or consociational states).

There are numerous examples of the consociational model of democracy, few of them successful (Lijphart, 1968). The Lebanon moved in quite a short time from being an exemplar for a model of consociational democracy to being a byword for instability, a microcosm of a disordered world. In the former Soviet Union the nationalities issue was presented in much pre-1990 commentary as the little local difficulty of a basically stable regime. The federal structure of the old Soviet Union was a reflection of the diverse national and ethnic make-up of the empire, but in practice federalism in the USSR was compromised by the pervasive and unifying power of the Communist Party of the Soviet Union (CPSU), by the dominance of the Russian Republic in the affairs of the Union, and by the power of ethnic Russians in the affairs of the autonomous republics and regions.

Since the dissolution of the USSR in 1991 the politics of nationality and ethnicity has changed dramatically. In Kazakhstan, which became independent in 1992, a process of 'Kazakhization' has taken place, consisting of a deliberate policy of nation-building complete with new myths of Russian conquest and colonization. Ethnic Russians (the former political and economic elite of the Kazakh Republic) are being marginalized by this process. The response of the Russian Republic to these developments, and to those affecting an estimated 25 million Russians living outside the republic, has been to emphasize the duty of Russia and its armed forces to protect the diaspora. In geopolitical terms the status of the Russian diaspora is significant because of the opportunity it affords the Russian Republic to interfere in the affairs of notionally independent states and thus to reconstruct a Russian imperium under the guise of the Confederation of Independent States (CIS). Since the electoral success of the ultranationalist Sergei Jirinovsky and the Liberal Democrats in the elections of 1993, the prospects for heightened ethnic tensions or civil and religious conflicts in the region have been greatly increased. Russia's martial response in late 1994 to the claims for greater autonomy and even full independence from the Russian Federation made by Chechenia was in part the result of domestic pressures on President Yeltsin to react firmly to secessionist rhetoric, and thus to portray himself as a true Russian nationalist and defender of the federation.

But the real burden of these developments is that what was once interpreted as the transitional quirks of a modernizing and potentially totalizing society must now be seen as part of the systematic deconstruction of the Soviet version of modernity and the revitalization of the cultural and political forms subsumed under Soviet hegemony. Now while there are specific historical reasons for the onset of the crisis in the former USSR and in the case of the subaltern cultures of the Soviet empire, 'dehomogenization' and 'dehegemonization' are also apparent in some Western societies in the throes of coming to terms with the politics of identity which Cable (1994) calls 'the world's new fissures'.

Far from being 'homogenized' or ordered by the pressures of globalization, national identities, ethnic and racial identities, local identities and gender identities in the West have burgeoned in recent years. This growth has been accompanied by the shift of the politics of identity from the sometimes glamorous but largely powerless margins of 'radical chic' in the West to a position much closer to the public centre of politics. In doing so it has gone some way to replace or overlay the more familiar politics of 'left' versus 'right', of mass political parties, which is producing increasing cynicism and disillusion among electorates (Cable, 1994; Gamble, 1993; Lash and Urry, 1994).

Ethnic and nationalist forces also carry a potentially lethal charge for the modern nation-state where such identities are translated into demands for 'infranational' separation or autonomy. Of course it is not always clear just how powerful a challenge is posed to the nation-state by those subnational groups who, as Friedman (1993) relates, are economically fully integrated into the larger system. Most such groups and movements are conventionally modern in their ideologies and aspirations. Much the same was true of African nationalism during the 1950s and 1960s, despite the impact of African socialism and Marxism on these forces once they had achieved power. In general, anti-colonial and nationalist movements did not draw upon some 'savage dream' of a tribal past to nourish their aspirations, but applied the formula prescribed by the culture of the world polity, which laid down appropriate paths of national development and proper goals for the nationalist enterprise (Meyer, 1980a; Meyer et al., 1987).

There is not much in the way of mould-breaking politics in these cases, and this is not surprising. Welsh, Scottish and Breton nationalism, long separated from a pre-civilized past and already modernized, would have difficulty invoking or imagining a culture out of time with the symbols of the nation-state. This would hold even for older brands of African nationalism whose leaders were often schooled in the elite institutions of the colonizer, or in the alternative path of the Soviet world view. By contrast, Polynesian islanders, Micronesians, Australian Aboriginals, even Native Americans may be much closer to such imaginings and thus to a total way of life.

If this seems a little fanciful, perhaps less so is the sense in which recent manifestations of the politics of identity – radical feminist challenges to the patriarchal structures of the nation-state, religious fundamentalism in the American South or in Egypt, and Inkatha's demands for a Zulu quasi-state in South Africa – are all intimations of what Martin Jacques (1994) calls the 'meltdown' of the nation-state. Jacques writes about the fragmentation of Italian politics and the threats to the fragile Italian state seen in the clamour for major institutional reform which gained force in the early 1990s and resulted in the election of a 'freedom coalition' lead by Silvio Berlusconi, whose most obvious credential for the electorate was that he was not part of the corrupted political class. Jacques's argument, perhaps over-stated given the powerful inertia in Italian politics, is that Italian politics and the Italian state are disintegrating. He is careful not to generalize from the Italian case to other European polities, while still pointing out the growing crisis of confidence in the governing class in all of them, but his analysis raises an intriguing prospect. At a time when the European Union has increased membership in the European proto-state through the addition of Sweden, Finland and Austria (though not Norway), seemingly one of the founder states of the Union is undergoing a process of restructuration. Now which is the more authentic image of contemporary European and world politics, or are they both equally valid?

In these dangerous days increasing attention is focused on the disintegration of the nation-state by ethnic civil war and through the politics of 'blood and belonging' (Ignatieff, 1994). Of course not all manifestations of the politics of identity take this form and, under-class rebellions in metropolitan cities like Los Angeles notwithstanding, the tendency in the core of the global system is still to celebrate or tolerate the flowering of new identities as part of the spirit of pluralism, or of the sort of universalism which allows anyone to play. For example, in Canada, itself riven by the separatist demands of the Francophone Québecois, the federal government has instituted a policy of voluntary ethnicity, whereby anyone claiming an ethnic identity must be treated as authentic by public authorities.

The idea of individuals inventing and reinventing ethnic identities to suit circumstance or fashion is profoundly at odds with the concept of ethnicity as expressing deep attachments among communities defined by struggle, history and language. Of course, designer ethnicity, political correctness and the politics of 'genderquake' may look like salvation compared with the carnage and chaos of Bosnia and Rwanda, or the pangs of South Africa's rebirth, but in some areas of conservative thinking these decentralizing and deconstructive forces are themselves the harbingers of great social disorder. Thus it is possible to interpret the notice seen in the windows of some Hispanic grocery stores in large American cities, to the effect that 'English [is] spoken here', as a death-knell for the notion of cultural hegemony, and evidence of a militant periphery at work in the centre, but it may be just someone's idea of a good joke.

In chapter 7, I want to explore some of the new fissures in world politics, paying close attention to the idea of a changing global order, including the decline of American strategic and cultural hegemony and the retraditionalization of cultures often referred to in the suggestion that the cultural battleground of the global system has shifted from superpower rivalry to a clash of civilizations.

7 Conflicts and Issues in the Global System

Introduction

The cultural phenomena reported in the previous chapter, and the globalizing trends examined throughout the book, clearly are capable of different interpretations. Without wishing to anticipate the analysis in chapter 8 on the 'epochal' nature of the changes in train, these turn on the ways in which the putative 'transformation' of modernity is to be understood. Most interpretations recognize that the transformation of modernity is a global reordering, in which the constitutive power of Western modernity is being reworked and 'dehegemonized', and the locus of economic power in the world is being shifted ever westwards. The dissolution of the communist version of modernity is sometimes taken as a quickener of the breakup of this global cultural hegemony and not an indication of its vitality (Wallerstein, 1991a; 1991b). As we have seen, accounts also differ as to whether the 'new-old' cultural phenomena of ethnic nationalism and the identity-forming power of global cultures are to be treated as harbingers of doom or of liberation.

One theme above all dominates discussion and that is the sense of growing systemic disorder. In this chapter and the next I will explore the idea of a 'new world disorder', bearing in mind that (1) it is important not to overstate the historical uniqueness of what is taking place (Smith, 1992) and, to make the point again, that (2) systemic disorder need not imply chaos (Morgan, 1986; Pascale, 1986). The relationships between entropy and order, transformation and stability are taken up directly in chapter 8. Here I want to begin by looking at the geopolitics of the global system, first of all by taking in the implications of a multipolar world for global stability and change, then by examining the question of global governance in a post-hegemonic era, and finally by examining some of the sites of conflict in the global system, particularly that of civilizational conflict.

Despite Francis Fukuyama's (1992) sanguine predictions on the triumph of the West and of Western liberal democracy as a global institution, there is continued doubt about the ideological cast of the global system, and about its orderliness. In part this is because while 'global' ideological conflict seems to have faded with the ending of the Cold War, new demons in the shape of fundamentalist mullahs, or warlords and drug barons straight out of a script for *Mad Max*, have come to challenge the 'peace dividends' purchased so dearly. Aside from the threats of inter-ethnic and religious conflicts, a world in which 'traditional weapons' can be carried in public places, and children are frisked for drugs at the entrances to schools, leaves very little room for equanimity about the future. Moreover, these conflicts and forces are no longer confined to the rim of the world, but have come to gnaw at the fringes of still modernizing civilizations – in Bosnia, in Georgia, in Egypt and in Turkey – and even appear in the post-historical centres of the world, like Germany, Italy, France, Britain and of course the United States. Such phenomena and events are worthy of consideration both in their own right and because they provide a convenient demonology in accounts of Western malaise. For the moment, however, I intend to look to the most obvious and momentous shift in world politics, the ending of the Cold War and the demise of the global institution of bipolarity.

Old and new world orders

The idea of a new world order, bruited most recently by American President George Bush during the buildup to the Gulf conflict in September 1990, stems from the ending of the Cold War and from changes in the cognate areas of 'bipolarity' and nuclear proliferation (Wagner, 1993). 'Bipolarity' refers to the particular distribution of power in the global system after the Second World War, in which many states were members of one of two hostile coalitions (blocs), each dominated by a superpower. It also refers to the nuclear hegemony exercised by these superpowers (Wagner, 1993).

It is convenient to think of bipolarity as a global institution because for a short period of world history it provided a context or frame of reference for most independent states, even for those countries who declared themselves formally non-aligned (Koslowski and Kratochwil, 1994; Wendt, 1994). Wallerstein (quoted in Ascherson, 1991) says that there was never a true bipolarity, only a bargain between unequal rivals, but even if this was true it still leaves the construction of bipolarity as a powerful constraint upon the identity and behaviour of actors. As a global institution the impact of bipolarity was short-lived but intense: indeed it is not too fanciful to suggest that, for the forty years or so of superpower domination of world politics, history was frozen if not stopped (Joffe, 1993). During the Cold War an international system which had been structured by the realist strategies of nation-states in shifting and unstable alliances was transformed into a politics of ideological blocs dominated by two superpowers that were champions of quite different world views. This transformation took different forms in the West and in the East. In the West the tenets of a state-centred international society still flourished, based on the global myth of the sovereignty of nations; in the East nationality was stifled under the harsh regime of Soviet modernization.

With the ending of bipolarity, History in Fukuyama's sense has returned with a vengeance, its stage now peopled by robustly historical figures like General Aideed in Somalia and Saddam Hussein in Iraq. Conflicts now flourish that were largely unthinkable in the period of brittle certainty that was the Cold War, like those in the former Yugoslavia or in the parts of Africa now 'freed' from the rigours of superpower tutelage. Perhaps it was inevitable that the blossoming of both old and new conflicts would occur first on the fringes of superpower influence in the old bipolar world, and in those parts of the old Soviet empire – the non-Russian nationalities – poorly integrated into the imperium. In the West the weakening of the bonds forged by the demands of the Cold War has been less dramatic and certainly less violent than in the East, although the reunification of Germany, the revamping of Italian politics and the rethinking of America's strategic role in the world are themes of great moment, not least for the future direction of European unity. I want to emphasize again that the collapse or erosion of larger structures of meaning, like the global institution of bipolarity, may result in confusion and chaos, in greater ambivalence and in ambiguities of identity, but can also produce new kinds of order and greater coherence as agents remake their identities increasingly conscious of different scripts. The dissolution of institutions and the redefinition of identities are thus to be seen as part of the same systemic phenomenon.

The 'old' order was constituted by the stable condition of bipolarity known as the Cold War, when antagonism between the superpowers and their cohorts consisted of an 'imaginary war' along the main frontiers which divided the hegemons in Europe and turned bloody only at the margins, in Asia and Africa. During this period of global order, colonialism virtually came to an end, partly as a consequence of the growth of nationalist movements nourished by superpower ambitions. Some Third World states even achieved a sort of power *vis-à-vis* the superpowers, by playing one off against the other in multilateral institutions like the UN, which were otherwise impotent as a result of superpower rivalry (Cammack et al., 1993).

The putative new world order (NWO) which looked set to replace it consists, or more accurately was said to consist, of a number of related elements. First, the voluntary withdrawal of the Soviet Union from its 'historical' world role was intended to leave it still intact and militarily capable, but benign as a player with global pretensions. As a result, the United States would be the only real superpower. Second, the prospects for lasting peace and prosperity in the NWO would be enhanced by revitalized bodies like the United Nations. Freed from the constraints of superpower rivalry the UN would play a more interventionist role in local conflicts, or in eradicating brutish conduct by individual regimes, with American-led coalitions of states acting to enforce the writ of the world community. Third, this globally sanctioned *pax Americana* would have a geo-economic dimension, carrying market liberalism to former state-socialist economies through multilateral institutions like the European Bank for Reconstruction and Development (EBRD), the IMF and the OECD. Overall the flow of world trade would continue to be liberalized through GATT and through the growing interconnectedness and interdependence of the world economy.

What is intriguing about this version of the NWO is that the West 'wins' but without thumbing its nose at the erstwhile enemy and without scrapping all of the stabilizing features of bipolarity. Neil Ascherson (1991) puts it neatly when he says that the idea seemed to be that 'weaponry would be reduced on both sides, more treaties on frontiers and dispute settlement would be signed, and Communist governments in Eastern Europe would grow steadily nicer to their subjects'. But of course history reasserted itself in a rather messier fashion, and modified bipolarity was shattered by the dissolution of the Soviet Union, leaving the United States to soldier on alone. Thus the West 'won' in Fukuyama's sense, but in doing so lost some of the need for its own unity and much of the rationale for American dominance. The implosion of the Soviet empire not only unbalanced world politics, but released an energy in the form of suppressed national identities which has proved remarkably discommoding to the idea of any newly ordered world. This genie will be very resistant to being put back in the bottle.

Hegemonic decline

For many observers America's leadership in the Gulf War presaged a new period of multilateral engagement with the world's problems under a benign hegemony. But a more cautious interpretation now counsels that the United States has neither the capacity nor the will to play the world's policeman. More radical interpretations like that of Immanuel Wallerstein paint a starker picture of hegemonic decline in which recent events, like the making of the Gulf War coalition and even the posturing over Haiti, are the final throes of a decaying hegemonic order and not evidence of its continued vitality. The strength of the NWO can be gauged by looking at the question of American hegemony and at the institution of multilateralism on which the legitimacy of any NWO so much depends.

The theme of America in crisis and of hegemonic decline is canvassed widely. In his celebrated book *The Rise and Fall of the Great Powers*, Paul Kennedy (1988) depicts the falling-off in American power as part of a cyclical pattern of growth and decline largely due to economic and technological factors. In this realist and curiously determinist account of the dynamics of growth and decline, global or regional domination goes to the strongest nation-state, given that the rationale of states is to compete with each other. What goes round eventually comes round: thus strong states flourish and may even become hegemonic, but in time they will be superseded by others, even stronger and more resourceful. Now there is no need here to debate the merits of Kennedy's view of the key actors or motive forces in world politics, or the cyclical rhythms which he sees at the heart of global politics, since the main question is the continued vitality of American hegemony. On this the evidence is complex and confused (Nye, 1989; Nau, 1990), and it is sometimes difficult to separate reasoned analysis from impassioned breast-beating on the part of those lamenting the loss of national power, or wishful thinking dressed up as macro-history on the part of those who see no virtues in a *pax Americana* or an Americanization of global culture.

From the 'declinist' side, the argument is put with some vigour. America remains a huge military power, but in a world no longer under threat from superpower conflict the possession of such might is not only meaningless to many people, but very costly. Moreover, in a multipolar world it is hard for the United States to play this part and to be accepted as the guardian of the 'free' world. This feeling extends to the growing number of American citizens who see costly engagements as contrary to the national interest, in a world rapidly overtaking the United States in economic terms. Of course periodic crises of confidence and the urge to disengage from a world role have been long-term features of American domestic politics, and periodically of foreign policy too, but in the past a sense of moral obligation as well as self-interest has tempered the urge to disengage. Ironically, the end of the Cold War seems to lighten the moral burden for the United States, and to deplete its power.

This is not just a matter of psychological impairment, some failure of national will or collective *Angst* directed at an ungrateful world: after all the USA was the driving force behind the Gulf War coalition, and also sent troops into Somalia in 1992 to secure the conditions for governance. Rather it stems from major changes in the distribution of economic power on a global scale (Cohen, 1993). Generally speaking, America has not responded well to these changes. It has an enormous trade deficit, most seriously with Japan and the dynamic economies of the Pacific Rim, and a budget deficit that is running at some $300 billion. Key industrial sectors, notably the automobile industry and electronics but also other areas of high-tech production, are suffering badly from Japanese competition, although there is now some evidence that the United States is beginning to redeem its position in hardware and software innovations for multi-media technology (Bowen, 1994). Throughout the period from 1960 to 1990, growth in US productivity lagged behind that of all the other members of the G-7 group of leading industrialized nations (Cohen, 1993, p. 117). In recent years the Japanese have invested about twice as much per capita in the United States as have American companies, whose financial and fiscal fragility continues to weaken investor confidence.

These measures of economic ill-health are passed off by apologists as part of the uncomfortable transition to a service-dominated post-industrial economy, rather than as an index of marked and irreversible decline, but the weight of evidence suggests that America's domination of the world economy – through the power of·the dollar and the speed with which American companies accomplished the innovation-to-market process – has been eroded substantially. But potentially more debilitating is the alleged moral and social decay now seen as endemic in American society. This decay is apparent in the deconstruction of the very idea of being 'American', in the blossoming of ethnic identities and the new raising of consciousness among 'indigenous peoples'. It is visible in the violent urban landscapes and the perceived shallowness of popular culture with its diet of sports, videos, game shows and rampant commercial populism. Of course these are arguments which might be applied to many of the 'core' states in the world system, with the American condition no more than a paradigm for the general decay of Western values, culture and economic dominance.

The 'inevitabilist' thrust of many of these arguments does need, however, to be treated with some caution. For one thing, they paint a picture of secular decline from which there is no escape. Of course it is difficult to counter arguments that rely upon cycles of growth and decline, because evidence of counter-cyclical revival can be dismissed as only minor interruptions in the grander cycle that leaves America, to adapt W. B. Yeats (1945), still slouching towards the apocalypse. Still, the rate of fall may not be quite so dizzzying as portrayed. At its most diffuse, what we call 'Americanism' – consumer values and the permissive cultures of individualism – is now an integral part of the globalized Western cultural account. Particular institutions, like American models of liberal education, have become and remain global cultural products, and American English is the new *lingua franca*. To be sure, these features of American cultural dominance are everywhere contested, and local politics of cultural resistance have sprung up around them. Nevertheless, the picture of a hegemon culturally vitiated and enervated beyond recall is too one-sided a picture.

In other respects, America's leading position in military power and its strategic reach remain a huge influence on the stability of the world order. The former Soviet Union is no longer a world player in this league, although the stability of its nuclear-capable parts is still a threat to global order. Recent events in the Persian Gulf and in Bosnia have demonstrated that both Japan and the European Union are still only economic players on the world stage and that they are barely competent actors in the geopolitics of their respective regions (Joffe, 1993; Funabashi, 1994). Despite the end of the Cold War, and the loss of 'mission' on a global scale that this entailed for the United States, it is clear that it is competent to act as the world's policeman, even in an era when its writ is manifestly more difficult to enforce and its willingness to abjure narrowly defined national interests is at a low ebb.

The fragmentation of the modern bipolar system and the diffusion of economic and political power across the world raise questions about the possibility of any new hegemonic power emerging, although China is sometimes bruited as a possible candidate (Huntington, 1993). For the United States, the realities of a disordered and more competitive world have necessitated a partial reappraisal of its global role.

Isolationism and economic protectionism still appeal to certain strains of down-home populist and fundamentalist thinking, exemplified by anti-politicians like Ross Perot, and possibly to the new Republican majorities in the Congress after the 1994 mid-term elections, but they are still largely unthinkable for an American President. America's commitment to the 'enlargement' of market democracy on a world scale and to the meting out of just deserts to various 'backlash states' – Cuba, North Korea, Iran, Iraq, Libya and Haiti – is tempered by the exigencies of a domestic politics still very sensitive about the commitment of US forces in overseas trouble spots, and by the stated intention to effect such a policy through 'assertive multinationalism' using various multilateralist agencies and periodic coalitions of allies.

Multilateralism and the new world order

The sort of global order mooted by President Bush relied heavily upon a particular vision of the post-communist world. At root it traded on the idea of cooperation with the Soviet Union and upon the ability of the United States to build a coalition against any aggressor by using the United Nations as a rallying point, or as a symbol of unity to legitimate direct action, as happened in the Gulf War. Since the breakup of the Soviet Union the first condition no longer holds, but while apparently strengthening the global position of the United States, it also removed the USSR (and for a time Russia) as a significant partner in creating and policing the NWO 'struggling to be born', as President Bush stated in 1990. The reappearance of Russian interest in brokering a solution to both the Bosnian conflict, and the Iraqi mini-crisis during 1994, reinstate this possibility, but also summon up the shade of a global politics based on spheres of influence.

In addition, the ending of the Cold War also left some of the constituent parts of the former USSR as potential sources of disorder and instability, a cauldron of strategic, nationalist, ethnic and territorial rivalries. In light of these considerations, it is not surprising that the United States should adopt a more cautious approach to the policing of world order than was characteristic of the heyday of *pax Americana*. In fact, the new approach is in keeping with the spirit if not the letter of America's commitment to multilateralism throughout the post-war years (Ruggie, 1993, p. 567), but there is a significant difference. As the only real superpower the United States is now much more reluctant to police the world 'or to act as its social worker' (Miller, 1992). As *The Economist* (19 June 1993) has said, this has created a world order 'in which America can sometimes lead, but in which it can also hide'. In this more cautious approach to the governance of the global order, recourse to multilateralist structures has assumed a growing importance both in security matters and in economic cooperation (Boutros-Ghali, 1993).

Multilateralism entails the 'coordination of the behaviour of states on the basis of generalised principles of conduct' (Ruggie, 1992, p. 562). Norms governing behaviour may be codified in different domains of interstate relations, including international regimes and international organizations, but they may also display a more 'diffuse reciprocity' which is not codified in any way. Principles of conduct include norms whereby trading regimes establish reciprocity in traded goods, or in which security regimes uphold non-aggression pacts. In the years since 1945, the range and diversity of multilateral institutions have increased markedly (Ruggie, 1992, p. 584), a phenomenon associated with the global *pax Americana* and the influence of the dominant American world view.

From the American standpoint the multilateralist agenda was pursued most directly and ambitiously in post-war Europe, through the North Atlantic Treaty Organization (NATO) and the various institutions of Western European integration – the European Coal and Steel Community (ECSC), the European Atomic Energy Authority (EURATOM) and of course the European Union. On a global scale, its commitment to the ideals of a liberal trading order and to the supraterritorial governance of global financial flows was pursued through bodies like the GATT, the IMF and the World Bank. It is important to note that America's commitment to multilateralism did not and does not extend to encouraging multilateralist institutions to operate as proto-governments or take on independent powers. Indeed the concept of a world society established on the basis of common identities and wrought by multilateral organizations like the United Nations or the European Union is obviously beyond the 'logic of anarchy' still espoused by both realist theoreticians and many national policy-makers (Buzan, 1993; Krasner, 1994).

Multilateral regimes clearly imply a good deal of 'complex interdependence', but often of a highly instrumental kind (Wendt, 1994). Such pragmatism can be seen even in the advanced multilateralism of the European Union, an institution now able to affect the lives of millions of 'national' citizens, but which is still a long way from being a community of affect. The necessity to establish a world civil society as the basis for a real world government remains completely problematic given both the constructed 'anarchy' of the world system of states and the continuing identity-securing power of the nation-state (Morgenthau, 1948; Bull, 1977; Bull and Watson, 1984). Recent multilateral organizations have generally been informed by a more modest intent than the creation of a world society. Implicitly at least, they have worked with a functional or neo-functional model of identity creation, attempting to fashion a regional, an international or even a world society in the absence of common cultures but an increasing number of functional links (Buzan, 1993, p. 336).

Usually the European Union is held up as the most developed attempt to create a *Gemeinschaft* by using *Gesellschaft* methods and to craft a civil society beyond the nation-state, and I have commented on the unity process in chapter 5. In addition the spread of transnational networks of non-governmental organizations (NGOs), voluntary associations and social movements provides some evidence of the increasing density of global civil society and the willingness of grassroots organizations and national bodies to legitimate forms of government beyond the nation-state. Global governance of the sort found in international law and in economic institutions like the GATT has already modified the sovereignty and decisional autonomy of states, for example by making the concept of human rights subject to non-state jurisdiction. Moreover, the globalization of human rights as a cultural script owes an increasing debt to the work of transnational NGOs like Amnesty, social movements and international regimes, rather than to the efforts of individual states (Byrsk, 1993).

Thus despite obvious limitations the search for peace, freedom and justice in the new world order relies heavily on multilateralist solutions to local and global conflicts and problems. In the words of former US Secretary of State, James Baker, organizations like the United Nations are 'the architecture for continued peaceful change' (quoted in Miller, 1992, p. 8). How should these claims be judged? John Ruggie points to the ubiquity and adaptiveness of multilateral institutions in areas like global ecology, for example the Earth Summit at Rio in 1990 (1922, p. 597), to the persistent efforts of the GATT to broker an open world trading order, and also to the relative success of multilateral nuclear non-proliferation. But on the debit side, perhaps with sufficient force to undermine the reality of an NWO, are forces injurious to multilateralism; let me deal with some of the most pressing.

First, nuclear non-proliferation seems one of the successes of the NWO, even triumphing over domestic crises in Russia and the

Ukraine. But the world also contains a number of states whose sense of national interest has pushed them to develop, or to try to develop, a military nuclear capability. These include Israel, Pakistan, China, Iraq and of course North Korea, whose pariah status and self-imposed exile from many of the usual channels of international discourse still make it a very dangerous outsider, playing out its own version of Cold-War brinkmanship (Colquehoun, 1993). Changes in the leadership of North Korea during 1994 following the death of Kim Il Sung may defuse tensions between it and South Korea in the longer term, but the prospects of a war to unify the Korean peninsula are still not completely remote.

Second, the secular movement of peoples from the periphery to the core of the world economy is exposing the fragility of new-found cosmopolitanism and official multiculturalism. Migration from parts of the old Third World, but increasingly from the new Fourth World, is taking place at a time when other historical forces are reminding the 'indigenous' peoples of the core of their own ethnicities. In Germany and in France, as well as in Algiers, the treatment of the universal foreigner is re-creating a politics of exclusion; old ghosts are stirring (Joffe, 1993). Even in the United States, the inclusiveness of the freedom rides and the late 1960s summer-of-love ethic is giving way to an exclusionary politics based on difference and the phenomenon of 'victim politics', a concept no longer confined to the traditionally excluded.

These problems may not be capable of solution by national governments, but they are hardly on the agenda of multinational and supranational bodies, save through the issues of 'refugees' and 'famine'. The Gulf War saw an unlikely alliance formed under United Nations auspices and American leadership, but the prospects for a repeat of this sort of mobilization as a standard feature of the NWO are very small: such cooperation may always be *sui generis* rather than paradigmatic. Thus at the Cairo population conference in 1994, the proceedings were dominated by an unlikely ecumenical alliance of Catholic and Islamic delegates opposed to birth control policies sponsored by the United Nations. The new-found spirit of cooperation among members of the UN Security Council spoken of by Secretary-General Boutros-Ghali is also full of difficulties which flow from the immanent tension between the desire for cooperation around general principles and the continued force of national, regional and even civilizational interests.

Third, the prospects for the democratization of the NWO also look bleak. Selective intervention on humanitarian grounds is more than matched by the difficulties of mobilizing sufficient enduring support for multilateral excursions. The promotion of freedom, justice and democratic institutions in countries as various as Nigeria, Russia, China, Burma and Syria still looks very remote. Haiti may yet stand as a monument to a US/UN-managed transition to a constitutional democracy, but the signs are not auspicious. Ethnic particularism has redrawn the map of the former Yugoslavia, and could still do so in the unitary post-apartheid state in South Africa. As far as the stability of the former state-socialist realm is concerned, the West now seems resigned to the fact that the 'fruits and perils of democracy' (O'Brien, 1993) will have to await the setting up of something that looks like full market capitalism – a lesson already taken to heart in parts of the Pacific Rim, where the authoritarian government of the 'intelligent island' of Singapore is generally fêted over its promotion of a high-tech economy.

In Africa, for long a part of the Cold-War board game, there have been momentous changes in the last few years. The one-party regimes and dictatorships, so redolent of Cold-War expediency, have given way to what in some cases (Chad or the Congo) resembles and in other cases (Zimbabwe and Eritrea) actually is a functioning multi-party democracy. On the other hand, military rule and social instability caused by tribalism and ethnic cleansing (Rwanda, Burundi), along with the generally worsening state of African economies, make many African countries parlous places to live in. In most Saharan and in some sub-Saharan states, like Comoros, Somalia and Eritrea, Islamic fundamentalism is a growing force and distinctly regime-threatening.

Civilizational conflict

For disciples of the idea of an NWO come at the 'end of History', this makes depressing reading. Instead of a world joyously taking up, or being constrained to enjoin with, the liberal-democratic rule of law and the ideals of economic liberalism, we stumble towards a different but perhaps more treacherous future. Of course, we may be conjuring demons where none exist, but even without hyperbole, this seems a world more on fire than the promise of the 'year of revolutions' in 1989 seemed to hold out. Michael Ignatieff (1994) argues that this is a new age of violence, with an empire destroyed and with the remaining superpower reduced to the role of a cautious bystander. Tribalism has been rediscovered, or in some cases simply invented without any recourse to an imagined past, and the new politics of identity is proving increasingly troublesome to conventional politics and its ground rules. We have also rediscovered the concept and the fear of civilizational conflict, and, more than the postmodern politics of identity or the gun culture of ethnic banditry, this spectre is offered by some observers as the defining conflict of the post-Cold-War age (Huntington, 1993).

Such at any rate is the argument of Samuel Huntington (1993) in a recent reworking of various *fin de siècle* themes. Unless applied solely to manners or civility, the concept of 'civilization' is a contested one these days, carrying repugnant overtones about the superiority of one culture over others (Robertson, 1992, pp. 115–16). I do not propose to deal with this aspect directly here; instead I want to address the civilizational challenges to the cultural hegemony of Western modernity, including the challenge to its narrowing of history to a treatment of the emergence and consolidation of *nation*-state forms and *national* identities.

Huntington argues that civilizational identities – he refers to the Western but also to Confucian, Japanese, Islamic, Hindu, Slavic-Orthodox, Latin American and possibly African – will be the principal sources of global politics in the post-Cold-War world, superseding the Western model of international politics based on the nation-state and the conflict of ideologies which informed the Cold War. Such conflicts are no longer relevant to a world rediscovering more fundamental identities, tribalism of course, but also the broadest levels of cultural identity that bind people together through the force of language, history, customs and religion: in other words, civilizations.

This cultural shift in global politics is due to a number of factors. The first is that civilizational differences are fundamental and far more enduring than modern political ideologies and particular regimes. Civilizations may rise and fall, merge or divide, but they are unlikely to disappear entirely. The 'fault lines', says Huntington, are always there, and with the ending of the Cold War and the faltering in the ascendancy of the Western cultural account they have been uncovered once again (1993, p. 29). Second, the compression of time and space as a facet of globalization contributes to the 'civilization-consciousness' of a growing number of people by expanding the opportunities to interact with, and presumably to feel badly about, members of another civilizational culture. These same processes and those of economic modernization have also served to weaken the bonds of locality and even of the nation-state, but without removing the need for elemental forms of identity and security. The upsurge in religious fundamentalism seen all over the world, indeed the revival in organized if sometimes unorthodox religion itself, is clear evidence of the continuing need for 'authentic' sources of meaning and identity (p. 26).

The status of the Western cultural account in all this is ambiguous and contradictory. For one thing, the diffusion of the values and artefacts of Western culture figures as a growing and convenient focus of cultural resistance: in Algeria, Muslim fundamentalists have ordered people to take down satellite dishes and thus cut themselves off from the pollution of Western culture. However, the means to effect this exorcism are themselves often the products of modern technology, like tanks, jet aeroplanes and automatic weapons, which again raises the question as to how far any society or culture can be immune to global currents. Finally, says Huntington, civilizational identities are important and will continue to be important because ethnicity and religion mark out who and what an individual 'is' more clearly than anything else. There are localized forms of this, perhaps breeding communalism and ethnic cleansing, but in Bosnia and the Muslim republics of the former USSR, as well as in German cities where phenotype serves as a marker for exclusion, these expressions of difference are merely local variants of larger civilizational themes.

Parts of this argument are persuasive, but the evidence cited by Huntington cannot be made to carry quite the burden placed upon it (Harries, 1993). For one thing, the awful and awesome façade of civilizations and their separation along historical and cultural fault lines may be a nostalgic shibboleth, a picture of a dream world. The more mundane fact is, as Fouad Ajami says, that 'furrows run across whole civilizations', just as they run across individuals, and this is the legacy of modernity (1993, p. 5). As Ajami says, in making itself the West made others as well, so where one civilization ends and another begins cannot be stipulated with any certainty. Thus the powerful movement in some regions to indigenize the Western cultural account, or completely to slough off Westernization and to fundamentalize identities, are themselves part of the dialectic of Western modernity (Robertson, 1992).

Even Islamic fundamentalism, often cited as a paradigm case of the search for authenticity in the face of the corrupting influence of Western modernity, does not spring fully armed from a clear-cut history and tradition of 'fundamentalism': indeed, the concept was unknown in Islam. It is better understood as part of the 'essentialization' of the 'other', or of 'local truth' rediscovered through global structures and global cultural scripts (Abaza and Stauth, 1990). Again, I want to stress that these points do not make identity politics any the less unsettling for those caught up in it. Robertson wishes to extend these insights to a consideration of the search for authenticity and fundamental truths undertaken by religious groups and social movements like feminists and ecologists, which still remain dependent on the modernity they reject in order to define their own sense of otherness (1992, pp. 168–9). This is a little like saying that without a victim there would be no murder, but it does underline the sense that both premodern and postmodern identities remain 'parasitic on modernity' (Rosenau and Bredemeier, 1993). Another gloss on the idea is found in Garrison Keillor's (1990) admission that 'ever since I left home and came to New York, I've known exactly who I am. *Ich bin ein* Minnesotan. In Minnesota, it's never really clear what that means, but living in Manhattan, I know exactly what Minnesotaness means.' So, rooting civilizational counter-cultures in the dialectic of the globalized Western tradition may not make their appearance any the less uncomfortable or disconcerting, but it does serve to locate the process as something more than an unreflexive and atavistic withdrawal from the world, appearing instead as one of the features of a contested globality. Even in Qom, it seems, the world is never that far away.

More prosaically, but arguably of greater immediate moment, is the sense in which the pull of civilizational identities runs up against the forces of both expediency and modernity. Huntington (1993) makes much of the vitality and the solidarity of pan-Islamic visions which invoke the image of a fundamentalist millennium in the spirit of Khomeini's Iran. But the reality is infinitely more prosaic and the interests more pragmatic. In March 1994, the victory of the pro-Islamic Welfare Party in municipal elections in Beyoglu (Pera) in Turkey and in other large municipalities was achieved on the basis of promises of efficient local government – clean air, clean streets and so on – rather than through a platform which challenged the secular state in Turkey. In a piece of *post hoc realpolitik* disguised as religious passion, Saddam Hussein invoked the fire of the holy war, the jihad, to scourge the 'Western' coalition and legitimate his annexation of Kuwait in 1990. On the streets of Amman, stateless Palestinians echoed the rhetoric and the Palestine Liberation Organization (PLO) almost went to the fire with him, but in fact the war pitted one Muslim government against another, and the list of Muslim opponents of Saddam outnumbered his supporters (Ajami, 1993; Kirkpatrick, 1993). Of course there was great ambivalence in the responses of these governments to a Western-led intervention in the Gulf, but the writ of national interests and respect for the sanctity of the territorial state ran stronger than the calls to tradition, and especially a tradition reforged in the heat of clerical passion in Iran. In Bosnia too it would be hard to present the conflicts as playing out the clash of civilizations, despite the region's historic frontier status in this respect and despite the rhetoric which has attempted to legitimate territorial claims. Non-Bosnian mujahideen, coming to the aid of their coreligionists, found them already steeped in the corrupted ways of the West and its fleshly pleasures.

Elsewhere in the Islamic world, for example in Egypt, Turkey or Algeria, the challenge of religious fundamentalism to more or less secularized, more or less legitimated and stable regimes feeds the spectre of civilizational conflicts and the collapse of Western modernity on its cultural margins. But the prospects of a clash of civilizations in Huntington's sense is mediated by the pervasive forces of the world economy and the global information culture, and most of all by the particularizing and secular force of the sovereign nation-state, the most important of the 'furrows' driven across civilizations by modernity. Even in Iran the millennium has been postponed, and in the post-Khomeini period the love affair with the Islamic past has been transmuted into something like an accommodation with the present. Sudan, with its military, fundamentalist regime, remains unrepentantly autarkic, but generally modernity remains a powerful cultural script even where – and here Huntington is quite right – its progress emphasizes its faults and reminds people of other less complex but more compelling imaginaries.

Ajami speaks of the profound weariness with utopias which characterizes the late-modern world where men (sic) 'want Sony, not soil' (Ohmae, 1993). The prospect of civilizational conflict raises the ante somewhat, suggesting that 'History' is far from dead and that a featureless, shallow postmodern landscape is some way off. But the big conflicts envisaged by Huntington are for the moment still conflicts of the mind, translated only occasionally into horrid acts. In the partial vacuum left by the ending of the Cold War, smaller, intensely visceral conflicts have come to lacerate the boredom at the 'end of History'. Generally, our attention is still directed upwards and outwards to issues like world poverty, free trade or global warming – issues which, however diluted, draw attention to a common humanity and a common future. Yet it remains a profoundly historical assertion that particular histories, particular destinies and particular ambitions still have force enough to augur descent and fall.

8 The World in a State of Chaos?

Introduction: the world in flames?

In chapter 1, referred to those authors who have spoken with almost biblical gravity of the 'epochal' changes now in train across the world. Their language is full of apocalyptic imagery, or else naïve enthusiasm for the 'megatrends' which are transforming the global system (Naisbitt and Aburdene, 1990). The themes of disorder, uncertainty and transformation run through these accounts, which differ only on whether the changes are to be feared or celebrated. Thus, depending on your source, the world is about to cross a 'great divide' (Drucker, 1993, p. 1), is poised on the brink of postmodernity (Borgmann, 1992; Harvey, 1989) or is due to erupt because of new fissures created by the politics of identity (Cable, 1994). From the personal to the global, change is in the air, whether seen in the self 'dismembered' by modernity, in the threats to established ways of life carried by 'integrated world capitalism' (Deleuze and Guattari, 1984), or in the clash of civilizational cultures.

It is tempting to treat this degree of fluidity as entirely new because of its intensity and magnitude. Yet the putative 'decline' of the West in general and of American hegemony in particular, along with the more or less bloody fragmentation of some identities and the harvesting of others, invites analogies with previous world-historical periods of large-scale social change. As Dennis Smith says, 'empires have crumbled before, market forces have been unleashed from old constraints of previous epochs, and the transition from relative order to relative instability has often marked out the furrows of historical change' (1992, p. 756). Even the plague was carried across seas and frontiers in the holds of trading ships; these days air travel just makes it quicker. The transformation of Westernized modernity, both 'internally' as a set of cultural scripts, and in terms of its definitional grip on the cultural currents of world history, appears in this larger time frame as just another transformation, albeit one in which the spatial coordinates are now truly global.

Order and disorder in the global system

The imagery of 'disorder' is closely tied in with the idea of systemic transformation. But I want to suggest that this 'disorder' is also a property of global systemness, in which challenges to dominant cultural scripts are a corollary of a systemic 'order' which itself was not *given*, but achieved as the outcome of reflexive practices by agents in their dealings with institutional scripts. What is often described as 'disorder' must be seen as an entirely systemic property of the dynamism of social systems, and not an infallible indicator of entropy and decay. Disordered systems, or those which would be described by mathematicians as 'chaotic', display unpredictable behaviours and constitute highly iterative, recursive and dynamic structures which change substantially over time. Such systems are characterized by discontinuous behaviour rather than by evolutionary continuity, and they are full of transformative potential (Gregersen and Sailer, 1993; Gleick, 1987; Leifer, 1989). Now it is clear that this kind of analysis requires dispensing with conventional, functionalist definitions of both system and order, and with the urge to dichotomize modernity and postmodernity, in favour of a messier account of the ways in which still powerful modern scripts nevertheless 'subsidize' a growing number of postmodern characters (Rosenau and Bredemeier, 1993), p. 345).

Recently, dominant treatments of the constitution of social systems have tended to stress their organic character. Social systems, for example formal organizations, are said to demonstrate a functional unity which is retained through processes of adaptation to their environment, or else environments 'naturally' select organizations with 'appropriate' capabilities for survival. Wholeness, harmony and clear, given 'goal states' are the characteristics of such systems. I have offered a critique of functionalist positions in chapter 3 and I will not rehearse those arguments again. My point is that functionalism treats the socially constructed nature of social systems as entirely unproblematic, and the intervention of agency is largely a matter of its contribution to system maintenance. But interpretations of the sort offered in this book, which treat constituents of the global system as socially constructed elements of wider social processes, are less concerned with the ostensible purposes of actions or ideologies than with how they are constructed and reconstructed (produced and reproduced) through different social processes and in various contexts, as a means to constitute systemness.

Much of the early work on the 'social construction of reality' was applied to individuals (Berger and Luckmann, 1966), but the reworking of these ideas by 'institutionalists' and by those sometimes called 'constructivists' (Hix, 1994; Wendt, 1992) has applied the analysis to a global level, trying to explain the emergence and spread of social institutions there (Thomas et al., 1987; Soysal, 1995). However, the burden of the analysis remains the same: social reality is constituted in and through social practice, wherein actors rely upon broad cultural scripts to supply the form and the rationale for all kinds of social arrangements. At the same time actors reinforce what is, after all, an act of imagining, by 'ritualizing, codifying and transmitting cultural products and the meanings they attach to them' (Barrett, 1992; and also Meyer et al., 1987; Ramirez, 1987). Such processes of institutionalization (Krasner, 1988) must not be seen as instantiating a teleologically defined 'goal state' or order, departure from which implies systemic ruin. Modern institutions of great cultural power, like the nation-state, which have shaped the global system by supplying rules and resources and providing contexts for action and identity formation, are nonetheless socially constructed 'realities' and themselves have to be reproduced. Deinstitutionalization, the erosion or loss of context and the transformation of identities may not be harbingers of chaos, but may be part of a dynamic restructuration of social life (Agnew, 1994; Wendt, 1994; Koslowski and Kratochwil, 1994).

In some cases of course the sheer speed of systemic change may create a 'vacuum of meaning'. Such a vacuum may have occurred in the former Soviet Union, despite the frantic attempts to reconstruct identities around the marketization of those societies (Stark, 1992; Jowitt, 1992). Jowitt talks about the lack of 'form' in such 'genesis environments', where the removal of the dominant institution of the socialist state has both left a legitimation gap and opened up the prospects for a completely new beginning (Offe, 1991). Stark, however, cautions against the tendency to treat all aspects of the situation as new, seeing in the fall of communism not the collapse of a single monolithic identity but the further transformation of scripts, which were already negotiated and ambiguous, by actors accustomed to manage uncertainty through improvising on established routines.

Now this may understate the destructive effects of the fall of communism on collective and individual identities, but it does underline two factors which are not just confined to the analysis of state-socialist systems but applicable to the processes of systemic transformation in general. The first is that disorder on this scale can be liberating for agents as well as dislocating in a systemic sense; the second is that what looks like (and in some ways may even be) chaos or the loss of grand narratives is better seen as a form of 'transformative practice' in which the 'introduction of new elements most typically combines with adaptations, rearrangements, permutations and reconfigurations of existing ... forms and meanings' (Stark, 1992, p. 300; Agh, 1991). So the use of terms like 'dislocation', 'uncertainty' and 'systemic disorder' is, as Friedman says, 'quite in order, so long as it is understood that disorder is itself systemic' (1993, p. 206).

Disorder in the global system should be seen as a property of a dynamic system and not just as a dysfunctional feature of equilibrium systems (Gregersen and Sailer, 1993). Arguing thus does not detract from the sense in which 'disordered events' (Rosenau and Bredemeier, 1993) may be experienced as profoundly disturbing by participants; but, in line with much recent thinking about the dynamism of non-social systems, it suggests that the systemness of the global system, indeed of all social systems, consists of a surface appearance of stability set in an energy or flux (Bohm, 1980). The idea of system as a flow and an energy rather than an 'order' redirects attention to the relations between actors and institutions and to the importance of practical consciousness in the reproduction of a system. As we have seen, relations can be generative (reproductive) and degenerative, as the identity of actors and the integrity of scripts are reproduced or modified through processes of cultural enactment, autopoietic self-reflection and reflexivity, all without loss of systemic energy.

Clearly, one must not overstretch the idea that both the constitution and dissolution of structures can be seen as 'systemic'. Friedman is instructive on this point (1993, pp. 208–10), saying that the dissolution of more encompassing structures (cultural scripts or institutions) can result in the creation of more coherent or whole identities among various units of the system. In turn this increases the scope for conflict and disorder, along with the accelerated dissipation of larger structures. Thus the redrawing of the world economy in which the locus of production shifts from core to periphery, and new regional powers emerge at the expense of older ones, also creates space for new identities to form, producing more discerning consumers, or militant 'green' activists, and this too is an indication of the energy in the system. The question is: 'how are the tolerances of the system revealed through this restructuration?'

Any response which argues that there are no tolerances, because there are no principles of organization, adopts a brutally postmodern interpretation of the constitution of social life, which is captured in Lyotard's (1984) conception of the 'fractal' (read 'discontinuous') nature of existence. But the argument throughout this book is that there are still powerful and enduring institutional scripts linked with the globalization of Western modernity. It is equally clear that the 'hegemony' of this account is under severe threat from a number of alternative presuppositions, and from the logic of its own development. Yet the prognosis has to be more cautious than that which predicts wholesale dissolution. A more fruitful way to proceed has been to chart the ways in which units in the global system come to understand and 'identify' themselves through reflexive monitoring of the contexts in which they are located. This is not quite the narcissism seen in autopoietic accounts of the self-reproduction of systems, since contexts are not simply extensions of self-identity. But it does allow both for an interpretation of systems as socially constructed, and for a way of understanding the transformation of individual and collective identities, which find the business of routine reproduction problematized by the growing complexity and availability of global scripts. Overall it would be appropriate to say that when institutions as contexts cease to generate meaning, and to provide a meaningful context for action in their own terms, they have been transformed.

Let me recap on some of the main points in this section. Any order in the global system, for example the dominance of neo-liberal ideologies, may produce disorder in local contexts, as individual and collective actors attempt to deal with global processes (Friedman, 1993). Collectively this accommodation may involve the absorption of local identities into the cultural mainstream, but it can also result in a search for more holistic or authentic identities, and new cultural principles which oppose and vitiate the force of global scripts. On a personal basis, the status of the individual subject, so central to the epistemology of modernity, may also undergo transformation as a result of this disorder, leading to a fragmentation of the individual subject, and a crisis of personality or selfhood. Clinical interpretations of this crisis point to the possible emergence of schizoid tendencies, or narcissistic degeneration, especially where the self has been separated from identity-supportive processes and structures. The 'dismembered' self can regain identity only through a search for new significatory criteria, in 'authentic' traditions and older cosmologies, or conceivably through forms of therapy which restore the 'centredness' of the self lost through 'fractal' experience of the disordered world. While such reidentifications may be 'functional' from the perspective of the individual subject, they can still be destructive or transformative from the standpoint of larger social structures and cultural scripts.

The transformation of modernity?

I will not recount the morphology of modernity in detail (Hall et al., 1992; Smart, 1993; Giddens, 1990; 1991a), but it is appropriate to pick out some of the main themes so as to evaluate claims about the transformation of modernity. The features of 'modernity', and of the Western cultural account as the paradigm form in which large parts of the world are 'modernized', consist of a set of philosophical principles and institutional forms. These principles include belief in the discovery of general principles of social order and of social life, belief in the progressive and liberating qualities of positivist science, regard for the ontological status of the individual as a social actor, and the rationalization of life through impersonal norms and rules governing behaviour. Modernity is also a set of institutions or 'institutional clusters' (Hall, 1992, p. 3), and these are capitalism as an expansionist economic order, industrialism as the mechanization of production on a large scale and the generic political form of the nation-state.

One of the cardinal features of a globalized modernity wrought under the Western cultural account has been the transformation of the relationships between space and time, which has altered the ontological status of territorial space and chronological time as frameworks for ordering social relations. Globalization dissolves the physical and psychological boundaries of place, and either liberates or threatens those identities in some way tied to particular locations. Increasingly, identities can be constructed 'out of place' and even out of chronological time. For Giddens, this aspect of modernity is critical since it allows for connections between social actors which are not constrained by time or place. These connections make palpable, or at least *virtual*, the idea of the world as a single place. The creation of intersocietal and trans-societal networks of individuals and collective actors at least intimates a global system which is more than the sum of its subglobal parts and certainly more than the sum of national societies. One of the consequences of this 'compression', as it is often called, is the 'relativization' of all sorts of identities, brought about by the growing permeability of national societies and localities, as well as other identities, to globalizing forces. At the same time, the scope for conflict over fundamentals carried in the 'collision between civilizational, societal and communal narratives' is markedly increased (Robertson, 1992, p. 140).

This much I have canvassed in previous chapters. In many respects the processes of globalization seem to work as quickeners in the playing out of modernity, although this is not a teleological process, and there is unlikely to be a neat denouement. Instead, there is a good deal of what Stuart Hall (1992) calls the 'contradictory' social experience of globalization, which alters the experience of space and time, produces ambivalence and not coherence of identity, and creates new cultural phenomena and sites for identity creation, which are not tied to place or established cultural traditions. In other cases the experience of globalizing processes has coagulated identities and drawn boundary markers where none existed previously, or else were not expressed politically. All this confirms the impression of movement, flux and change, or of disorder: but does it signify a 'crisis' of modernity, and, if so, how is this interpreted?

Postmodernity and the crisis of modernity

The concept of *postmodern* is elusive and full of ambiguity. I want to distinguish three main ways in which it is used, emphasizing the last (Case, 1993; Parker, 1993; O'Sullivan, 1993). The first usage is as a philosophical critique of foundationalist ideas about the philosophy of knowledge; the second as an aesthetic strategy which, among other things, seeks to relativize scientific discourse; and the third, most germane to the concerns of this chapter, as denoting some form of epochal cultural transition and seen in the features of the external world (Parker, 1993). Discussions of the 'crisis of modernity' employ all these uses, although many of those labelled 'postmodernists' equivocate over the claim that postmodernity signifies the end of modernism (Lyotard, 1984). Some even argue that there is little or no meaning to the concept 'postmodern' (Baudrillard, 1981).

Authors disagree too about the disjunctive nature of postmodernity, with some, notably Foucault, preferring the idea that we are in the midst of a period of 'epistemic transition' where postmodernity as the complete antithesis of true or real representations of knowledge, or even of pretensions to this, is not realized in existing systems of Western knowledge, which remain 'parasitic on modernity' (Heller and Feher, 1988). On one point, however, all agree: there can be no totalizing theory and no holistic experience, for difference, as both a philosophical and a linguistic reference, is everything (Bayard, 1994; Derrida, 1976). As a result the Enlightenment project as a philosphical tradition languishes. The 'big' philosophical questions which so troubled Enlightenment thinkers – the nature of 'man', the 'objective kernel' of the self and the general quality of existence – are all ruled inadmissible or irrelevant. Logocentrism, implying fixed philosophical meanings and universal definitions, is fallacious, and the knowledge forms which purported to offer an intellectual foundation for these truths are rendered as 'mere constructs' – for knowledge too must be deconstructed.

Knowledge and experience are thus relativized, and the crisis of modernity appears both as a faltering in the philosophical project defined by the concepts of rationality, progress and the unified self, and in the universalist pretensions of Western moral philosophy and civil law. It also manifests itself as a critique of the main principles of modernization, those of liberal perfectibility and human emancipation (Reise, 1992). So the crisis is thoroughly systemic in terms of its threat to the Western cultural account as a global script or meta-narrative (Lyotard, 1984) and extends to questions of identity, particularly to the question of the definition and maintenance of selfhood under conditions of increasing contingency and risk.

In a detailed defence of the Enlightenment project against what he sees as the nihilism and 'conservative obscurantism' of postmodernist scepticism, Jürgen Habermas (1987; 1989) also acknowledges the failure of some of the main narratives of Western modernity, like the welfare state, to sustain a plausible and confident vision of the future. At the same time he also deprecates the lack of faith in ethical universalism, seeing moral relativism as a danger to the emancipatory potential of modernity. Much of the writing of 'postmodernists' is, says Habermas (1984), really anti-modern, in the sense that it discards the ideals of universal truth and progress, and dismisses the overarching goal of a moral community founded on communicative competence and the ability of subjects to recognize and to act on 'truth claims'.

In his examination of the transformation of the public sphere Habermas paints a very bleak picture of postmodernity, complete with reference to the neutered public realm and the passive consuming self also found in other characterizations of postmodern dystopia. As always, pessimism is qualified by his continued faith in the emancipatory potential of modernity, to be realized through a refurbished public sphere peopled by 'linguistically competent' and creative actors (Johnson, 1994; Villa, 1992). In similar vein, Bauman's (1987; 1992) treatment of a modernity in which men and women are made anomic and rootless in a highly bureaucratized institutional order (the modern state) also intimates the prospect of an even shallower and meaningless postmodernity, where ambiguity and ambivalence result from attempts by individuals to come to terms with the rapidly changing world around them. They do this through 'natural' guile, strategies of make do and mend, and increasingly through the sanitized wares of various expert systems or forms of social engineering. Now in a world of expert systems and of metaphorical and actual 'safe sex', ambivalence can be resolved by such 'legislators' but at the expense of independence and authentic 'self-identities' (Bauman, 1987; 1992). Such resolution may also involve and even require the loss (or unlearning) of collective memory and its replacement by official or institutionalized histories and forms of accounting (Halbwachs, 1950).

But does it have to be like this? In Anthony Giddens's work, by contrast, the late-modern self is not just a frantic seeker after mail-order identities, bombarded and bemused by the techniques of niche marketing, or reassured by the promise of a self 'centred' through exposure to Erhard seminars training (EST), primal rage therapy or assertiveness training (Lackey, 1992). Fripperies these may seem, but we should suspend our disbelief, for they all are part of a late-modern hermeneutic and the exotic tools for an aesthetic reinterpretation of selfhood. It is true that this is the risk society, but even here there is still room for the reflexive construction of the self. The modern juggernaut can be ridden, and it is both possible and morally acceptable to enjoy the ride without too much *Angst* about the world we have lost, or about the identities which may have been discarded along the way. Giddens acknowledges that this experience may be intensely dislocating, leading some to attempt an escape into a more 'solid' past and others into a search for identity through magic, or by romanticizing the primitive and the communal, but on the whole this is not the subject of too much hand-wringing (Giddens, 1990; 1991a; 1993).

For some critics, like Habermas or Bauman, the fluxive and directionless character of social and cultural change symbolizes the pathological character of postmodernity. But these features hold few

fears for Giddens, because identities are not simply swallowed in the
flux of late-modern cultural excess and dilation, or lost in an aestheticization of life that reduces 'big' issues to 'language games' and
morality to entertainment values (Mongardini, 1992). Here is where
Giddens departs from the apparently similar observations of other
critics of postmodernism, preferring the idea that social relations,
while obviously more fluid and riskier, have been released from the
constraints of time and place, and are not just 'hopelessly plural' in
the sense conveyed by Bauman (McLennan, 1992, p. 342). Life is not
a supermarket of meanings, each as bland as the next, and individuals are not merely passive consumers, witless neophiliacs or victims
of the 'three-minute culture'. In globalized late modernity, the proliferation of information through the growing sophistication and
availability of technology affords an efficient means for 'regaining
control of time' (Mongardini, 1992, p. 59), supplying resources for
increased reflexivity and thus for apparent control. Individuals are
caught up in events and processes quite beyond their immediate control, and at the same time are more equipped to identify and to
understand the sources of their insecurity.

Of course, knowing that one is not and probably never can be fully
'in control' may itself contribute to the sense of 'ontological insecurity', and may even breed a sort of species insecurity. Where the
denizens of traditional societies were literally resigned to their fate,
and moderns achieved a limited security through applying rational
solutions to identified and often 'local' problems, the late-modern self
can find no refuge in either the cosmos or ignorance. Thus a sense
of *powerlessness* always lurks as the corollary of *empowerment* in
a world in which access to 'knowledge' even removes the haven of
ignorance. In such an environment, what looks like empowerment
or the freedom to search for new sources of meaning – in 'lifestyle'
politics, in religion, in work, or in control of one's body through the
use of cosmetic plastic surgery and personal trainers – may only be
forms of therapy. But for some at least, therapeutic 'solutions' are
all that can be expected, and Marin County psychobabble is as good
as it is likely to get. And there is always the fun side: the poster in
a New York gym offering the advice 'No pecs – no sex' may not be
politically correct, but it has the distinct advantage of not giving way
to *Angst* and weary pessimism. Even so, many such accommodations
do appear less like reflexivity – even a highly aesthetic sort of reflexivity – and more like frantic reactions bred of uncertainty and anxiety. In this they are hardly celebrations of the contingent quality of
life, but more like the delusions of the anorexic or the bulimic who

believe that they are somehow still in control. Quiet desperation on this scale may also trigger a search for fundamentals, or produce resignation which tips over into decadence and narcissism. This is certainly the bog-standard image of the postmodern world and it is one which Giddens, as well as Habermas, finds repugnant and unwarranted, though for different reasons.

Why? Because they both believe that change need not be an empty process, consuming the wholeness of modernity, rationality and the centred self. If modernity 'dissolves' truth or, as Vattimo (1988) says, 'the idea of truth', it also allows for new and multiple truths to emerge, including the truth that disorientation need not be feared even where uncertainties abound. Thus for Giddens, the aim of the reflexive project is to accomplish some form of unity from the fragmentation and disorientation of late-modern life. To accomplish this task, individuals must reappropriate fragments of knowledge, using increasingly accessible and comprehensible 'expert systems' to come to terms with and form coherent narratives about the world they live in and about their own lives. Only thus can they be set on a path to self-actualization and self-development. The manifest dangers of the risk society are balanced by the 'knowledge' of areas of life once thought inaccessible to ordinary people and also by the the fact that freedom of choice and the celebration of difference are given greater scope and legitimacy. As Lackey points out, 'the uncertainty and antinomy of modernity, while a source of unabashed anxiety, provide the framework for both the self's strength and the transformation to a new social order, freedom of choice' (1992, p. 182; see also Masini, 1993).

This is a substantial claim, clearly distancing Giddens from 'conventional' treatments of the shallowness and anxiety-generating aspects of postmodern life. Giddens's late-modern individual, or even Rorty's (1992) celebration of the aesthetic dimensions of postmodernity as the basis for a new communitarian ethic that celebrates the poetically contingent quality of life, are a long way from Foucault's 'fractured' self, or the vigorous nihilism of Michael Douglas's male 'victim' in the motion picture *Falling Down*.

But just why Giddens believes that a non-pathological form of identity politics should emerge in response to or out of the growing tide of cultural relativism and insecurity, as opposed to the 'totality of fragments' envisaged by Pred and Watts (1992), or more robustly 'historical' forms of identity politics, is not made clear (Swanson, 1992). In the cynical 1990s such optimism might seem as dated as the chanting of mantras, or invoking the 'spirit of Woodstock'.

However, few commentators now doubt that 'life-political' questions for matters of personal identity are central to the crisis of modernity, and the connections between what Giddens calls the 'situated practices of individuals' and the properties of increasingly large-scale, even global systems serve to increase the scope for a politics of identity.

In much of the debate over 'reflexive modernization', questions of lifestyle politics, identity and globalization are completely intertwined. Lifestyle changes are often based upon the rapidly changing character of economic relations, for example those that *Time* magazine describes as the new 'corporate clearances' of the 1990s, in which millions of workers are being removed from the work environments and the jobs that gave them a 'context, a sense of self-worth and a kind of identity' (*Time International*, 1993, and see Gray, 1994; Handy, 1994). These changes contribute to dilemmas of identity that have to be dealt with reflexively in order to sustain coherent self-narratives, and to prevent a growing contingency making us more insecure, or even mad. But this is a tall order, and may be less appealing than offers of 'redemptive politics' as surrogates for those whole and solidary identities – for example those of social class and trade unionism, or the nuclear family unit – which have been mauled in recent decades. Since the effect of many globalizing processes is to destructure modernity, it is individuals who have to confront rapid change, often stripped of the comforting solidarity of place and class, or the certainties of 'normal' gender roles. What sort of politics is likely to emerge in such conditions?

The critical difference between modern and postmodern politics is that the achievement of 'personhood', or of any identity, becomes largely a matter of cultural manufacture rather than having ontological status in a moral and political space already defined by world-historical forces and institutionalized as a global script. Faced only with the prospect of ever more contingent futures, the individual comes to terms with, and even triumphs over, the 'loss' of culture and history by reinventing herself. A person is 'whole' only in the reflective awareness of the possibility of any number of 'selves', none of which is any more 'real' than any other; and the search for 'truth', as Gellner (1992) has pointed out, is either pragmatically set aside in favour of the solipsism 'don't worry – be happy!' or itself reinvented through some redemptive formula, promising salvation. What passes for politics in such a world turns on the expression and management of differences that are just convenient summaries of shifting identities, which are neither authentic nor inauthentic but just 'are', or rather are just 'made'.

But this may be an altogether too refined or too cynical a view of the politics of postmodernity. For one thing, the charge of being thought of or seen as 'inauthentic' is still a very powerful one; and in James Clifford's (1988) words, in an interconnected, globalized world 'one is always to varying degrees "inauthentic", caught between cultures, implicated in others.' In such a world difference is not just a guise put on for the sake of convenience or fashion or out of boredom, but an expression of fundamental cleavages. Thus being caught between cultural spaces increases the scope for resistance and critique, and for the celebration of the other, but it also permits a more brutal politics based on exclusion of the inauthentic. In Fukuyama's (1992) world this is not a problem, since the question of inauthenticity is made nugatory by the claim that differences, while irritating, are likely to be transient, and where not transient, at least manageable.

Of course, where nothing is enduring, nothing can be construed as authentic or make any claim to universal authority. A postmodern politics of difference augurs either a benign anarchy, which is discriminating of neither political demand nor method, or what Cohen and Arato (1992), echoing Habermas, call a politics of 'democratic will-formation' which is not reliant upon conventional forms of political representation and brokerage, or outdated political ideologies. The latter vision, while appealing in the same way as Habermas's politics of communicative competence or Giddens's (1993) politics of self-actualization, may still be just a tad utopian. A politics based upon difference, whether of race, gender, able-bodiedness, local identity, or indeed anything at all, might be appropriated for emancipatory ends, but is also capable of service in more suspect causes. Primarily this is because it is grounded in nothing more compelling than the legitimation of difference, rather than in institutional scripts which give meaning and legitimacy to certain kinds of behaviours rather than others. So the key issue is how such a politics can be sustained without realizing its own worst nightmare. Pathological strains of the politics of difference include a rabid pluralism, complete with demand overload; the imposition of some new 'geoculture' which endorses apparently liberating but actually totalitarian forms of political correctness; and the need to rely upon a bureaucratically mediated 'freedom' in the form of a statist or suprastatist regulated consensus.

Noel O'Sullivan says that a politics of diversity is sustainable, but only in the convenient and administratively sanctioned and controlled form that he calls a 'politics of security', which is emptied of moral considerations and any concern with the substantive aspects of empowerment and democracy (1993, pp. 38–9). This is the pathological image of both modern and postmodern visions of emancipatory politics. An officially sanctioned entitlement to be heard, or to have access to services as 'rights', supersedes the idea of a politics of diversity sustained, but also contained, by general, moral considerations of civility (O'Sullivan, 1993; Gray, 1988). Elements of these new forms of politics are to be found, for example, in the transformative non-politics of some brands of feminism, which have sought to 'undo' concepts like 'citizenship' and reveal their 'gendered' bias. Formal democracy, or liberal democracy of the sort said by Fukuyama (1991) to have 'triumphed' with the fall of communism, is itself directly challenged by these 'post-historical' forces, which have tried to subsume or convert the languages and concerns of liberal discourse with new scripts, like patriarchy (Moi, 1991).

Evidence for growth in the appeal of these 'new' forms of politics and ideologies is patchy. In the West, usual politics and usual politicians seem to be held in growing cynical regard, single-issue protest movements abound and the aestheticization of even mainstream politics accelerates with the electoral success of the image-dominated campaign of the Forza Italia party in Italy. The language of inclusion and of the legitimation of difference has achieved the status of lore in countries like the USA, further transforming the public philosophy of interest group liberalism and elevating political correctness to the status of a potential new orthodoxy. And yet elections still turn on economic issues, and people generally ride the 'juggernaut' of insecurity and threats to identity without abandoning usual politics entirely. In the East, the revolutions of 1989 drew upon some of the main themes in the modernist narrative – justice, freedom, community and sovereignty – as well as upon the repertoire of modern political protest, and there was little in the way of postmodern ennui or scepticism to be seen (Johnson, 1994; Habermas, 1990). Because of these factors, some commentators feel that the 'unease' and dislocation so central to the thesis of insecurity and identity ambivalence may be no more than a product of fevered intellectual imagination, and the cynicism of 'Generation X' just the 1990s equivalent of the 1960s phenomenon of the weekend hippie (Swanson, 1992).

So the question of systemic transformation remains difficult to pin down. However, the merit of postmodern thinking about the incremental and epochal changes in train is that it does offer an intimation of the limits of modernity and a 'symptomatology' of its ills. In the contested and indeterminate forms and processes of global systemness, we can glimpse the transformative potential of a dynamic system.

9 Conclusion

To end at the beginning. Of late, the idea of the world being made one place is widely canvassed. There is a frisson of global consciousness in the speeches of politicians and in various specialist narratives, including those of the social sciences, and apparent too in popular discourse. As to the latter, awareness may be no more developed than the consciousness of subscribers to satellite TV channels, who are experiencing *virtual* globality; for while we may be consumers of global products, we still cling to, or else remain nostalgic about, things parochial. There is, however, much evidence to support the rule-of-thumb definitions of globalization set out in earlier chapters, that processes which are operating at a global 'level' do affect local behaviours and local identities. To this extent many people are 'constrained to identify' with the global system, even where identification takes the form of a conscious rejection of globalized cultural and material products (Robertson, 1992).

The perception of global constraints can affect national politics and local opinion in all sorts of ways. For example, in the run-up to the general election in the United Kingdom in 1992, the Conservative administration benefited from a widespread perception that worsening economic conditions were not the fault of the British government, but due to general and 'uncontrollable' shifts in the world economy. But Roland Robertson is also right to say that consciousness of global trends need not imply endorsement of, or even acquiescence in, such trends. Despite the fact that global consumer cultures are often linked with things American, many citizens of the

United States have rarely been comfortable with cosmopolitanism, and of late there seems to be a growing desire to withdraw a little further away from the *otherness* of the globalized world they have played a considerable part in making. Warren Howe (1994) writes that the United States has abandoned its plans to replace measurements in feet and pounds with the international decimal system. Television weather forecasters no longer give the temperature in both Fahrenheit and Celsius, and foreign-language instruction has been stopped in all American state schools, at least as a standard part of the curriculum.

The tensions between global forces and national institutions and sensibilities are not new. In his book *Preparing for the Twenty-First Century*, Paul Kennedy quotes *The Economist* of October 1930 to the effect that the 'all-embracing unit' of the world economy constitutes an 'antithetical tendency' to the otherwise nationally organized social life of 'humanity' (1993, p. 332), and the dynamism of capitalism as a world system has been based on that same antinomy (Gamble, 1993). In its present form the global system exhibits the same tension, but it is thrown into greater relief by the sharp acceleration in certain social and economic trends, and in technological innovations which could scarcely have been imagined in 1930.

First, there is the reordering of the world economy, from what Lash and Urry (1994, p. 322) and Offe (1985) described as 'organized capitalism' to an increasingly general form of 'disorganized capitalism', wherein flows of capital, goods and services, and above all of communications, have become truly global, completely breaking down the idea of societalist forms of capitalism. In this process, the collapse of the main systemic alternative to capitalism, in the form of state socialism, is seen by some as a key factor in the creation of a global system of disorganized capitalism. This is not to say that national and local factors do not continue to affect the character of the emergent 'post-industrial' or 'post-capitalist' world economy and to impart a peculiarly local feel to regimes of 'reflexive accumulation', because it is also clear that local cultural traditions, different public philosophies and patterns of government regulation all produce variation in the institutionalization of this new global script (Lash and Urry, 1994).

Second, and most critically, is the extent to which the new global cultural economy is becoming an information economy, with communication structures operating largely free of particular jurisdictions, or having the capacity to do so. The 'informatizing' of the world economy has had dramatic effects upon the autonomy and behaviour of institutions like financial markets, and has begun a revolution in how work and leisure are organized, as well as in changing the meaning that such 'industrial' concepts have for individuals in the 'post-industrial' world (Handy, 1994). Local particularisms may survive and even flourish under these conditions, but the overall effect of the routine availability of 500 terrestrial and satellite TV channels and interactive television will be to attenuate the hold exercised by localities over the cultural imagination of individuals, even where the same technology allows for local and individual customizing of global products.

Third, the decolonization of large parts of the globe in the last forty years has underwritten the continuing importance of political nationalism and the enduring power of the myths of statehood in a globalizing world. Whereas decolonization was a part of the global process of modernization, the collapse of the Soviet empire and the further sundering of the world into nationalities and warring ethnies is evidence of the undoing of the modernist narrative. In all this the position of the nation-state looks increasingly fragile, bearing in mind the problems that face national governments in regulating the flows and networks of the information economy, and the challenges posed to its integrity by the new-found audacity of subnational movements, of localities and of indigenous peoples. It also faces a growing redundancy because of the operation of multilateral and supranational institutions of governance, and from transnational policy networks which are changing the pragmatic accommodations and the ties of affect between national governments and some organized interests.

Fourth, there are the threats to humankind as a whole, or to significant parts of it, which are due to: (1) changes and imbalances in the demographic make-up of the planet, which have seen the ageing of populations in the richer and technologically sophisticated First World, and a population explosion in the Third and Fourth Worlds; (2) the increased prospects for environmental disaster, as the developing world denudes natural resources like the rainforest in order to fuel economic development, and thus increases the likelihood of destructive climate changes; and (3) the availability of weapons of mass destruction, even in the aftermath of the Cold War, and the public 'success' of nuclear non-proliferation. The prospect of 'outlaw' states like North Korea, Libya or Iran possessing cheap atomic weapons due to advances in fusion technology exacerbates the sense of personal and global insecurity (Kennedy, 1993).

These trends underscore the oneness of the globe by exposing our vulnerability to certain kinds of risk, almost regardless of where we are located physically and to some degree heedless of our status. It is true also that a common humanity is laid bare by such risks, but it would be sanguine to believe that therein lies the possibility of succour. The processes of globalization have both compressed our sense of the world and broadened our experience of it, through the increased mobility of 'objects' (material goods) and 'subjects' (people). This is true whether we are travellers in fact or, as receivers of electronic images, just travellers in the imagination (Lash and Urry, 1994). Through the various forms of telecomedia, we 'know' the world more intimately than our grandparents would have thought possible, although our sense of where we are located in it may be much less secure. Transnational electronic communications break free of particular territories, spanning and dissolving time and space, and thus erode the intimate particularity of places.

This is not just a matter of the ease with which it is now possible to become a traveller or a sojourner, or even of the accessibility of 'global' consumer products. It is also because the physical environment, even the idea of nature itself, has been generalized and sanitized, torn or educated out of the symbology of local and national identities, and made into a resource or commodity, a heritage, or a space to be preserved. In this we may have chosen, perhaps unwittingly, to rewrite history just as surely as if we had reinvented the past for ideological purposes or propaganda. For as Dennis Cosgrove (1994) says, rather than being scientifically defined objects or locations, 'nature, landscape and environment are semiotic signifiers, deeply embedded in the cultural constitution of ... nations and integral to the distinctive identities of ... peoples.' As a consequence the politics of place (Hershkovitz, 1993) and the meaning of landscape have assumed a growing significance in the redefinition of usual politics in the West, as well as in the 'geographical and sociological imaginations' (p. 396).

Throughout this book I have cautioned against facile acceptance of the idea that global trends are producing a homogenized global cultural space, principally because such a claim confuses the globalization of flows and the creation of global or world spaces – in big cities or computer conferences – with the globalization of meaning structures. The reality is much more confused and the consequences of globalization still inchoate. While it is true that it has become increasingly difficult to 'remember' place as a context in relation to which identity is formed and maintained, in a world in which people and things are increasingly mobile, it is also apparent that technology can now provide some immediate sensory reminders of home for strangers in a strange land. For those minded, it is now possible to buy computer software which will deliver part or all of the Bible, not only in national languages, but in local dialects and patois too. Scratch the panoramic pictures of sagebrush, heather, or mountain landscapes in some issues of *Sunset* magazine and a not unpleasant aroma is released, a fleeting evocation of these landscapes and other 'blue remembered hills'. These things are exercises in nostalgia marketing, but that is beside the point, which is that we should be careful not to assume the homogenizing power of new technologies, or to underestimate the ability of local subjects to use them to recall, to underwrite or even to reinvent their own sense of belonging.

Cosmopolitanism too can sit easily on those who maintain a strong sense of belonging to a locality to which they are linked by ties of family, work and culture. Middle-class educated Italians have no difficulty in remembering their roots and ties in the intensely local identities of Genoa, Siena or Palermo, even though they may be members of an 'executive club' of frequent air travellers. The point is that subjects of all kinds are simultaneously globalized and localized through such exposure and uses: how could it be otherwise when the flows of cultural influence are so tortuous and contradictory? In Japan, the making of a new cultural milieu draws upon Hollywood traditions in the television and cinematographic arts, as well as embracing the aesthetics of postmodern design cultures to produce 'its own version of the 1990s' (Hiney, 1994) exemplified in the vivid images of *Manga* cartoons. These cartoons take the quintessentially American art form of the animated cartoon and transform it into a statement of Japanese cultural revolt. The results are a world away from the archetypal American 'toon', but depict a post-industrial socioscape which is also the antithesis of at least three other versions of Japanese culture: the sense that it is or was just a poor imitation or joke version of American culture, the stereotype of tea gardens and the samurai spirit, and the essentially modernist image of company anthems and clever gadgets. At the same time, as Hiney says, the provenance of the *Manga* culture lies firmly with Kubrick's *A Clockwork Orange* and the Rolling Stones' 'Streetfighting man'.

This is the stuff of global systemness. Of course, by canvassing such a wide range of illustrative materials to try to understand how the global system is possible and how it is being transformed, there is always some danger of over-extension or of eclecticism. But the multi-dimensionality of globalization cannot be grasped either by disciplinary parsimony or a literal respect for concepts like 'level of analysis'. A multi-dimensional approach looks to the connections between agency and institutions across conventional levels of analysis to find the expressions of global systemness. This is not a matter of uncovering functionally required goal states, or discovering that the behaviour of agents or system parts is functional almost by default, or in effect; rather it consists in what Mouzelis (1989) calls the 'truism' that all social conduct presupposes structure and that structures in turn are reproduced through practice. In other words, the global system, like all social systems, has to be continuously remade, and in that remaking lies the scope for further reflexive action by agents, and for systemic transformation. In this book I have tried to suggest ways in which action-centred concepts like structuration can be used in conjunction with forms of institutionalist analysis strongly influenced by social constructionism to come to terms with the idea of global systemness.

One of the complaints about adopting structurationist analysis is the claim that it is excessively abstract, but it seems to me that this is a 'fault' remediable by more empirical work (Whittington, 1992) applied, as Giddens suggests, to concrete circumstances. Some of this is already available in work on sovereignty as a social construction (George, 1994), systemic change in the former Soviet Union (Koslowski and Kratochwil, 1994), the concept of territoriality (Ruggie, 1993) and the autonomy of managerial agency (Whittington, 1992). The initiation, establishment and persistence of institutional scripts, and the reproductive and transformative practices of agents, may require long-term research and the careful reconstruction of events and processes, using a battery of investigative tools, but they are amenable to study. Much recent work having its provenance in forms of world-system analysis is particularly active in this area (Thomas et al., 1987; Soysal, 1995), and the significance of transnational networks of interaction, and the local reception of global cultural products, are priority areas for research (Axford and Boyce, 1994; Hannerz, 1992b).

Clearly, the multi-dimensionality of relationships in the global system adds to the difficulties of investigation, especially where non-local or non-face-to-face relationships are examined; but in a globalized world, despatialized relationships and networks of only 'virtual presence' which are also 'out of time' must be increasingly prime candidates for research. Because of this it is also necessary to amend the idea that an actor-sensitive approach to the analysis of social life, one which stresses social integration, depends upon the phenomenon of face-to-face interaction. Agents are no less social practitioners in the absence of copresence, although it is arguable that some kinds of social relationships, perhaps family life, are not sustainable under such conditions. But to insist on such a limited conception of agency would make the individual largely powerless in many social relationships which are organized across large distances, and thus nugatory in the transformation of larger structures, though not in their reproduction. Both Giddens (1993) and his critic Mouzelis (1993) point out that face-to-face relations need not imply a lack of capacity to influence what the latter refers to as 'macro-actions', and this seems an obvious point when applied to the deliberations of strategically endowed actors like Cabinet committees, staff officers or the boards of multinational companies. Whether this reasoning extends to agents who are not the equivalent of two-star generals is more questionable. But in either case the key point may not be the distances involved, but the understanding of and access to appropriate resources and rules. For example, during the money markets crisis of 1992, strategically placed dealers were able to intervene dramatically using computer technology to assert the dominance of market forces. And of course power is relational, so that, although not everyone is a two-star general, they may be empowered in different ways and in different contexts. The management guru Tom Peters (1990) writes of a conductor on the Union Pacific railroad achieving more autonomy from routine management control by being put 'in charge' of a computer terminal in his cab. Decisions which had once to be passed to a supervisor at regional headquarters now fall within the remit of the conductor because he can get access to relevant information directly. More abstractly, the message here has to be that structure is reliant upon practice and that social integration, through what Giddens calls 'mediated connection', is an important part of the constitution of global systemness and the autonomy of agents.

Which returns us to the question of reflexivity. The significance of reflexive modernization has been emphasized throughout this book. This concept underlines the modified action orientation of the argument, by suggesting that mastery of the self is a primary task for agency in the global system. Furthermore, under global conditions still heavily subsidized by the Western cultural account, institutional reflexivity, or the culturally sanctioned expectation that agents can and should perform a critical monitoring function, legitimates the status of the individual as both a self-analyst and a social critic. Looked at in this way it is possible to treat the growing contingency of lifestyles affected by global forces with a degree of optimism. This is because while individuals must rely upon the comforting mediation provided by expert systems, a growing contingency pushes them to be more creative, more adventurous and more demanding, and thus expands the horizons for individual emancipation and self-realization. Such conditions also improve the prospects for a politics of personal choice which is not just angry, introverted or narcissistic, but reflexive. However, some important caveats must be introduced.

The first replays doubts expressed above about the ability of individual subjects to exercise choice. Rules and resources may be in plentiful supply, but they still have to be accessed and used (Whittington, 1992, pp. 706–7). In this respect the 'situatedness' of actors in particular identities, say as women, members of an ethnic minority or some other marginal group, may make the exercise of strategic choice no more than a gesture. The same would be true of access to the sorts of technical facilities which could transform mundane activities like shopping, or contribute to the creation of a 'teledemocracy' by putting an interactive terminal in every home. In the postmodern hyperspace, competent consumers just might be the equivalent of active citizens, but they still need skills appropriate to their station, and a sense of personal efficacy in order to exercise them.

Moreover, the possibilities for greater control by individuals over their lives could be more than matched by the technical capacities of the corporation, the state or the superstate to effect a pervasive and discreet surveillance of a mass culture which is now more visual than literary or verbal (Lash and Urry, 1994, p. 324; Giddens, 1985). Webster and Robins (1989) mourn the passing of the book culture and of the private and critical activity of reading in a way reminiscent of Marshall McLuhan's critique of the passionless and undemanding outputs of television, which are consumed all too passively. But in this they may be too pessimistic as well as a touch elitist, for the *samizdat* of the imagination can function equally well using a modem and a screen: only the aesthetics and sensual qualities of the medium may be judged inferior to the printed page. There is more than an echo here of the concern felt by Maurice Halbwachs as long ago as 1950, when he attributed to industrial modernization a cardinal part in the destruction of the collective memories of localities and groups. Extended to the cultural hyperspaces and cyberspaces of postmodernity these sentiments might be as compelling. Halbwachs's fear of the impact of modernization on the ability of subjects to 'remember' who they are is magnified by a vision of postmodernity in which there are no reference points in the past (and no need for them) and in which cultural forms are as fleeting and as erasable as a computer file (Douglas, 1987).

These are important qualifications on the emancipatory potential of a politics of choice and reflexivity. In other respects too Lash and Urry's stress on the liberating potential of aesthetic reflexivity may understate the importance of access to appropriate resources in the creation of a politics of identity. For example, the reworking of identities as part of the reflexive project may do little more than glamorize the 'victim' status of those subject to entrenched forms of exclusion and closure, as in the recently fashionable politics of 'victimization' seen in the United States.

The second caveat raises an issue examined in chapters 6 and 8. The 'excess of contingency' noted by Lash, or seen in Beck's 'risk society', may not produce a benign and emancipatory politics of identity. Indeed the flight from meta-narratives shows incredulity towards the Enlightenment project of emancipation altogether (Villa, 1992). Individuals and groups may not embrace change in the manner prescribed, but look for solutions to identity problems which involve a flight from reflexivity, seeking refuge in what Lash and Urry distinguish as the community of 'the we' and meeting identity needs through communitarianism and fundamentalism (1994, p. 315). The processes of modernization and globalization have released, or in some versions separated, the individual from the shared meanings and rootedness of traditional pasts and often from the places in which these meanings were stored. The outcome may be subjects who are empowered and in control, or selves which are atomized and rootless.

In either case the individual is often cast adrift from the 'shared meaning and background practices of the "we" ' (p. 315). In certain circumstances communities or networks can be invented reflexively, out of choice and not, in Bourdieu's sense, out of *habit*. The latter springs from an individual's *unreflective* rootedness in 'immediate' communities and in 'real' places. The idea of reflexivity owes much to the Enlightenment tradition of subjecting conduct to abstract, general rules governing behaviour, and Lash and Urry's gloss on this usage involves a critical subject making an aesthetic judgement about the suitability or efficacy of creating particular identities to suit changing circumstances and to meet changing 'needs'. But the idea of 'habitus', or of Heidegger's 'being-in-the-world', to which Lash and Urry also refer, admits no reflexivity, no choice and no invention. The 'we' conjured here is the 'we' of palpable communities and tribes (neo-tribes) in which culture is the jumble of shared meanings that bind people to place and to the past (pp. 316–18). While it is true that the yearning to re-create this sort of community amid the fragments of postmodern life can yield relatively benign, if mildly exotic, 'neo-tribes' – of New Age travellers, or urban tepee dwellers – it is also the justification for the exclusion of the 'inauthentic', for ethnic cleansing in Bosnia, for racial attacks and for the dogmas of 'survivalism' found in parts of the United States.

So the third caveat questions the assumption that reflexivity is characteristic of a world increasingly uncertain and risk-laden and where institutional reflexivity is being rewritten as a global script in the course of challenges to the Western cultural account which sustained it. Inevitably the available evidence is capable of different interpretations. The thrusting of life-political issues to the forefront of the political agenda in the West is still legitimated by the civil traditions of Western liberalism and humanism even where, as in some forms of feminist discourse, their rhetoric challenges the validity of that account and its implicit masculine assumptions (O'Sullivan, 1993). A politics of identity rooted in the cultural sphere, and based on a celebration of difference, looks to deconstruct the universalist tenets of liberalism and individualism by treating them as oppressive texts (Foucault, 1984; Derrida, 1976; Wallerstein, 1991a; 1991b) and by challenging the status of those other foundational myths of Western modernity – abstract universalism, rationality and the nation-state. On the face of it, this looks more like the triumph of particularism than of universalism, of parochialism rather than globalism, and in the political realm the casualties may be big governments, mass political parties and the institutions of representative government in mass democracies. Since forms of democratic rule that combine the universalism of Enlightenment philosophy and the demands of postmodern identity politics are hard to find, who now inherits the earth (Mouffe, 1993)?

Civilizational or pan-cultural conflicts also seem less distant, even if they are still largely imagined, and the 'culture of violence' *in* cities, *by* both indigent and bored youth, *on the part* of the have-nots everywhere, is much discussed in intellectual circles and among the literati (Stone, 1994). Yet for all this, it is proper to be a little cautious and to qualify the apocalyptic mood, for the 'jihad against McWorld' is only bloody occasionally (Barber, 1992). The transformation of modernity and its dehegemonization as a cultural script is nowhere complete, and though the West may not have triumphed, neither has it crumbled. Rather, like the fate of the modern nation-state, it has been 'hollowed out' as a global cultural script and the future is rife with possibilities. Recent essays by Michael Ignatieff (1994) and Eric Hobsbawm (1994) which paint a lurid picture of the tribalizing of the world, depict an 'undoing' or disintegration of the

Western cultural account. These jeremiads place the temper of the global system beyond any kind of reflexivity and on the brink of ruin.

But other positions are more optimistic on the shape of things to come. They canvass the idea of a postmodern space of flows that is rich in new global cultures, where individuals reinvent themselves as a way of coming to terms with the growing interpenetration and aestheticization of politics, economics and culture. In this world, spaces replace places as contexts for identity formation and for many of the routines of living, but not entirely, since agents can reimagine place, perhaps through the creation of *virtual* places like the common rooms of the *virtual* university, the *virtual* family reunion or the *virtual* town meeting. Set against these visions of the global future, Francis Fukuyama's (1992) insistence on an end to the long march of History and the triumph of modernity is much less pluralistic and contested. However, even Fukuyama is willing to allow the possibility that the 'last man' may slough off his historical role, start again and – whisper it – reinvent himself. So the idea with which this book began, that of seeing the world as a single place, must now acknowledge that the singularity of the global system is continuously subject to the interpretative practices of agents in the making and remaking of the conditions of their existence – and that *systemness* implies no more, but significantly, no less than this.

References

Abaza, M. and Stauth, G. 1990: Occidental reason, orientalism, Islamic fundamentalism: a critique. In M. Albrow and E. King (eds), *Globalization, Knowledge and Society*. London: Sage.

Abdel-Haq, Mohammed K. 1993: *The Relationship between Islamic Banking Theory and Practice*. PhD Thesis, Oxford Brookes University.

Abu-Lughod, Janet 1989: *Before European Hegemony: the world system A.D. 1250–1350*. New York: Oxford University Press.

Abu-Lughod, Janet 1991: Writing against culture. In R. G. Fox (ed.), *Recapturing Anthropology: working in the present*. Santa Fe, New Mexico: School of America Research Press.

Adatto, Kiku 1990: *Sound-Bite Democracy: network evening news presidential campaign coverage 1968 and 1988*. Research Paper R-2, Joan Sorenson Barone Centre on the Press, Politics and Public Policy. Cambridge: Harvard University.

Addo, Herb 1984: On the crisis in the Marxist theory of imperialism. *Contemporary Marxism*, 9, Fall, 123–48.

Agh, Attila 1991: The transition to democracy in Central Europe: a comparative view. *Journal of Public Policy*, 11(2), 13–151.

Aglietta, M. 1979: *A Theory of Capitalist Regulation*. London: New Left Books.

Agnew, John 1994: The territorial trap: the geographical assumptions of international relations theory. *Review of International Political Economy*, 1(1), 55–71.

Ajami, Fouad 1993: The summoning. *Foreign Affairs*, 72(4), 2–9.

Almond, Gabriel and Verba, Sydney 1963: *Civic Culture*. Boston: Little Brown.

Amin, Samir 1972: Underdevelopment and dependence in Black Africa. *Journal of Modern African Studies*, 10, 503–24.

Amin, Samir 1980: *Class and Nation*. New York: Monthly Review Press.

Anderson, Benedict 1983: *Imagined Communities*. London: Verso.

Anderson, Perry 1974: *Lineages of the Absolutist State*. London: New Left Books.

Ang, Ien 1990: Culture and communication: towards an ethnographic critique of media consumption in the transnational media system. *European Journal of Communication*, 5(2–3), 239–60.

Antal, Ariane B. and Merkens, Hans 1993: Cultures and fictions in transition: challenges facing managers and employees in East German companies. *Journal of General Management*, 19(1), 76–86.

Appadurai, Arjun 1990: Disjuncture and difference in the global cultural economy. In M. Featherstone (ed.), *Global Culture: nationalism, globalization and modernity*. London: Sage.

Appadurai, Arjun 1993: *The Production of Locality*. Paper to the ASA IV Decennial Conference, Oxford, July.

Appelbaum, Richard and Henderson, Jeff (eds) 1992: *State and Society in the Pacific Rim*. London: Sage.

Arato, Andrew 1985: Soviet society as a world-system. *Telos*, 65, 178–87.

Archer, Margaret S. 1988: *Culture and Agency: the place of culture in social theory*. Cambridge: Cambridge University Press.

Ardener, Edward 1989: The construction of history: 'vestiges of creation'. In E. Tonkin, M. MacDonald and M. Chapman (eds), *History and Ethnicity*. London: Routledge.

Arnason, Johan 1990: Nationalism, globalization and modernity. In M. Featherstone (ed.), *Global Culture: nationalism, globalization and modernity*. London: Sage.

Arrighi, Giovanni 1982: A crisis of hegemony. In S. Amin, G. Arrighi, A. G. Frank and I. Wallerstein (eds), *Dynamics of Global Crisis*. London and Basingstoke: Macmillan.

Arrighi, Giovanni, Hopkins, Terrence K. and Wallerstein, Immanuel 1989: *Antisystemic Movements*. London: Verso.

Ascherson, Neal 1991: The new disorder. *The Independent on Sunday*, 17 February, 8–9.

Axford, Barrie, 1987: The United Kingdom. In J. Sigler (ed.), *An International Handbook of Race and Race Relations*. Westport: Greenwood Press.

Axford, Barrie 1993: *Dirty Politics* (review). *Media, Culture and Society*, 15, 507–10.

Axford, Barrie 1994: *Multiple Truths and Postmodern Imaginings: new ways of reading European unity*. Paper to the Conference of the International Society for the Study of European Ideas, Graz.

Axford, Barrie and Boyce, Brigitte 1994: *Changing Rules of the Game: new ways of reading European unity*. Paper to the ESRC/COST-A7 Conference on the Evolution of Rules for the Single European Market, Exeter, September.

Axford, Barrie and Deacon, David 1982: *The Theme of the State in Comparative Macro-History*. Paper to the Political Sociology Panel of the Annual Conference of the Political Studies Association of the UK, University of Kent.

Axford, Barrie and Deacon, David 1984: *World System Analysis and State Theory: the need for paradigm reorientation*. Paper to the World Systems Panel of the Annual Conference of the Political Studies Association of the UK, University of Southampton, 3–5 April.

Axford, Barrie, Deacon, David, Shaw, Brian and Turner, John 1991: The single European market and small businesses: evaluations of and responses to a changing environment. *European Research*, 2(July), 1–6.

Bachrach, Peter 1967: *The Political Theory of Democratic Elitism*. Boston: Little Brown.

Badie, Bertrand and Birnbaum, Pierre 1983: *The Sociology of the State*. Chicago: University of Chicago Press.

Bahro, Rudolf 1981: *The Alternative in Eastern Europe*. London: Verso.

Baldwin-Edwards, Martin and Schain, Martin 1994: The politics of immigration-introduction. *West European Politics*, 17(2), 1–17.

Balibar, Etienne, 1991: Es gibt keinen Staat in Europa: racism and politics in Europe today. *New Left Review*, 186, 5–20.

Barber, Bruce 1992: Jihad against McWorld. *Atlantic Monthly*, 269 (March), 53–63.

Barone, C. 1983: Dependency, Marxist theory, and salvaging the idea of capitalism in South Korea. *Review of Radical Political Economics*, 15(1), 41–67.

Barrett, Deborah 1992: *Reproducing People as a Public Concern*. Unpublished doctoral proposal, Stanford University.

Barry, Brian 1970: *Sociologists, Economists and Democracy*. London: Collier Macmillan.

Bartlett, Charles A., Doz, Y. and Hedlund, G. (eds) 1990: *Managing the Global Firm*. London: Routledge.

Bartlett, Charles A. and Ghoshal, S. 1989: *Managing Across Borders: the transnational solution*. London: Hutchinson Business Books.

Bartlett, Charles A. and Ghoshal, S. 1992: What is a global manager? *Harvard Business Review*, September–October, 124–32.

Bate, Steve P. 1994: *Strategies for Cultural Change*. London: Butterworth-Heinemann.

Baudrillard, Jean 1981: *For a Critique of the Political Economy of the Sign*. St Louis: Telos Press.

Baudrillard, Jean 1983: *Simulations*. New York: Semiotext.

Bauman, Zygmunt 1987: *Legislators and Interpreters*. Cambridge: Polity.

Bauman, Zygmunt 1990: Modernity and ambivalence. In M. Featherstone (ed.), *Global Culture*. London: Sage.

Bauman, Zygmunt 1992: *Intimations of Postmodernity*. London: Routledge.

Bayard, Caroline 1994: *A Postmodern Reading of European Identities and Polities: a provisional cartography of Europe and postmodernity*. Paper to the Conference of the International Society for the Study of European Ideas, Graz.

Beck, Ulrich 1992a: *Risk Society: towards a new modernity*. London: Sage.

Beck, Ulrich 1992b: From industrial society to risk society: questions of survival, structure and ecological enlightenment. *Theory, Culture and Society*, 9, 97–123.

Beck, Ulrich, Giddens, Anthony and Lash, Scott 1994: *Reflexive Modernization*. Cambridge: Polity.

Bellah, R., Madson, R., Swidler, A. and Tipton, S. 1985: *Habits of the Heart*. Berkeley, CA: University of California Press.

Benington, John and Harvey, Janet 1994: *Spheres or Tiers? The significance of transnational local authority networks*. In *Published Proceedings of the Annual Conference of the Political Studies Association of the UK*, vol. 2.

Berger, Peter and Luckmann, Thomas 1966: *The Social Construction of Reality*. Harmondsworth: Penguin.

Bergesen, Albert 1980a: From utilitarianism to globology: the shift from the individual to the world as a whole as the primordial unit of analysis. In A. Bergesen (ed.), *Studies of the Modern World-System*. New York: Academic Press.

Bergesen, Albert (ed.) 1980b: *Studies of the Modern World-System*. New York: Academic Press.

Bergesen, Albert 1982: The emerging science of the world-system. *International Social Science Journal*, 34(1), 23–37.

Bergesen, Albert (1990): Turning world-system theory on its head. *Media, Culture and Society*, 7(2–3), 67–83.

Bhaba, H. (ed.) 1990: *Nation and Narration*. London: Routledge.

Bhaskar, Roy 1976: Two philosophies of science. *New Left Review*, 94.

Bhaskar, Roy 1979: *The Possibility of Naturalism*. Brighton: Harvester.

Binder, Leonard (ed.) 1971: *Crises and Sequences in Political Development*. Princeton: Princeton University Press.

Bohm, D. 1980: *Wholeness and the Implicate Order*. London: Routledge and Kegan Paul.

Borgmann, Albert 1992: *Crossing the Postmodern Divide*. Chicago: University of Chicago Press.

Boulding, Kenneth E. 1956: General systems theory – the skeleton of science. *Management Science*, 2, 197–208.

Bourdieu, Pierre 1977: *Outline of a Theory of Practice*. Cambridge: Cambridge University Press.

Bourdieu, Pierre 1984: *Distinction*. London: Routledge.

Bourdieu, Pierre 1990: *The Logic of Practice*. Palo Alto: Stanford University Press.

Boutros-Ghali, Boutros 1993: UN peace-keeping in a new era: a new chance for peace. *The World Today*, April, 66–9.

Bowen, David 1994: *Multimedia: now and down the line*. London: Bowerdean.

Boyce, Brigitte 1994: Interest representation in the European Community, European integration and the concept of Europeanism. *History of European Ideas*, 19(1–3), 153–9.

Boyne, Roy 1990: Culture and the world system. In M. Featherstone (ed.), *Global Culture: nationalism, globalization and modernity*. London: Sage.

Braudel, Fernand 1972: *The Mediterranean and the Mediterranean World in the Age of Philip II*. 2 vols. New York: Harper and Row.

Braudel, Fernand 1975: *Capitalism and Material Life 1400–1800*. New York: Harper and Row.

Braudel, Fernand 1977: *Afterthoughts on Material Civilization and Capitalism*. Baltimore: Johns Hopkins University Press.

Brenner, Robert 1977: The origins of capitalist development: a critique of neo-Smithian Marxism. *New Left Review*, 104, 25–92.

Brier, Alan and Axford, Barrie 1975: The theme of race in British social and political research. In I. Crewe (ed.), *The Political Sociology Yearbook. Volume 2: The Politics of Race*. London: Croom Helm.

Bryant, Christopher and Mokrzycki, Edmund 1994: *The New Great Transformation? Change and continuity in East-Central Europe.* London: Routledge.

Bukharin, Nicolai 1917: *Imperialism and World Economy.* New York: Merlin Press (1972).

Bull, Hedley 1977: *The Anarchical Society: a study of order in world politics.* New York: Columbia University Press.

Bull, Hedley and Watson, Ian 1984: *The Expansion of International Society.* Oxford: Oxford University Press.

Burke, Kenneth 1970: *The Rhetoric of Religion.* Berkeley, CA: University of California Press.

Burns, Tom and Stalker, George M. 1961: *The Management of Innovation.* London: Tavistock.

Buzan, Barry 1993: From international system to international society: structural realism and regime theory meet the English School. *International Organisation*, 47(3), 328–52.

Byrsk, Alison 1993: From above and below: social movements, the international system and human rights in Argentina. *Comparative Political Studies*, 26(3), 259–85S.

Cable, Vincent 1994: *The World's New Fissures.* London: Demos/RIIA.

Callinicos, Alex 1989: *Against Postmodernism.* Cambridge: Polity.

Cammack, Paul 1992: The new institutionalism: predatory rule, institutional persistence, and macro-social change. *Economy and Society*, 21(4), 397–427.

Cammack, Paul, Pool, David and Tordoff, William 1993: *Third World Politics: a comparative introduction.* 2nd edn. London: Macmillan.

Campanella, Miriam 1992: The effects of globalization and turbulence on policy-making processes. *Government and Opposition*, 28(3), 190–202.

Caporaso, James (ed.), 1987: *A Changing International Division of Labour.* Boulder, CO: Lynne Rienner.

Cardoso, Fernando H. 1993: North–South relations in the present context: a new dependency? In Martin Carnoy, Manuel Castells, Stephen Cohen and Fernando H. Cardoso (eds), *The New Global Economy in the Information Age.* Basingstoke: Penn State Press.

Cardoso, Fernando, H. and Faletto, Enzo 1979: *Dependency and Development in Latin America.* Berkeley, CA: University of California Press.

Carnoy, Martin 1983: *The State and Political Theory.* Princeton: Princeton University Press.

Carnoy, Martin 1993: Multinationals in a changing world economy: whither the nation-state? In M. Carnoy, M. Castells, S. Cohen and F. H. Cardoso (eds), *The New Global Economy in the Information Age: reflections on our changing world*. Basingstoke: Penn State Press.

Carnoy, Martin, Castells, Manuel, Cohen, Stephen and Cardoso, Fernando H. 1993: *The New Global Economy in the Information Age*. Basingstoke: Penn State Press.

Carr, Edward H. 1939: *The Twenty Years Crisis, 1919–1939*. London: Macmillan.

Carter, E., Donald, J. and Squires, J. (eds) 1993: *Space and Place: theories of identity and location*. London: Lawrence and Wishart.

Case, Peter 1993: *Postmodernism and the Reflexive Project: Christine's reflections*. Oxford Brookes University: Thamesman Publications, Occasional Paper and Seminar Series.

Castells, Manuel 1989: High technology and the new international division of labour. *International Labour Review*, October.

Castells, Manuel 1993: The informational economy and the new international division of labour. In Martin Carnoy, Manuel Castells, Stephen Cohen and Fernando H. Cardoso (eds), *The New Global Economy in the Information Age*. Basingstoke: Penn State Press.

Castells, Manuel and Laserna, Roberto 1989: The new dependency: technological change and socio-economic restructuring in Latin America. *Sociological Forum*, 4(4), 535–60.

Castoriades, C. 1987: *The Imaginary Institution of Society*. Cambridge: Cambridge University Press.

Cerny, Philip 1990: *The Changing Architecture of Politics: structure, agency and the future of the state*. London: Sage.

Chapman, M. 1992: *Defining Culture: a social anthropological perspective*. Paper to the UK AIB Conference, Brighton.

Chase-Dunn, Christopher 1979: Comparative research on world-system characteristics. *International Studies Quarterly*, 23(4), 610–23.

Chase-Dunn, Christopher 1981: Interstate system of capitalist world-economy: one logic or two. *International Studies Quarterly*, 25(1), 19–42.

Chase-Dunn, Christopher 1988: Comparing world-systems: towards a theory of semi-peripheral development. *Comparative Civilizations Review*, Fall.

Chase-Dunn, Christopher 1989: *Global Formation: structures of the world economy*. Oxford: Blackwell.

Choate, Pat 1990: *Agents of Influence*. New York: Knopf.

Clegg, Stewart 1989: *Modern Organizations: organization studies in a postmodern world*. London: Sage.

Clegg, Stewart 1992: Modern and postmodern organisations. *Sociology Review*, April, 24–8.

Clifford, James 1988: *The Predicament of Culture: twentieth century ethnography, literature, and art*. Cambridge, MA: Harvard University Press.

Cohen, I. J. 1989: *Structuration Theory: Anthony Giddens and the constitution of social life*. London: St Martin's Press.

Cohen, Jerry L. and Arato, Andrew 1992: *Civil Society and Political Theory*. Boston: MIT Press.

Cohen, Stephen S. 1993: Geo-economics: lessons from America's mistakes. In Martin Carnoy, Manuel Castells, Stephen Cohen and Fernando H. Cardoso (eds), *The New Global Economy in the Information Age*. Basingstoke: Penn State Press.

Colchester, Nicholas and Buchan, David 1990: *Europe Relaunched*. London: Economist Books/Hutchinson.

Collins, Richard 1990: National culture: a contradiction in terms? In R. Collins (ed.), *Television, Policy and Culture*. London: Unwin Hyman.

Collinson, David 1992: *Managing the Shopfloor: subjectivity, masculinity and workplace culture*. Berlin: Walter de Gruyter.

Colquehoun, Keith 1993: North Korea as a dangerous outsider. *The World Today*, November, 210–14.

Cosgrove, Dennis 1994: Terrains of power. *The Times Higher Education Supplement* 11 March, 18–19.

Coulson-Thomas, Charles 1992: *Transforming the Company*. London: Kogan Page.

Cox, Robert 1987: *Production, Power and World Order: social forces in the making of history*. New York: Columbia University Press.

Craven, P. and Wellman, B. 1974: The network city. In M. P. Effrat (ed.), *The Community*. New York: Free Press.

Deal, Terrence and Kennedy, Allan A. 1988: *Corporate Cultures*. Harmondsworth: Penguin.

Deleuze, G. and Guattari, Felix 1984: *Anti-Oedipus: capitalism and schizophrenia*. New York: Athlone Press.

Der Derian, James and Shapiro, Michael J. (eds) 1989: *International/Intertextual Relations: postmodern readings of world politics*. Lexington, MA: Lexington Books.

Derrida, Jacques 1976: *Of Grammatology*. Baltimore: Johns Hopkins University Press.

Dessler, David 1989: What's at stake in the agent–structure debate? *International Organisation*, 43(3), 431–73.

De Swann, Abram 1989: Platform Holland: Dutch society in the context of global cultural relations. *International Spectator*, XLIII(11), 718–22.

Deutsch, Karl 1953: *Nationalism and Social Communication: an inquiry into the foundations of nationality*. Cambridge, MA: MIT Press.

Deutsch, Karl 1957: *Political Community and the North Atlantic Area*. Princeton: Princeton University Press.

Deutsch, Karl 1961: *Social mobilization and political development. American Political Science Review*, 60 (September), 463–515.

Donald, J. 1988: How English is it? *New Formations*, 6.

Dos Santos, T. 1970: The structure of dependence. *American Economic Review*, 60 (May), 231–6.

Douglas, M. 1987: *How Institutions Think*. London: Routledge.

Drucker, Peter F. 1989: *The New Realities*. London: Butterworth.

Drucker, Peter F. 1993: *Post-Capitalist Society*. London: Butterworth-Heinemann.

Dryzek, John S., Clark, Margaret L. and McKenzie, Gary 1989: Subject and system in international interaction. *International Organisation*, 43(3), 477–503.

Dunleavy, Patrick and O'Leary, Brendan 1987: *Theories of the State: the politics of liberal democracy*. London: Macmillan.

Durkheim, Emile 1962: *Socialism*. New York: Collier.

Eisenstadt, Samuel N. 1987: *European Civilization in a Comparative Perspective*. Oslo: Norwegian University Press.

Elias, Norbert 1978: *The Civilizing Process. Volume 1: The History of Manners*. New York: Pantheon Books.

Emirbayer, Mustafa and Goodwin, Jeff 1994: Network analysis, culture and the problem of agency. *American Journal of Sociology*, 99(6), 1411–54.

Emmanuel, A. 1972: *Unequal Exchange: a study of the imperialism of trade*. New York: Monthly Review Press.

Enloe, Cynthia, 1989: *Bananas, Beaches and Bases: making feminist sense out of international politics*. Berkeley, CA: University of California Press.

Evans, Peter R., Rueschmeyer, D. and Skocpol, Theda (eds) 1985: *Bringing the State Back In*. Cambridge: Cambridge University Press.

Featherstone, Kevin 1994: Saint or sinner? Jean Monnet and the 'democratic deficit' in the European Community. *Journal of Common Market Studies*, June, 149–70.

Featherstone, Mike 1990: Global culture: an introduction. *Theory, Culture and Society*, 7, 2–3.

Foucault, Michel 1972: *The Archeology of Knowledge*. London: Tavistock.

Foucault, Michel 1984: What is Enlightenment? In P. Rabinow (ed.), *The Foucault Reader*. New York: Pantheon Books.

Foucault, Michel 1990: *The History of Sexuality*. Harmondsworth: Penguin Books.

Frank, André Gunder 1969a: *Latin America: underdevelopment or revolution?* New York: Monthly Review Press.

Frank, André Gunder 1969b: *Capitalism and Underdevelopment in Latin America*. New York: Monthly Review Press.

Frank, André Gunder 1978: *Dependent Accumulation and Under-development*. New York: Monthly Review Press.

Frankel, Boris 1983: *Beyond the State? Dominant theories and socialist strategies*. London: Macmillan.

Freeman, John 1990: *Banking on Democracy? International finance and the possibilities for popular sovereignty*. Mimeograph, University of Minnesota.

Frieden, Jeffrey A. 1991: Invested interests: the politics of national economic policies in a world of global finance. *International Organisation*, 45(1), 425–51.

Friedman, Jonathan 1989: Culture, identity and world process. *Review*, 12(1), 51–69.

Friedman, Jonathan 1990: Being in the world: globalization and localization. In M. Featherstone (ed.), *Global Culture: nationalism, globalization and modernity*. London: Sage.

Friedman, Jonathan 1993: Order and disorder in global systems: a sketch. *Social Research*, 60(2), 205–34.

Friedman, Jonathan 1994: *Cultural Identity and Global Processes*. London: Sage.

Fuchs, Stephan 1991: Systems Theory (review). *Contemporary Sociology*, May, 454–5.

Fukuyama, Francis 1991: Liberal democracy as a global phenomenon. *Political Science & Politics*, December, 659–64.

Fukuyama, Francis 1992: *The End of History and the Last Man*. London: Hamish Hamilton.

Funabashi, Yoichi 1994: Japan and the new world order. *Foreign Affairs*, 74(5), 59–74.

Gamble, Andrew 1993: Shaping a new world order: political capacities and policy challenges. *Government and Opposition*, 28(3), 325–39.

Garfinkel, Harold 1984: *Studies in Ethnomethodology*. Cambridge: Polity.

Geertz, Clifford 1963: *Old Societies and New States*. New York: Free Press.

Geertz, Clifford 1973: *On the Interpretation of Culture*. New York: Basic Books.

Gellner, Ernest 1992: Squaring the ménage à trois. *Times Literary Supplement*, 21(7).

Gellner, Ernest 1993: *Nations and Nationalism*. Ithaca: Cornell University Press.

George, Jim 1994: *Discourses of Global Politics: a critical (re)introduction to international relations*. Boulder, CO: Lynne Rienner.

Giddens, Anthony 1981: *A Contemporary Critique of Historical Materialism*. London: Macmillan.

Giddens, Anthony 1984: *The Constitution of Society*. Cambridge: Polity.

Giddens, Anthony 1985: *The Nation-State and Violence*. Cambridge: Polity.

Giddens, Anthony 1990: *The Consequences of Modernity*. Cambridge: Polity.

Giddens, Anthony 1991a: *Modernity and Self-Identity*. Cambridge: Polity.

Giddens, Anthony 1991b: Structuration theory: past, present and future. In C. Bryant and D. Jary (eds), *Giddens' Theory of Structuration*. London: Routledge.

Giddens, Anthony 1993: *New Rules of Sociological Method*. 2nd edn. Cambridge: Polity.

Gill, Stephen 1994: *Opportunities and Obstacles to the Emergence of a New Multilateralism*. Paper for the International Symposium on Sources of Innovation in Multilateralism, Lausanne.

Gill, Stephen and Law, David 1988: *The Global Political Economy; perspectives, problems and policies*. Brighton: Harvester Wheatsheaf.

Gilpin, Robert 1981: *War and Change in World Politics*. Cambridge: Cambridge University Press.

Gilpin, Robert 1987: *The Political Economy of International Relations*. Princeton: Princeton University Press.

Gleick, J. 1987: *Chaos: making a new science*. New York: Viking.

Glyn, Andrew and Sutcliffe, Bob 1992: Global and leaderless. In R. Miliband and J. Seville (eds), *Socialist Register*.

Goldstein, Morris, Mathieson, Donald and Lane, Timothy 1991: *Determinants and Systemic Consequences of International Capital Flows*. International Monetary Fund.

Gouldner, Alvin 1970: *Coming Crisis of Western Sociology.* New York: Basic Books.

Gouldner, Alvin 1980: *The Two Marxisms: contradictions and anomalies in the development of theory.* London: Macmillan.

Gourevitch, Peter 1986: *Politics in Hard Times.* Ithaca: Cornell University Press.

Gowa, Joanne 1984: State power, state policy: explaining the decision to close the gold window. *Politics and Society*, 13(1), 91–117.

Grant, Wyn 1987: *Business and Politics in Britain.* London: Macmillan.

Gray, John 1988: The politics of cultural diversity. *Salisbury Review*, 7, 38–44.

Gray, John 1994: Into the abyss. *Sunday Times*, News Review, 30 October.

Greenwood, John, Grote, J. R. and Ronit, Karstin 1992: *Organized Interests in the European Community.* London: Sage.

Greenwood, John and Ronit, Karstin 1994: Interest groups in the European Community: newly emerging dynamics and forms. *West European Politics*, 17(1), 31–52.

Gregersen, Hal and Sailer, Lee 1993: Chaos theory and its implications for social science research. *Human Relations*, 46(7), 777–801.

Gusterson, Hugh 1993: Realism and the international order after the Cold War. *Social Research*, 60(2), 279–300.

Haas, Ernst B. 1961: International integration: the European and the universal process. *International Organisation*, 3, 366–78.

Hass, Peter M. 1992: Introduction: epistemic communities and international policy coordination. *International Organisation*, 46(1), 1–37.

Habermas, Jürgen 1970: *Towards a Rational Society.* Boston: Beacon Press.

Habermas, Jürgen 1971: *Knowledge and Human Interests.* Boston: Beacon Press.

Habermas, Jürgen 1972: *Legitimation Crisis.* London: Heinemann.

Habermas, Jürgen 1973: *Theory and Practice.* Boston: Beacon Press.

Habermas, Jürgen 1984: *The Theory of Communicative Action*, vol. 1. Cambridge: Polity.

Habermas, Jürgen 1987: *The Philosophical Discourse of Modernity.* Cambridge: Polity.

Habermas, Jürgen 1989: *The New Conservatism.* Cambridge: Polity.

Habermas, Jürgen 1990: What does socialism mean today? *New Left Review*, 183, 3–21.

Halbwachs, Maurice 1950: *The Collective Memory*. New York: Harper and Row.

Hall, Stuart 1992: The question of cultural identity. In S. Hall, D. Held and A. McGrew (eds), *Modernity and its Futures*. Cambridge: Open University/Polity.

Hall, Stuart, Held, David and McGrew, Tony (eds) 1992: *Modernity and its Futures*. Cambridge: Open University and Polity Press.

Halliday, Fred 1989: Theorising the International. *Economy and Society*, 18(3), 346–60.

Hall-Jamieson, Kathleen 1992: *Dirty Politics: deception, distraction and democracy*. Oxford: Oxford University Press.

Hammer, Michael and Champy, James 1993: *Reengineering the Corporation: a manifesto for business revolution*. London: Nicholas Brearley.

Handy, Charles 1989: *The Age of Unreason*. London: Arrow.

Handy, Charles 1994: *The Empty Raincoat*. London: Hutchinson.

Hannerz, Ulf 1989: Notes on the global ecumene. *Public Culture*, 1(2).

Hannerz, Ulf 1990: Cosmopolitans and locals in world culture. In M. Featherstone (ed.), *Global Culture: nationalism, globalization and modernity*. London: Sage.

Hannerz, Ulf 1992a: The global ecumene as a network of networks. In A. Kuper (ed.), *Conceptualising Society*. London: Routledge.

Hannerz, Ulf 1992b: *Cultural Complexity: studies in the social organization of meaning*. New York: Columbia University Press.

Harries, Owen 1993: The collapse of 'the West'. *Foreign Affairs*, 72(4), 41–3.

Harris, Nigel 1986: *The End of the Third World*. Harmondsworth: Penguin.

Harvey, David 1989: *The Condition of Postmodernity: an inquiry into the conditions of cultural change*. Oxford: Basil Blackwell.

Hebdige, Dick 1989: After the masses. In S. Hall and M. Jacques (eds), *New Times*. London: Lawrence and Wishart.

Heintz, Peter 1982: Introduction: a sociological code for the description of world society and its change. *International Social Science Journal*, 34(1), 11–22.

Held, David 1991: Democracy, the nation-state and the global system. In D. Held (ed.), *Political Theory Today*. Cambridge: Polity.

Held, David 1992: Democracy: from city-states to cosmopolitan order? *Political Studies*, 42, special issue, 10–40.

Held, David and McGrew, Anthony 1993: Globalization and the liberal democratic state. *Government and Opposition*, 28(3), 261–85.

Heller, Agnes and Feher, Ferenc 1988: *The Postmodern Political Condition*. New York: Columbia University Press.

Hershkovitz, Linda 1993: Tiananmen Square and the politics of place. *Political Geography*, 12(5), 395–420.

Hindess, Barry and Hirst, Paul Q. 1975: *Pre-Capitalist Modes of Production*. London: Routledge and Kegan Paul.

Hiney, Tom 1994: Tokyo? Yo! *The Sunday Times, Style and Travel*, 2 January, 14–15.

Hirst, Paul Q. and Thompson, Grahame 1992: The problem of 'globalization': international economic relations, national economic management and the formation of trading blocs. *Economy and Society*, 21(4), 357–97.

Hix, Simon 1994: The study of the European Community: the challenge to comparative approaches. *West European Politics*, 17(1), 1–29.

Hobsbawm, Eric 1990: *Nations and Nationalism since 1780: programme, myth, reality*. Cambridge: Cambridge University Press.

Hobsbawm, Eric 1994: *The Age of Extremes: the short twentieth century 1914–1991*. London: Michael Joseph.

Hobsbawm, Eric and Ranger, Terrence 1983: *The Invention of Tradition*. Cambridge: Cambridge University Press.

Hobson, Joseph A. 1902: *Imperialism: a study*. London: Allen and Unwin.

Hockenos, Paul, 1993: *Free to Hate: the rise of the right in post-communist Eastern Europe*. London: Routledge.

Howe, Warren 1994: Too foreign for US. *The Sunday Times, Style and Travel*, 19 June, 11.

Howell, Signe 1991: The meaning of art. In S. Hiller (ed.), *The Myth of Primitivism*. London: Routledge.

Howell, Signe 1993: *Whose Global Culture? Some profound primitive influences upon the civilized world*. Paper to the ASA 1V Decennial Conference, Oxford, July.

Hu, Yao-Su 1992: Global or stateless corporations are national firms with international operations. *California Management Review*, 34(2), 107.

Huntington, Samuel 1993: The clash of civilizations. *Foreign Affairs*, 72(3), 22–50.

Ignatieff, Michael 1994: *Blood and Belonging*. London: BBC Publications.

Jacques, Martin 1994: Battleground of Europe's future. *Sunday Times, The Culture*, 27 March, 8–11.

Jameson, Frederick 1991: *Postmodernism or the Cultural Logic of Late Capitalism*. London: Verso.

Jerome, Robert W. (ed.) 1992: *World Trade at the Crossroads: the Uruguay Round, GATT and beyond*. London: University Press of America.

Jessop, Bob 1982: *The Capitalist State*. Oxford: Martin Robertson.

Jessop, Bob 1987: *Economy, State and Law in Autopoietic Theory*. Essex Papers in Politics and Government, 42.

Jessop, Bob 1990: *State Theory: putting the capitalist state in its place*. Cambridge: Polity.

Joffe, Josef 1993: The new Europe: yesterday's ghosts. *Foreign Affairs*, 72(1), 29–43.

Johnson, James 1994: Public sphere, postmodernism and polemic. *American Political Science Review*, 88(2), 427–30.

Johnstone, Iain 1994: Workers united. *The Independent on Sunday*, 8 May, 15.

Jowitt, Ken 1992: *New World Disorder: the Leninist distinction*. Berkeley, CA: University of California Press.

Kapstein, Ethan B. 1991–2: 'We are us': the myth of the multinational. *National Interest*, 26 (Winter), 55–62.

Katznelson, Ira 1981: Lenin or Weber? Choices in Marxist theories of politics. *Political Studies*, 29(4), 632–40.

Katznelson, Ira 1992: The state to the rescue? Political science and history reconnect. *Social Research*, 59(4), 719–37.

Keane, John 1991: *The Media and Democracy*. Cambridge: Polity.

Kegley, Charles W. Jr and Wittkopf, Eugene R. 1993: *World Politics: trend and transformation*. 4th edn. New York: St Martin's Press.

Keillor, Garrison 1986: *Lake Wobegon Days*. London: Faber and Faber.

Keillor, Garrison 1990: Who do you think you are? In *We Are Still Married*. London: Faber and Faber.

Kennedy, Paul 1988: *The Rise and Fall of the Great Powers: economic change and military conflict 1500–2000*. London: Fontana.

Kennedy, Paul 1993: *Preparing for the Twenty-First Century*. London: HarperCollins.

Keohane, Robert O. 1983: Theory of world politics: structural realism and beyond. In A. Finifter (ed.), *Political Science: the state of the discipline*. Washington: American Political Science Association.

Keohane, Robert O. 1984: *After Hegemony: cooperation and discord in the world political economy*. Princeton: Princeton University Press.

Keohane, Robert O. and Nye, Joseph S. 1977: *Power and Interdependence*. Boston: Little Brown.

Keohane, Robert O. and Nye, Joseph S. 1988: Complex interdependence, transnational relations and realism: alternative perspectives on world politics. In C. W. Kegley Jr and E. R. Wittkopf (eds), *The Global Agenda*. 2nd edn. Random House.

King, A. D. (ed.) 1991: *Culture, Globalization and the World-System: contemporary conditions for the representation of identity*. London: Macmillan.

Kirkpatrick, Jeanne 1993: The modernizing imperative: tradition and change. *Foreign Affairs*, 72(4), 22–4.

Kohler-Koch, Beate 1994: Changing patterns of interest group intermediation in the European Community. *Government and Opposition*, 29(2), 166–80.

Kondratieff, N. D. 1979 (1926): The long waves in economic life. *Review*, 2(4), 519–64.

Koslowski, Rey and Kratochwil, Friedrich V. 1994: Understanding change in international politics: the Soviet empire's demise and the international system. *International Organisation*, 48(2), 213–47.

Krasner, Stephen 1988: Sovereignty: an institutional perspective. *Comparative Political Studies*, 21 (Spring), 66–94.

Krasner, Stephen 1994: International political economy: abiding discord. *Review of International Political Economy*, 1(1), 13–19.

Kuhn, Thomas 1970: *The Structure of Scientific Revolutions*. Chicago: University of Chicago Press.

Kumar, Krishan 1992: The 1989 revolutions and the idea of Europe. *Political Studies*, 40(3), 434–62.

Kunda, Gideon 1992: *Engineering Culture: control and commitment in a high-tech corporation*. Philadelphia: Temple University Press.

Lackey, Chad 1992: Giddens' *Modernity and Self-Identity* (review). *Berkeley Journal of Sociology*, 37, 181–5.

Laclau, Ernesto 1988: Building a New Left: an interview with Ernesto Laclau. *Strategies*, 1(1), 10–28.

Laclau, Ernesto and Mouffe, Chantal 1987: Post-Marxism without apologies. *New Left Review*, 166, 79–106.

Landsberg, M. 1979: Export-led industrialization in the Third World: manufacturing imperialism. *Review of Radical Political Economics*, 11(4), 50–63.

Lang, James 1980: In search of the world-system. *Contemporary Sociology*, 11 (May), 260–6.

Lash, Scott 1993: Reflexive modernization: the aesthetic dimension. *Theory, Culture and Society*, 10(1), 1–25.

Lash, Scott and Urry, John 1987: *The End of Organized Capitalism*. Cambridge: Polity.

Lash, Scott and Urry, John 1994: *Economies of Signs and Space*. London: Sage.

Layder, Derek 1994: *Understanding Social Theory*. London: Sage.

Leifer, Robert 1989: Understanding organisational transformation using a dissipative structure model. *Human Relations*, 42, 899–916.

Lenin, Vladimir I. 1975: *Imperialism, the Highest Stage of Capitalism*. Moscow. Foreign Language Press.

Lerner, Daniel 1958: *The Passing of Traditional Society*. New York: Free Press.

Lijphart, Arend 1968: *The Politics of Accommodation: pluralism and democracy in the Netherlands*. Berkeley, CA: University of California Press.

Lindberg, Leon N. and Scheingold, Steven A. 1970: *Europe's Would-be Polity: patterns of change in the European Community*. Englewood Cliffs, NJ: Prentice-Hall.

Lipietz, A. 1987: *Mirages and Miracles*. London: Verso.

Lipset, Seymour M. 1959: *Political Man*. London: Heinemann.

Lipset, Seymour M. and Rokkan, Stein 1968: *Party Systems and Voter Alignments*. New Haven: Yale University Press.

Lipset, Seymour M., Seong, Kyoung R. and Torres, John C. 1993: A comparative analysis of the social requisites of democracy. *International Social Science Journal*, 136.

Lodge, Juliet 1993: Transforming the democratic deficit. *Journal of Common Market Studies*, 32(3), 343–69.

Luhmann, Niklas 1982a: *The Differentiation of Society*. New York: Columbia University Press.

Luhmann, Niklas 1982b: The world society as a social system. *International Journal of General Systems*, 8(3), 131–8.

Luke, Timothy 1985: On the nature of Soviet society. *Telos*, 65, 187–96.

Luxemburg, Rosa 1951: *The Accumulation of Capital*. London: Routledge and Kegan Paul.

Lyotard, François 1984: *The Postmodern Condition*. Minneapolis: University of Minnesota Press.

MacCannell, David 1992: *Empty Meeting Grounds: tourist papers*. London: Routledge.

MacDonald, Sharon 1993: Identity complexes in Western Europe: social anthropological perspectives. In S. MacDonald (ed.), *Inside European Identities: ethnography in Western Europe*. Oxford: Berg.

Mann, Michael 1986: *The Sources of Social Power. Volume 1: A History of Power from the Beginning to AD 1760*. Cambridge: Cambridge University Press.

March, James G. and Olsen, Johan P. 1984: The new institutionalism: organizational factors in American political life. *American Political Science Review*, 78 (September), 734–49.

Marcus, G. E. and Fischer, M. M. J. 1986: *Anthropology as Cultural Critique*. Chicago: University of Chicago Press.

Marsh, David and Rhodes, Rod 1992: *Policy Networks in British Government*. Oxford: Oxford University Press.

Masini, Eleonara M. 1993: Futures studies and the trends towards unity and diversity. *International Social Science Journal*, 137, 323–31.

Massey, Doreen 1991: A global sense of place. *Marxism Today*, June, 25–6.

Mattelhart, A. 1983: *Transnationals and the Third World*. South Hadley: Bergin and Garvey.

Maturana, Humberto and Varela, Francisco 1980: *Autopoiesis and Cognition: the realization of the living*. London: Riedl.

Mauss, Marcel 1979a: Body techniques. In *Sociology and Psychology*. London: Routledge.

Mauss, Marcel 1979b: A category of the human mind: the notion of the person, the notion of the 'self'. In *Sociology and Psychology*. London: Routledge.

Mazey, Sonia P. and Richardson, Jeremy J. 1993: *Lobbying in the European Community*. Oxford: Oxford University Press.

McCarthy, Thomas 1978: *The Critical Theory of Jürgen Habermas*. London: Hutchinson.

McGrew, Anthony 1992: A global society? In S. Hall, D. Held and A. McGrew (eds), *Modernity and its Futures*. Open University/Polity.

McLennan, Gregor 1992: The Enlightenment project revisited. In S. Hall, D. Held and A. McGrew (eds), *Modernity and its Futures*. Cambridge: Open University/Polity.

Mearsheimer, John 1990: Back to the future: instability in Europe after the Cold War. *International Security*, 15(3), 5–57.

Meehan, Elizabeth, 1993: *Citizenship and the European Community*. London: Sage.

Mendes, Candido 1992: The quest for globality: interdisciplinary endeavour in the social and natural sciences. *International Social Science Journal*, 42, 607–14.

Meštrović, Stjepan J. 1994: *The Balkanization of the West: the confluence of postmodernism and postcommunism*. London: Routledge.

Meyer, John W. 1980a: The world polity and the authority of the nation-state. In A. Bergesen (ed.), *Studies of the Modern World-System*. New York: Academic Press.

Meyer, John W. 1980b: In search of the world-system. *Contemporary Sociology*, 11 May, 260–6.

Meyer, John W., Ramirez, Francesco and Boli, John 1987: Ontology and rationalization in the Western cultural account. In George Thomas, John Meyer, Franco Ramirez and John Boli (eds), *Institutional Structure: constituting state, society and the individual*. Beverly Hills, CA: Sage.

Middlemass, Keith 1993: The informal politics of the European Community. *Political Quarterly*, 64(2), 126–37.

Miliband, Ralph 1985: State power and social classes. *New Left Review*, 138, 57–70.

Miller, T. B. 1992: A new world order? *The World Today*, January, 7–9.

Milward, Alan S. with Brennan, S. and Romereo, Frederico 1992: *The European Rescue of the Nation-State*. London: Routledge.

Minc, Alain 1992: *The Great European Illusion: business in the wider community*. Oxford: Blackwell.

Modelski, George 1978: The long cycle of global politics and the nation-state. *Comparative Studies in Society and History*, 20(2), 214–35.

Modelski, George 1983: Long cycles of world leadership. In W. R. Thompson (ed.), *Contending Approaches to World System Analysis*. Beverly Hills, CA: Sage.

Modelski, George 1988: *Sea Power in Global Politics 1494–1943*. Washington: University of Washington Press.

Modelski, George 1990: Is world politics evolutionary learning? *International Organisation*, 44(1), 1–24.

Moi, Toril 1991: *Sexual Textual Politics*. London: Routledge.

Mongardini, Carlo 1992: The ideology of postmodernity. *Theory, Culture and Society*, 9, 55–65.

Moravcsik, Anthony 1991: Negotiating the Single European Act: national interests and conventional statecraft in the European Community. In R. Keohane and S. Hoffman (eds), *The New European Community: decision making and institutional change*. Boulder, CO: Westview Press.

Morgan, Gareth 1986: *Images of Organization*. London: Sage.

Morgenthau, Hans 1948: *Politics among Nations*. New York: Knopf.

Morley, David 1992: Electronic communities and domestic rituals. In M. Skovmand and K. C. Schroder (eds), *Media Cultures: reappraising transnational media*. London: Routledge.

Mouffe, Chantal 1993: *The Return of the Political*. London: Verso.

Mouzelis, Nicos 1989: Restructuring structuration theory. *Theory, Culture and Society*, 6, 613–35.

Mouzelis, Nicos 1993: Evolution and democracy: Talcott Parsons and the collapse of Eastern European regimes. *Theory, Culture and Society*, 10, 145–51.

Naisbitt, John and Aburdene, Patricia 1990: *Megatrends 2000*. London: Pan.

Nau, Henry R. 1990: *The Myth of America's Decline: leading the world economy into the 1990s*. Oxford: Oxford University Press.

Nettl, Peter 1968: The state as a conceptual variable. *World Politics*, 20 July.

Nicholson-Lord, David 1993: Civilization for sale. *The Independent on Sunday*, 12 December, 21–2.

Nordlinger, Eric 1981: *The Autonomy of the Democratic State*. Cambridge, MA: Harvard University Press.

Nye, Joseph S. Jr 1989: *Bound to Lead: the changing nature of American power*. New York: Basic Books.

O'Brien, Conor C. 1993: The fruit and peril of democracy. *The Independent*, 8 October, 26.

O'Donnell, Guillarmo, Schmitter, Philip and Whitehead, Laurence (eds) 1986: *Transitions from Authoritarian Rule: prospects for democracy*. Baltimore: Johns Hopkins University Press.

O'Neill, John 1990: AIDs as a globalizing panic. *Theory, Culture and Society*, 7, 329–42.

O'Sullivan, Noel 1993: Political integration, the limited state, and the philosophy of postmodernism. *Political Studies*, 41(4), 21–42.

Offe, Claus 1985: *Disorganized Capitalism*. Cambridge: Polity.

Offe, Claus 1991: Capitalism by democratic design? Facing the triple transition in East Central Europe. *Social Research*, 58(4), 866–92.

Ogbonna, E. 1993: Managing organisational culture: fantasy or reality. *Human Resource Management*, 3(2), 42–54.

Ohmae, Kenichi 1990: *Borderless World: power and strategy in the interlinked economy*. London: Collins.

Ohmae, Kenichi 1993: The rise of the region-state. *Foreign Affairs*, 72(3), 78–87.

Olson, Mancur Jr 1965: *The Logic of Collective Action: public goods and the theory of groups*. Cambridge, MA: Harvard University Press.

Parekh, Bhiku 1994: Discourses on national identity. *Political Studies*, 42(3), 492–504.

Parker, Martin 1993: Post-modern organisations or post-modern organisation theory. *Organisation Studies*, 13(1), 1–17.

Parker, Martin 1994: *Organisational Citizenship and Modernist Emancipation*. Paper to the Conference on Modernity–Postmodernity: from the personal to the global, Oxford, September.

Parsons, Talcott 1966: *Sociological Theory and Modern Society*. New York: Free Press.

Parsons, Talcott 1968: *The Structure of Social Action*. 2nd edn. New York: Free Press.

Parsons, Talcott 1971: *The System of Modern Societies*. New York: Prentice-Hall.

Parsons, Talcott and Shills, Edward 1951: *Towards a General Theory of Action*. Cambridge, MA: Harvard University Press.

Pascale, Richard 1986: *Managing on the Edge*. Harmondsworth: Penguin.

Peet, Richard 1991: *Global Capitalism: theories of societal development*. London: Routledge.

Peters, Tom 1987: *Thriving on Chaos*. London: Pan.

Peters, Tom 1990: The forces of order versus market anarchists. In *The World in 1991*. London: Economist Publications, 118–21.

Peters, Tom and Waterman, Richard 1982: In *Search of Excellence*. New York: Harper and Row.

Peterson, V. S. and Runyan, A. S. 1993: *Global Gender Issues*. Boulder, CO: Westview.

Pieterse, Jan N. 1993: Fukuyama and liberal democracy: the ends of history. *Economy and Society*, 22(2), 218–31.

Piore, Michael J. and Sabel, Charles 1984: *The Second Industrial Divide*. New York: Basic Books.

Porter, Michael 1990: *The Competitive Advantage of Nations*. London: Macmillan.

Powell, Walter W. 1991: Neither market nor hierarchy: network forms of organization. In G. Thompson, J. Frances, R. Levacic and J. Mitchell (eds), *Markets, Hierarchies and Networks*. London: Sage.

Prahalad, C. K. and Doz, Y. L. 1987: *The Multinational Mission*. New York: Free Press.

Prahalad, C. K. and Hamel, Gary 1990: The core competences of the organization. *Harvard Business Review*, May–June, 79–91.

Pred, Allan and Watts, Michael J. 1992: *Reworking Modernity, Capitalism and Symbolic Discontent*. Newark, NJ: Rutgers University Press.

Prigogine, Ilya 1984: *Order out of Chaos*. New York: Random House.

Purcell, Randall B. (ed.) 1989: *The Newly Industrializing Countries in the World Economy: challenges for US policy*. Boulder, CO: Lynne Rienner.

Rabinow, Paul 1993: *A Critical Curiosity: reflections on hyper-modern places*. Paper to IVth Decennial Conference of the Association of Social Anthropology, Oxford.

Ramirez, Francisco 1987: Institutional analysis. In George Thomas, John Meyer, Francisco Ramirez and John Boli (eds), *Institutional Structure: constituting state, society and the individual*. Beverly Hills, CA: Sage.

Rapkin, David 1983: The inadequacy of a single logic: integrating political and material approaches to the world system. In W. R. Thompson (ed.), *Contending Approaches to World System Analysis*. London: Sage.

Reich, Robert 1992: *The Work of Nations*. New York: Vintage.

Reise, Utz 1992: Postmodern culture: symptom, critique, or solution to the crisis of modernity? An East German perspective. *New German Critique*, 57 (Fall), 157–70.

Rhodes, Rod A. W. 1994: The hollowing out of the state: the changing nature of the public service in Britain. *The Political Quarterly*, 65(2), 138–52.

Roberts, Adam 1993: Humanitarian war: military intervention and human rights. *International Affairs*, 69(3), 429–49.

Robertson, Roland 1992: *Globalization: social theory and global culture*. London: Sage.

Robertson, Roland and Lechner, Frank 1985: Modernization, globalization and the problem of culture in world-systems theory. *Theory, Culture and Society*, 2(3).

Robins, Kevin 1991: Tradition and translation: national culture in its global context. In J. Corner and S. Harvey (eds), *Enterprise and Heritage: crosscurrents of national culture*. London: Routledge.

Robins, Kevin 1994: The politics of silence: the meaning community and the uses of media in the new Europe. *New Formations*, 21 (Winter), 80–102.

Rogin, Michael P. 1971: Liberal society and the Indian question. *Politics and Society*, 1(3), 269–313.

Rorty, Richard 1992: Cosmopolitanism without emancipation: a response to Lyotard. In S. Lash and J. Friedman (eds), *Modernity and Identity*. Oxford: Blackwell.

Rosamond, Ben 1993: National labour organisations and European integration: British trade unions and 1992. *Political Studies*, 41(3), 420–35.

Rosenau, James (ed.) 1967: *Domestic Sources of Foreign Policy*. New York: Free Press.

Rosenau, James 1988: The state in an era of cascading politics:

wavering concept, widening competence, withering colossus, or weathering change? *Comparative Political Studies*, 21(1), 44.

Rosenau, James 1990: *Turbulence in World Politics: a theory of change and continuity*. Princeton: Princeton University Press.

Rosenau, Pauline V. and Bredemeier, Harry 1993: Modern and postmodern conceptions of social order. *Social Research*, 60(2), 337–62.

Rostow, Walt W. 1960: *The Stages of Economic Growth: a non-communist manifesto*. Cambridge: Cambridge University Press.

Ruggie, John 1992: Multilateralism: the anatomy of an institution. *International Organisation*, 46(3), 561–99.

Ruggie, John 1993: Territoriality and beyond: problematising modernity in international relations. *International Organisation*, 47(1), 149–74.

Sagan, Eli 1992: The politics of the impossible: or, whatever happened to evolutionary theory? *Social Research*, 59(4), 739–58.

Salt, John 1991: South–north migration in Europe today. *Economic Affairs*, June, 15–17.

Sassen, Saskia 1992: *The Global City: New York, London, Tokyo*. Princeton: Princeton University Press.

Schlesinger, Philip 1991: Media, the political order and national identity. *Media, Culture and Society*, 13(3), 297–308.

Schmitter, Philip and Streeck, Wolfgang 1991a: Organised interests and the European Community in 1992. In N. Ornstein and N. Perlman (eds), *Political Power and Social Change*. Washington, DC: AEI Press.

Schmitter, Philip and Streeck, Wolfgang 1991b: From national corporatism to transnational pluralism: organised interests in the single European market. *Politics and Society*, 20(2), 133–64.

Scholte, Jan 1994: *Supraterritoriality. postmodernity*. Paper to the Conference on Modernity–Postmodernity: from the personal to the global, Oxford, September.

Schou, Soren 1992: Postwar Americanization and the revitalization of European culture. In M. Skovmand and K. C. Schroder (eds), *Media Cultures: reappraising transnational media*. London: Routledge.

Schumpeter, Joseph 1952: *The Sociology of Imperialism*. New York: Kelly.

Searle, John 1965: *Speech Acts: an essay in the philosophy of language*. Cambridge: Cambridge University Press.

Sen, Amartya 1991: *On Ethics and Economics*. Oxford: Blackwell.

Sensat, Julius Jr 1979: *Habermas and Marxism: an appraisal*. London: Sage.

Silber, Gus 1994: The many tribes of Mandelaland. *The Sunday Times Magazine*, 27 March, 64–8.

Sklair, Leslie 1991: *The Sociology of the Global System*. Baltimore: Johns Hopkins University Press.

Skocpol, Theda 1977: Wallerstein's world capitalist system: a theoretical and historical critique. *The American Journal of Sociology*, 82(5), 1075–90.

Skocpol, Theda 1978: *States and Social Revolutions*. Cambridge: Cambridge University Press.

Skocpol, Theda, 1980: Gouldner at his best (review). *Contemporary Sociology*, 11, 194–5.

Skocpol, Theda 1981: Political response to capitalist crisis: neo-Marxist theories of the state and the case of the New Deal. *Politics and Society*, 10(2), 155–201.

Skocpol, Theda 1985: Bringing the state back in: strategies of analysis in current research. In Peter R. Evans, D. Rueschmeyer and Theda Skocpol (eds), *Bringing the State Back In*. Cambridge: Cambridge University Press.

Skowronek, Stephen 1982: *Building a New American State: the expansion of national administrative capacities 1877–1920*. Cambridge: Cambridge University Press.

Smart, Barry 1993: *Postmodernity*. London: Routledge.

Smelser, Neil 1959: *Social Change in the Industrial Revolution*. London: Routledge and Kegan Paul.

Smith, Anthony 1973: *The Concept of Social Change*. London: Routledge and Kegan Paul.

Smith, Anthony 1990: The supersession of nationalism? *International Journal of Comparative Sociology*, 31(2), 1–32.

Smith, Dennis 1992: Modernity, postmodernity and the new Middle Ages (review). *The Sociological Review*, 38(2), 754–71.

Soysal, Yasemin 1995: *Limits of Citizenship in the Contemporary Nation-State System*. Chicago: University of Chicago Press.

Spero, Joan E. 1991: Guiding global finance. *Foreign Policy*, 73 (Winter).

Stark, David 1992: From system identity to organisational diversity: analysing social change in Eastern Europe. *Contemporary Sociology*, 21(3), 299–304.

Stein, Arthur 1990: *Why Nations Cooperate*. Ithaca: Cornell University Press.

Stone, Norman 1994: A plague on the West. *The Sunday Times*, 17 April, 10, 9–10.

Story, Jonathan (ed.) 1993: *The New Europe: politics, government and economy since 1945*. Oxford: Blackwell.

Strang, David 1991: European political expansion: realist and institutional accounts. *International Organisation*, 45(2), 143–63.

Strange, Susan 1986: *Casino Capitalism*. Oxford: Blackwell.

Strange, Susan 1988: *States and Markets*. London: Pinter.

Swanson, Guy E. 1992: Modernity and the postmodern. *Theory, Culture and Society*, 9, 142–51.

Taylor, Charles 1989: *The Sources of the Self: the making of modern identity*. Cambridge: Cambridge University Press.

Teubner, Gunter (ed.) 1988: *Autopoietic Law: a new approach to law and society*. Berlin: de Gruyter.

Thomas, George, Meyer, John W., Ramirez, Francisco and John Boli (eds) 1987: *Institutional Structure: constituting state, society and the individual*. Beverly Hills, CA: Sage.

Thompson, John B. 1993: The theory of the public sphere (review article). *Theory, Culture and Society*, 10, 173–89.

Thompson, Kenneth 1992: Social pluralism and postmodernity. In S. Hall, D. Held and A. McGrew (eds), *Modernity and its Futures*. Cambridge: Open University/Polity.

Tickner, Anne J. 1992: *Gender and International Relations: feminist perspectives on achieving global security*. New York: Columbia University Press.

Time International 1993: Whatever Happened to the Great American Job? 2 November, p. 14.

Touraine, Alain 1991: What does democracy mean today? *International Social Science Journal*, 128, 259–68.

Trimberger, Ellen 1978: *Revolution from Above: military bureaucrats and development in Japan, Turkey, Egypt and Peru*. New York: Transaction Books.

UNCTAD 1993: *World Investment Report 1993: transnational corporations and integrated international production*.

Urry, John 1990: *The Tourist Gaze*. London: Sage.

Urry, John 1991: Time and space in Giddens' social theory. In C. Bryant and D. Jary (eds), *Giddens' Theory of Structuration*. London: Routledge.

Usborne, David 1993: Wiggers just wannabe black. *The Independent on Sunday*, 22 August, 10.

Vattimo, G. 1988: *The End of Modernity*. Cambridge: Polity.

Villa, Dana R. 1992: Postmodernism and the public sphere. *American Political Science Review*, 86(3), 712–21.

Vogler, John 1992: Regimes and global commons. In A. G. McGrew and P. Lewis (eds), *Global Politics*. Cambridge: Polity.

Von Bertalanffy, Ludwig 1968: *General Systems Theory: foundations, development, applications*. New York: Braziller.

Wagner, R. Harrison 1993: What was bipolarity? *International Organisation*, 47(1), 77–107.

Walker, R. B. J. 1993: *Inside/Outside: international relations as political theory*. Cambridge: Cambridge University Press.

Wallace, Helen 1993: European governance in turbulent times. *Journal of Common Market Studies*, 31(3), 293–303.

Wallerstein, Immanuel 1974: *The Modern World-System. Volume I*. New York: Academic Press.

Wallerstein, Immanuel 1979a: *The Modern World-System. Volume II: Mercantilism and the Consolidation of the European World Economy*. New York: Academic Press.

Wallerstein, Immanuel 1979b: *The Capitalist World Economy*. Cambridge: Cambridge University Press.

Wallerstein, Immanuel 1983: *Historical Capitalism*. London: Verso.

Wallerstein, Immanuel 1984: *The Politics of the World Economy*. Cambridge: Cambridge University Press.

Wallerstein, Immanuel 1989: The capitalist world-economy: middle-run prospects. *Alternatives*, 14(3).

Wallerstein, Immanuel 1991a: The lessons of the 1980s. In I. Wallerstein (ed.), *Geopolitics and Geoculture*. Cambridge: Cambridge University Press.

Wallerstein, Immanuel 1991b: Culture as the ideological battleground of the modern world-system. In I. Wallerstein (ed.), *Geopolitics and Geoculture*. Cambridge: Cambridge University Press.

Wallerstein, Immanuel (ed.) 1991c: *Geopolitics and Geoculture*. Cambridge: Cambridge University Press.

Wallerstein, Immanuel 1994: The agonies of liberalism: what hope progress? *New Left Review*, 204, 3–18.

Waltz, Kenneth M. 1954: *Man, the State, and War*. New York: Columbia University Press.

Waltz, Kenneth M. 1979: *Theory of International Politics*. Reading, MA: Addison-Wesley.

Waltz, Kenneth M. 1991: Realist thought and neorealist theory. In R. L. Rothstein (ed.), *The Evolution of Theory in International Relations*. Columbia, SC: University of Southern Carolina Press.

Warren, B. 1980: *Imperialism: pioneer of capitalism*. London: New Left Books.

Weber, Max 1976: *The Protestant Ethic and the Spirit of Capitalism*. London: Allen and Unwin.

Weber, Max 1978: *Economy and Society*. Berkeley, CA: University of California Press.

Webster, Frank and Robins, Kevin 1989: Plan and control: towards a cultural history of the information society. *Theory and Society*, 18, 323–51.

Weick, Karl E. 1979: *The Social Psychology of Organizing*. Reading, MA: Addison-Wesley.

Wellman, Barry and Berkovitz, S. D. 1988: *Social Structure: a network approach*. Cambridge: Cambridge University Press.

Wendt, Alexander E. 1987: The agent–structure problem in international relations theory. *International Organisation*, 41, 335–70.

Wendt, Alexander E. 1992: Anarchy is what states make of it: social construction of power politics. *International Organisation*, 46(2), 392–425.

Wendt, Alexander E. 1994: Collective identity formation and the international state. *American Political Science Review*, 88(2), 384–99.

Whittington, Richard 1992: Putting Giddens into action: social system and managerial agency. *Journal of Management Studies*, 29(6), 693–709.

Wildish, Clive and Case, Peter 1994: Studies of globalization: the unspeakable in search of the uneatable. In B. Axford and G. Browning (eds), *Modernity and Postmodernity: mapping the terrain*. no. 4. Oxford: Thamesman Publications.

Worsley, Peter 1970: *The Trumpet shall Sound*. London: Paladin.

Worsley, Peter 1984: *The Three Worlds. culture and development*. London: Weidenfeld and Nicolson.

Worsley, Peter 1990: Models of the modern world-system. *Theory, Culture and Society*, 7(2–3), 83–95.

Wrong, Dennis 1992: Disaggregating the idea of capitalism. *Theory, Culture and Society*, 9,147–58.

Yeats, W. B. 1945: The second coming. In C. J. Lewis and L. A. G. Strong (eds), *An Anthology*. Frome: Methuen.

Young, Oran 1986: International regimes: towards a new theory of institutions. *World Politics*, 39 (October), 104–22.

Zaslavsky, Victor 1985: The Soviet world-system. *Telos*, 65, 3.

Zazlavsky, Victor 1994: Russia and the problem of democratic transition. *Telos*, 96, 26–53.

Zeleny, M. (ed.) 1981: *Autopoiesis: a theory of living organization*. New York: North Holland Elsevier.

Zolberg, Aristide R. 1984: 'World' and 'System': a misalliance. In W. R. Thompson (ed.), *Contending Approaches in World-System Analysis*. London: Sage.

Zolo, Danilo 1990–1: Autopoieis: critique of a postmodern paradigm. *Telos*, 86, 3–33.

Index